$53 ^{00}

Critical Essays on

ISAAC BASHEVIS SINGER

CRITICAL ESSAYS
ON
AMERICAN LITERATURE

James Nagel, General Editor
University of Georgia, Athens

Critical Essays on
ISAAC BASHEVIS SINGER

edited by

GRACE FARRELL

G. K. Hall & Co.
An Imprint of Simon & Schuster Macmillan
New York

Prentice Hall International
London Mexico City New Delhi Singapore Sydney Toronto

G. K. Hall & Co.
An Imprint of Simon & Schuster Macmillan
1633 Broadway
New York, NY 10019

Library of Congress Cataloging-in-Publication Data

Critical essays on Isaac Bashevis Singer / edited by Grace Farrell.
    p. cm.—(Critical essays on American literature)
   Includes bibliographical references and index.
   ISBN 0-7838-0028-2 (alk. paper)
   1. Singer, Isaac Bashevis, 1904–   —Criticism and interpretation.
I. Farrell, Grace. II. Series.
PJ5129.S49Z63   1996
839'.0933—dc20   95-23576
                                       CIP

---

10   9   8   7   6   5   4   3   2   1

Printed in the United States of America

For Giancarlo
il mio marito

Contents

♦

NEW ESSAYS

General Editor's Note

♦

This series seeks to anthologize the most important criticism on a wide variety of topics and writers in American literature. Our readers will find in various volumes not only a generous selection of reprinted articles and reviews but original essays, bibliographies, manuscript sections, and other materials brought to public attention for the first time. This volume, *Critical Essays on Isaac Bashevis Singer*, is the most comprehensive collection of essays ever published on one of the most important modern writers in the United States. It contains both a sizable gathering of early reviews and a broad selection of more recent scholarship. Among the authors of reprinted articles and reviews are Irving Howe, Susan Sontag, Ted Hughes, Ruth R. Wisse, and Leslie Fiedler. In addition to a substantial introduction by Grace Farrell, this volume includes original essays commissioned specifically for publication here, new studies by David H. Hirsch on Abraham Cahan and Singer, Alida Allison on Singer's stories for children, Joseph Sherman on Singer and homosexuality, and Nancy Berkowitz Bate on the role of women in Singer's fiction. We are confident that this book will make a permanent and significant contribution to the study of American literature.

JAMES NAGEL
University of Georgia

Publisher's Note

◆

Producing a volume that contains both newly commissioned and reprinted material presents the publisher with the challenge of balancing the desire to achieve stylistic consistency with the need to preserve the integrity of works first published elsewhere. In the Critical Essays series, essays commissioned especially for a particular volume are edited to be consistent with G. K. Hall's house style; reprinted essays appear in the style in which they were first published, with only typographical errors corrected. Consequently, shifts in style from one essay to another are the result of our efforts to be faithful to each text as it was originally published.

Acknowledgments

♦

I wish to thank my colleagues at Butler University for their support in preparation of this book. It was an enormous task that could not have been completed without all sorts of help from many generous people, including Paul Yu, provost of the university; Bill Walsh, acting Dean, and Margriet Lacy, dean of the College of Arts and Sciences; Shirley Daniell, Eileen Cornelius, Sharon Lewis, and Renée Reed, who offered crucial technical support including typing, mailing, tracking down addresses, and obtaining copies of less-than-readily available material; my colleagues in the English Department; my students Jean Saunders and John Cone; and Nancy Bate, who volunteered hours of patient proofreading. Among my friends, fellow Singer scholars, and colleagues in the profession at large who offered encouragement and sometimes aid in gaining reprint permission, I am most grateful to my editor James Nagel, the late Irving Howe, Leslie Fiedler, Edward Alexander, Daniel Walden, Joseph Landis, Ben Siegel, Richard Burgin, Maier Deshell, Grace Darby at the *New Yorker*, and Rose Cervino and Phyllis Collago at the *New York Times*. My gratitude as always to my children, Matthew and Elizabeth.

GRACE FARRELL
Butler University

Introduction

GRACE FARRELL

His was a voice unique in American letters. Isaac Bashevis Singer—Jewish émigré from Poland, Yiddish-speaking Hasid—captivated an American and then a world readership with fiction that seemed both exotic, in its evocation of Eastern European *shtetl* life, and familiar, in its poignant depiction of loss and recovery, exile and redemption. Never easily placed within any tradition, always an outsider, Singer was doubly distanced from his American readers, who knew him only through translation, and from his Yiddish readers, who found their *shtetl* milieu transformed by both a modernist sensibility and an archaic, folkloric imagination.

Born near Warsaw on 21 November 1904, into a pious Hasidic household—which he would imaginatively portray in his memoir *In My Father's Court*—Singer was educated at local *cheders*, religious primary schools, and in his father's study house in Warsaw. When World War I forced his mother to flee the city, Singer continued his education in Bilgoray, studying the Talmud and modern Hebrew, which he in turn taught in private homes. During this period, he became immersed in the rural Hasidic folk culture that would permeate his work. He studied the Kabbalah, read Spinoza, and studied German and Polish. In 1921, Singer enrolled in Warsaw's Tachkemoni Rabbinical Seminary, but he returned to Bilgoray the following year to teach Hebrew.

Singer began his literary career writing for a Hebrew newspaper and proofreading for *Literarishe bleter*, a journal that his older brother, novelist Israel Joshua Singer, co-edited. In 1925, Singer made his fiction debut in Yiddish with a short story, "Oyf der elter" ("In Old Age"), which won a prize in *Literarishe bleter*'s literary contest. It was published under the pseudonym "Tse" and, in 1935, was reprinted in the *Jewish Daily Forward*. His second published story, "Nerot" ("Candles") appeared in 1925 in *Ha-yon*. Other early works include "Vayber" ("Women"), published that same year in *Literarishe bleter*; "Eyniklekh" ("Grandchildren"), published in *Varshever shriftn* (1926–27); "Verter oder bilder" ("Words or Images"), an essay published in *Literarishe bleter* (1927); and "Oyfn oylemhatoye" ("In the World of Chaos"), published in *Di yidishe velt* (1928). "Two Corpses Go Dancing," published in Yiddish in 1943 and in English in 1968 in *The Seance and Other*

Stories, is one of a number of variations that Singer wrote on "In the World of Chaos."

In 1932, Singer edited, with Aaron Zeitlin, a magazine called *Globus*, which printed several of Singer's short stories, including "A Zokn" ("The Old Man"), later translated and included in *Gimpel the Fool and Other Stories* (1959). In 1933 *Globus* serialized Singer's first novel, *Satan in Goray*, which was published in book form by the Warsaw P. E. N. Club in 1935. In these early years, Singer also began a series of translations into Yiddish, which, by 1935, included Knut Hamsun's *Pan* and *Victoria*, Remarque's *All Quiet on the Western Front*, and Mann's *The Magic Mountain*.

With help from his brother, Singer emigrated in May 1935 to New York by way of Paris, where he wrote for *Parizer haynt*. In New York he wrote for the *Jewish Daily Forward* under the pen names I. Warshawsky and D. Segal. In 1943 *Satan in Goray and Other Tales* was published in New York in Yiddish, and in the mid-forties Singer's fiction began appearing regularly. "Zaydlus der ershter" ("Zeidlus the Pope"), "Ser kurtser fraytik" ("Short Friday"), "Der roye veeyne-nire" ("The Unseen"), "The Spinoza of Market Street," "The Little Shoemakers," and "The Wife-Killer" all appeared in Yiddish in these years. In 1945, "Gimpl tam" ("Gimpel the Fool"), perhaps Singer's most famous story, was published in *Yidisher kemfer*.[1]

REVIEWS

It was in the 1950s that a range of Singer's work—long and short novels, a novella, and a collection of short stories—was brought before an English-speaking public. In 1950, after a three-year Yiddish serialization in the *Forward*, *The Family Moskat* was translated. The reviews of this novel introduced a debate concerning Singer's portrayal of Jews that has persisted over the decades. Although Richard Plant, who found the novel "reminiscent of Turgenev and Balzac," credited Singer for "never trying to romanticize Chassidic and Polish-Jewish life into something quaint and folkloristic,"[2] Nathan Rothman found Singer's "astringent portrait" of Jews facing the Holocaust like the "flaying of a prophet"; he cautioned that "those readers who can plow through the thick and moody substance of this novel will find themselves haunted by an after image not easily blinked away."[3] Joshua Kunitz, with reference to post-holocaustal literature "all aglow with an unconquerable affirmation," wondered with regret "why so little of all this is reflected or foreshadowed" in *The Family Moskat*.[4] Throughout his career, Singer would be criticized, particularly by scholars of Yiddish, for not continuing the tradition of sentiment established by that literature.[5] On the other hand, his supporters would praise him, as Eugene Goodheart put it, for being ". . . free of the parochial pieties of the Yiddish writer."[6]

Although for the most part this long, intergenerational saga was reviewed positively, it was his short story "Gimpl tam" that became the critical breakthrough for Singer. In 1952, when preparing an anthology of Yiddish literature, Eliezer Greenberg read "Gimpl tam" to Irving Howe, who asked Saul Bellow to translate it. Howe sent it to *Partisan Review*, and it appeared there in May 1953. As Singer put it, "I considered myself unknown to American readers. Then in 1953 *Partisan Review* published 'Gimpel the Fool,' in a translation by Saul Bellow. This story brought me so much popularity—somehow I have the strange feeling that all the literary people in America read that one issue of *Partisan Review*."[7] During the fifties and thereafter, his work appeared widely in English in magazines such as *Partisan Review*, *Commentary*, the *New Yorker*, *Harper's*, and *Esquire*. Two years after its appearance in *Partisan Review*, "Gimpel the Fool" was called "a classic of Yiddish literature" by the *Saturday Review*.[8]

In 1955, when Jacob Sloan's translation of *Satan in Goray* appeared, it was hailed by the *New York Times* as "poetically conceived. . . . Beautifully written by one of the masters of Yiddish prose, and beautifully translated, *Satan in Goray* is folk material transmuted into literature."[9] With comparisons to Flaubert and Turgenev, Irving Howe called it "a remarkable book, brilliant, enigmatic, and [deserving] the attention of anyone interested in modern literature." He cited Singer's ability "to hold such contrary elements as the miraculous and the skeptical, the moral and the exotic in a delicate tension. . . . He brings to play upon Jewish life a mind that delights in everything that is antique and curious yet is drenched with the assumptions of modern psychology."[10] As a stylist, Judd Teller remarked, Singer is "a careful, meticulous craftsman. His images are precise, his effects are deliberate, and when he uses, as he often does, obsolete and archaic Yiddish, it is by choice, to create an atmosphere, and not for lack of linguistic resources."[11]

Exuberant praise continued with the publication of *Gimpel the Fool and Other Stories* in 1957. The *New York Times* wrote: "Isaac Bashevis Singer is the last of the great Yiddish fiction writers. His novels, *The Family Moskat* and *Satan in Goray*, were hailed as major literary creations, but it is in *Gimpel the Fool and Other Stories* that Singer takes his place with the epic storytellers, transcending geographical and chronological boundaries."[12] With reference to Hawthorne, Paul Lauter discussed Singer's drawing upon "folk superstition and lore for the imps and prodigies of his sophisticated morality tales" and called the title story Singer's "masterpiece." Gimpel is Everyman, "a kind of hobo Patriarch, an archetype of "Beckett's bums, of Joyce's Bloom, of Bellow's Augie March . . ."[13]

The immediate translation of *The Magician of Lublin*, serialized in the *Forward* in 1959 and published in English in 1960, was indicative of Singer's increasing popularity with non-Yiddish speakers. "Singer's finest work," praised Stanley Edgar Hyman;[14] "the least satisfactory," Milton Hindus would conclude shortly thereafter.[15] In the *Herald Tribune*, Milton Rugoff wrote, *"The Magician of Lublin* casts a spell. There is in it a mixture of realism and fantasy, and a power to evoke the people and places of nineteenth-century Polish Jewry that loads every page with rare pleasures and unexpected rewards."[16] With insight unmatched until later scholars would tackle the novel in much greater detail, Francis King wrote, "In a small, delicate way this is an extraordinary novel, the apparent tranquillity of its surface, shining with optimism and good humour, concealing an inner chasm of violence and despair. The life of nineteenth-century Polish Jewry is recreated with a beautiful freshness and clarity; but from time to time this realistic picture is, as it were, gently stretched outwards until it achieves a grotesque or menacing distortion."[17]

Irving Howe found that "the book is not quite so dazzling as *Satan in Goray*, but it does represent Singer at fairly close to his best, particularly in his gifts for evoking the textures of sensuous life and for driving straight to those moments of tension and inner division which reveal the souls of his characters. But while there is no difficulty in making out what happens in the book, there is a real question as to what it all signifies."[18] We can only understand what it all means, Howe concluded, if we consider the ending of *The Magician* in modernist terms, as ironic and unresolved.

Howe seemed to be having difficulty justifying what he found to be Singer's "indulging in his repertoire of tricks."[19] In his review of *The Spinoza of Market Street and Other Stories* the following year, he drew back from his initial enthusiastic appraisals and articulated a reservation concerning Singer's work—its apparent lack of development: "Singer seems almost perfect within his stringent limits, but it is a perfection of stasis. . . . Within his narrow limits Singer is a genius. . . . Yet, [he] seems to be mired in his own originality."[20] While, with characteristic forthrightness, Howe questioned his own demand for "development" as a critical yardstick, other critics continued to heap praise upon Singer: "The greatest contemporary Yiddish writer, perhaps the greatest Yiddish writer of all time," wrote Eugene Goodheart for the *Saturday Review*.[21] Herbert Kupferberg wrote for the *Herald Tribune*, "Thus wisdom and foolishness, evil and good walk side by side through Mr. Singer's lost world. Or is it really lost? Certainly it gleams with brightness and brims with life in this richly imaginative, evocative and original set of stories."[22] David Lodge commented that "few adjustments would be necessary to set [these stories] in the late thirteenth and early fourteenth centuries . . . one has a sense that these stories have had a long, anonymous history in popular culture before receiving the finish of a sophisticated craftsman."[23] However, while not ceasing to honor the folk context of Singer's fiction, Goodheart, like Howe and Kazin before him and many a critic after him, linked Singer "through his irony, lyricism, grotesque fantasy, and sense of the absurd"[24] with modernism.

By this time, Singer's *oeuvre* in English was large enough to warrant retrospective reviews, and the first was published in 1962 by Milton Hindus, who differed with Howe's reassessment of Singer: "What Howe calls Singer's 'narrow,' 'stringent' limitations are precisely the source of his power, his 'genius.' Singer never loses sight of the fact that his forte is the imaginative transportation of reality, and if this is a limitation it is one only in Goethe's sense when he said that it is 'only by conscious self-limitation that mastery reveals itself.' "[25]

With the publication of *The Slave* in 1962, praise for Singer's work again reached its pre-*Magician* heights. "One of the great literary giants of our age," declared the *Jewish Spectator*.[26] Jean Stafford wrote, "He is a spellbinder as clever as Scheherazade; he arrests the reader at once, transports him to a far place and a far, improbable time and does not let him go until the end."[27] Reviewers had consistently commented on the technical virtuosity of Singer's style, and now David Boroff called Singer "a peerless story teller . . . There is about him a bardic quality that gives *The Slave* the strength and authority of a timeless folk tale. But Singer is no *naif* with a conjurer's gift for recreating the past . . . few writers since Shakespeare have been able to evoke so harrowingly the nightmare world of savage animals . . . and of man's kinship with them."[28] Later Ted Hughes would call it "a burningly radiant, intensely beautiful book."[29]

A new note, however, cropped up in William Barrett's brief, anonymous review for the *Atlantic Monthly*, one that would persist throughout Singer's career. "Singer's art," Barrett wrote, "has the simplicity of artlessness itself. Without any literary tricks, and using the simplest of language, he brings the whole life of that remote world, with its primitive and superstitious peasantry, haunted and vision-filled Jews, as vividly before us as this morning's dawn."[30] So arose another question that would follow Singer: was he the consciously meticulous craftsman or the naive and naturally gifted storyteller?

Implicitly addressing the issue of development raised by Irving Howe, Stanley Edgar Hyman articulated a progression in ideas in Singer's work from the depiction of evil in *Satan in Goray* through the withdrawal from that evil by withdrawal from the world in *The Magician of Lublin* to a transcendence through love in *The Slave*: "As it denies *Satan in Goray*, *The Slave* reverses *The Magician of Lublin*. Conversion now is *into* the world, *into* the embrace of nations. The highest value is human attachment rather than asceticism, ethics rather than observance. Jacob is Yasha reborn, but where Yasha suffered like Job, to glorify God, Jacob suffers like Moses, to prepare him to free those held in bondage."[31] In his review essay published the following year, poet Ted Hughes also differed with Howe's conclusions regarding Singer's lack of development. "Looking over his novels in their chronological order," Hughes wrote, "the first apparent thing is the enormous and one might say successful development of his vision."[32]

Although, in his review of *Short Friday and Other Stories* (1964), Stanley Edgar Hyman declared that "Singer is more than a writer; he is a literature.

. . . Everywhere in the book are marvels and delights,"[33] Warren Miller complained that "the tendency has been to protect, not to examine, to cozen, not criticize." Singer is praised by the ignorant: "For those who suffer nostalgia for what they've never known, Singer is a little genre painter offering heartwarming portraits."[34] Miller's implication, that the non-Jew simply cannot understand nor evaluate Singer's work, has been at issue throughout Singer criticism. Paddy Chayefsky declared that it did not matter if one knew little of the Yiddish literary tradition because Singer was outside any tradition.[35]

As these early reviews grappled with the appropriate context in which to place Singer, the American immigrant who wrote in Yiddish but seemed not to be a Yiddishist, the issue of his modernism kept emerging. It reshaped itself in existential terms in Ted Hughes's April 1965 review essay. He discussed Singer's genius as that which prevents his disintegration into either piety or despair. His vision brings him to the existential wasteland typified by modernism and then moves beyond it to rebuild his faith. He transforms Hasidic tradition into a source of universal significance. Hughes praised Singer for his poetic imagination and concluded that "his powerful, wise, deep, full-face paragraphs make almost every other modern fiction seem by comparison labored, shallow, overloaded with alien and undigested junk, too fancy, fuddled, not quite squared up to life."[36]

The latter half of the decade of the sixties brought a great deal of success for Singer. In 1965 *The Family Moskat* was reissued to respectable reviews. In 1966 Singer began serialization in the *Forward* of what would later be translated and published as *Enemies, A Love Story*. His first in a long series of children's books, *Zlateh the Goat*, illustrated by Maurice Sendak, was published and won for Singer his first Newbery Award. Irving Howe edited and introduced a selection of Singer's stories. In 1966, Singer brought out his first collection of quasi-fictional memoirs, *In My Father's Court*, previously published in Yiddish in 1956. The last years of the 1960s brought Singer two more Newbery Awards and American Library Association notations for his children's stories and a nomination for the National Book Award for *The Manor*. With the publication by the *New Yorker* of "The Slaughterer," collected in *The Seance and Other Stories*, Singer began an association with that magazine that lasted until his death.

In a hostile essay the year before the English publication of *In My Father's Court*, Jacob Glatstein had written, "it is a good thing for Bashevis' world reputation that he published his memoirs only in a Yiddish newpaper. Rarely has a writer committed to publication such trivial, common-place and egocentric effusions."[37] But the English-speaking American press praised the collection. Alfred Kazin wrote that Singer "looks back, presents life as a dream, even as a dream within a dream. . . . Yet each detail is an example of the power of literature to transform experience into myth, to give to the irrecoverable, the unbelievable past, its present status as legend."[38] But while Kazin admitted that the work "seems anecdotal and unconnected,"[39] Albert H. Friedlander found it to be "one of the truly outstanding books in its genre."[40] Jules Chametzky praised the book as both "the record of a most gifted man's spiritual and emotional growth" and a glimpse "into the workshop of an artist."[41] How, Chametzky asks, is Singer's past—the lost past of lost Jewry—to be reclaimed in literature? "How to reclaim the indispensable past—*this* past—without false sentimentality, without frozen and conventional responses, and without dishonor to the dead? That, I think, is the true nature of the 'literary' experiment Singer assays in this memoir. The last word in the book is 'love,' and it is with love, dignity and restraint that Singer walks his difficult tightrope and achieves the miracle of art."[42]

A year later, Chametzky also wrote one of the most insightful reviews of *The Manor*, another of the growing number of reviews that, following the lead of Ted Hughes, placed Singer in the context of existentialism. "In all of Singer's work," wrote Chametzky, "I find a profound sense, by implication, of the contemporary void—one that begins at the moment of recognition noted above—and a bodying forth of the knowledge that its negotiation requires the most delicate, and perilous, balance between worlds lost and found, known and unknown."[43] In the *New Yorker* review of *The Manor* and *The Estate*, L. E. Sissman again raised the issue of translation, concluding that only as Singer becomes increasingly fluent with English vernacular and continues to control his translations will this "writer of the first importance . . . carry his own gift of style, the mechanics of his vision, across the bridge from Poland to America."[44] *The Seance and Other Stories* received mixed reviews. "Singer's touch remains firm and sure," wrote the *Times Literary Supplement*,[45] but the *New York Times Book Review*, in an essay that made a rather baffling reference to Singer as "a sort of Jewish Sholom Aleichem," charged that "too often his stories are merely interested in describing a kind of fiddler-on-the-roof Poland."[46]

The decade of the seventies began with Singer's first National Book Award, given for his children's book *A Day of Pleasure*, and, before the decade ended, he was to receive another National Book Award and the Nobel Prize for Literature. Along with several works for children and a second volume of memoirs, his story collections in the seventies included *A Friend of Kafka*, *A Crown of Feathers*, *Passions*, and *Old Love*, and his novels included *Enemies, A Love Story*, and *Shosha*.

Time lauded *A Friend of Kafka and Other Stories* as "miraculous creations . . . in the highest artistic tradition, true stories,"[47] while the *New York Times* could only complain that an entire collection of Singer's stories might suffer from "the possible dilution of magic performed in quantity."[48] This reference to the repetitiousness of Singer's stories had been made in the past by more than one reviewer and is at the heart of Irving Howe's concern with the lack of development in Singer's work. In reviewing *A Crown of Feathers and Other Stories*, for which Singer won in 1973 his second National Book

Award, Michael Wood defended him, mentioning that more than half of the stories in this collection had contemporary, rather than *shtetl*, settings, and noted "a remarkable range of styles and tones, from farcical to macabre, through mocking and tender and earnest." Wood discussed Singer's ability to evoke the distances of "moral and cultural space" that separate people.[49]

Writing of another kind of distance—the space between the present and the remembered past—Nero Condini, in a review of *Passions* for *the Village Voice*, wrote that Singer's characters are defeated by "nostalgia for a world of meaning that is the center of Jewish life." He also articulated renewed criticism of Singer's repetition. *Passions*, he wrote, "is a recapitulation of all that precedes it," and Singer seems compelled to write one single book: "His stories are a long biography of himself, the good, famous Yiddish writer. It's a joke, isn't it? Let us rather say that Singer, whose art is oral at its origin, has the amiable, excusable defect of the good ranconteur: He repeats a lot, as bards of old."[50]

Charles E. Vernoff's review of *Passions* for *America* renewed the discussion of another thread running through the history of Singer's reviews. He itemized specific elements of Singer's narrative skill in sustaining intensity through understatement and credibility through first-person narration.[51] Roger Sale, on the other hand, writing in the *New York Times*, placed Singer in an oral, storytelling tradition and repeatedly described him as if he were a medium of cultural transmission, the naive storyteller of William Barrett's early review. Singer is a reporter of material so rich, Sale contends, that it does not need an artist to shape it: "When life itself grants all this, why invent? . . . it is life, not an author, that does the essential shaping."[52] But, as Michael Wilding would later put it in a review of *The Image*, "This is to underestimate Singer's very real achievement in bringing these materials to life. Is his source, in fact, any richer than anyone else's? Isn't all life a rich source? Isn't it a mark of his creativity that he gives the impression of a marvelous fund of material—when it is only from what he has made of his material that such an impression can be received? The creativity is so rich, the storytelling so fertile, that we then postulate a pre-existent source."[53]

In his review of *Old Love*, Robert Alter found a disturbing violence undistanced by the folkloric techniques of the earlier tales and concluded that what is most praiseworthy in Singer's *oeuvre* is often overlooked—stories of innocence and simplicity, celebrations of life and love "in the middle of our terrible century."[54] Richard Burgin declared himself "baffled by those critics who relentlessly stress Singer's devotion to traditional literary and 'moral' values while ignoring the meanings that are apparent behind the surface simplicity." Focusing on ontological issues, Burgin maintained that the problem of knowledge itself is at issue in Singer's work, both as theme and technique. His fiction creates a world stressed by "two fields of tension: the continuity of concrete detail and the world of deception, ambiguity, and misconception. . . . [Singer] manages to dramatize eternal paradoxes in a wholly contemporary fashion without making us overly aware of it."[55]

The novels of the seventies received mixed reviews. While *Enemies, A Love Story* was seen by the *Atlantic Monthly* as somewhat contrived, with a plot that verged on farce,[56] the *Times Literary Supplement* disagreed, citing how Singer resists "launching into all-out farce" and concluded that "this is a fine addition to a legendary body of work."[57] The *New York Times* called it "bleak, obsessive."[58] In the *New York Review of Books*, Thomas Edwards wrote that Singer "elevates this farce situation into tragicomedy." Contextualizing the novel in a non-Jewish tradition, Edwards described Herman as "a very special kind of picaro, and as a character who tries to invent his own life, fabricating through deceit a counterreality for himself to occupy."[59] Lis Harris praised *Shosha* as "more evocatively other-worldly than usual," a ghostly fairy tale of a capricious love that links the modern narrator with his old-world past just before it is obliterated in the Holocaust.[60] But Leon Wieseltier referred to *Shosha's* "obituary spirit," and called it another "mordant retrieval . . . a stunted novel about stunted lives."[61]

Wieseltier's essay reviewing *Shosha*, a reissue of *Gimpel the Fool and Other Stories*, and Singer's second selection of memoirs, *A Young Man in Search of Love*, was intensely hostile and reiterated much of the negative criticism that had been directed towards Singer from Yiddishists. Wieseltier contended that Singer not only introduces a profusion of philosophical notions to take the place of faith, but his characters do not always understand them (and by implication, neither does their author). He accused Singer of enjoying the spectacle of Jewish suffering and indulging a fascination with sin, and of a "proud and bilious indifference to the character of piety that further vitiates Singer's thirst for its collapse." He pointed out Singer's misogyny: "Singer seems to detest women. . . . they are . . . no more than creation's most savory forms of pork."[62] Disparaging Singer's non-Yiddish readers, Wieseltier concluded that Singer hates and undermines Jewish tradition, that "he has taken an extraordinary vengeance in literature: a joyless, acid portrait of Jewish life surrendered to demons and doubt . . . [one which] agrees nicely with that facile infatuation with the demonic that currently prevails in American culture . . ."[63]

Robert Alter's review of *Old Love* summarized the critical consensus of Singer by decade's end:

A great writer with a decidedly uneven production, who does not work equally well in all the fictional genres he has tried, who exhibits a dangerous tendency to repeat himself, and whose recent books lack the peculiar strengths of his earlier work.

This consensus, which strikes me as eminently justified, reflects a decided preference for the tales dealing with prewar Polish Jewry over the stories with a contemporary and New World or Israeli setting; views Singer as primarily a writer of short fiction and not as a novelist; and among the novels finds the large family chronicles like *The Family Moskat* and *The Estate* least interesting, the novels like *Satan in Goray* and *The Magician of Lublin*, which read like sustained fables, the most arresting.[64]

The decade of the eighties through Singer's death in 1991 saw the publication of additional children's stories, another volume of memoirs, and *The Collected Stories*. New novels included *The Penitent*, *The King of the Fields*, and *Scum*, and, posthumously, *The Certificate* and *Meshugah*. New story collections included *The Image* and *The Death of Methuselah*. In 1989, the American Academy and Institute of Arts and Letters bestowed on Singer its highest award, the Gold Medal.

The reviews of his last novels were mixed. *The Penitent*, which had been serialized in the *Forward* in 1974, "ought not to have been translated at all," according to Harold Bloom.[65] Writing for the *Times Literary Supplement*, Thomas Sutcliffe found it a book in which "Singer allows the attractions of faith and its ugliness to exist side by side," an "honest and compassionate book, with its own complex hero."[66] But Stefan Kanfer wrote that *The Penitent* "exhibits Singer's narrative mastery, but none of his compassion . . . As in the past, Singer fuses two styles: the fabulist confined to his *shtetl* and the modernist who regards the universe as a stark and enigmatic combat zone."[67] But Bloom maintained that "it is a very unpleasant work, without any redeeming esthetic merit or human quality."[68]

The King of the Fields was also a disappointment, "more reminiscent of a bad-imitation *Clan of the Cave Bear* than anything in the Nobel Prize–winner's beguiling canon."[69] *Scum* received more moderate reviews. The *Los Angeles Times* concluded that it is "not quite as surprising or sharp-edged as some of Singer's more recent books, and it's not quite as sublime as Singer's most enchanting and enduring work. Even so, *Scum* is still vintage stuff: robust, assured, passionate, richly peopled and driven by the stopwatch pacing that is the unremarked strength of Singer's storytelling."[70] The *New York Times* approached it as a deft and skillful recreation of the pre-Holocaust Polish-Jewish communty.[71] And John Bayley, for the *London Review of Books*, read it paired with the autobiographies, concluding that "all the old animation is there, and the joy in belonging heart and soul to this great and vital race, but there is melancholy too: the sense of limitation, the recognition of his impotence—his powerlessness to be an original artist and a man outside his race."[72] Clive Sinclair speculated that the novel may have been written in the 1950s, when Singer was writing both old-fashioned family sagas and modernist stories. He suspected that the translation was done directly from a serialized version without "any authorial reconsideration. There are uncharacteristically crude devices . . ."[73]

From the late fifties onward, Singer had been careful to control his

English translations. But in the last years of his life, when his health had failed, several new translations appeared, and posthumous publications are now appearing. It is not yet known, but it is important to know, how involved Singer was in publication and translation decisions. As Sinclair put it, "There is much of Singer's work that remains untranslated. Presumably, that will change now that he is dead. It is important to know when these 'new' novels were conceived, and whether their author considered that publication in book form would enhance his reputation. . . . Fortunately, *Scum*, though no masterpiece, is interesting enough for this to do no harm."[74]

The last collections of stories fared much better. David Leavitt wrote that *The Image and Other Stories* "splendidly confirms [Singer's] achievement." In it are "magnificent achievements" and "stunning prose."[75] ". . . rich and valuable," Zachary Leader of the *Times Literary Supplement* called it.[76] The frequent use of Singer's familiar framing device—a Singer-like character is told a story—was found repetitious by some reviewers. Leavitt called it "a bit of a cheat," particularly when it relieves the author of the responsibility of having created in some instances (such as "The Bond") misogynistic or sadomasochistic stories. An author who poses as a mere listener exempts himself from making moral judgments. As Michael Wilding put it, "The Bond" is "a vicious and dangerous piece, and the strategy of framing it in no way exonerates Singer from the responsibility of reproducing it."[77] However, Leader saw in the listener-narrator an appropriate distancing device that could mute sentiment "particularly in the more disturbing or violent stories."[78] Janet Hadda saw the narrative device itself as Singer's real subject matter—the "belletristic version of himself," a passionate story collector who serves as a screen through which a vanished world is remembered.[79]

The *Times Literary Supplement* called *The Death of Methuselah and Other Stories*, rather patronizingly, a "remarkable collection . . . [which] demonstrates the universality of Singer's 'little world.' "[80] In his review of the collection, Jay Cantor renewed the issue of Singer's misogyny: "Disorder is too often, and too sourly, identified with the failings of his women characters, their real, or imagined lack of fidelity. Repeated in many of the stories, this obsession seems crabbed, unequal to the metaphysical weight that Singer wants to give it."[81]

Posthumous publication of *The Certificate* and *Meshugah*, both of which had earlier been serialized in the *Forward*, gave Singer's readers a reminder of his quintessential narrator—a Singer look-alike beset by a trio or more of women on his melancholic and angst-filled journey through life. "Singer is the most magical of writers," wrote Lore Dickstein for the *New York Times*, "transforming reality into art with seemingly effortless sleight of hand. His deceptively spare prose has a pristine clarity that is stunning in its impact. . . . Isaac Bashevis Singer lives."[82]

ESSAYS

Throughout the history of Singer studies, "Gimpel the Fool" has held the place of honor, and the first critical essay on Singer, Alfred Kazin's "The Saint as Schlemiel," placed "Gimpel" within the lengendary Jewish arche-type—the saint as *schlemiel*—and compared Singer's story with those of I. J. Peretz and Sholem Aleichem. He then extracted Singer from that tradition to place him in an even larger context, and in so doing Kazin addressed the appeal of the Yiddish teller of folk tales to the modernist readers in his English-speaking audience. The attempt to locate Singer firmly within a tradition would provide an ongoing discussion from Kazin, through, notably, Eugene Goodheart, Max Schulz, Leslie Fiedler, Joseph Landis, and Dan Miron. Kazin wrote "Singer's work *does* stem from the Jewish village, the Jewish seminary, the compact (not closed) Jewish society of Eastern Europe. He does not use the symbols which so many modern writers pass on to each other. For Singer it is not only his materials that are 'Jewish'; the world is so. Yet within this world he has found emancipation and universality—through his faith in imagination."[83]

The decade of the sixties saw, in its inauguration, a reassessment by Irving Howe of his initial, rather ardent support of Singer; in its middle came a recommendation by Edmund Wilson that Singer be considered for the Nobel Prize,[84] and by its end a monograph and two collections of critical essays were devoted to Singer. An early, important essay by Eugene Goodheart discussed Singer as "an alien figure" in the Yiddish literary tradi-tion.[85] That tradition involves social criticism, while Singer practices a quietism that is "a sort of passive nihilism"; it uses sentimentality, while Singer, utilizing the perspectives of demons, remains distanced from the suffering of his characters; it maintains a clarity of moral vision, while Singer subverts conventional morality and embodies modernist ambiguity.[86] Irving Howe had discussed Singer's modernism in terms of the reader, who is left unsettled and anxious by stories that "neither round out the cycle of their intentions nor posit a coherent and ordered universe."[87] His world is the modern world of arbitrariness, injustice, and pointless suffering.

Another important and persistent issue concerning the ability to evalu-ate an author known only in translation was raised by Milton Hindus. He pointed out that the English text of *The Family Moskat* ends with the oft quoted line, "Death is the Messiah. That's the real truth," while the Yiddish text, continuing on for a dozen more pages, makes the ending far more ambiguous. English readers can only see the work "through a clouded glass."[88] Dan Jacobson rehearsed the many difficulties of literary translation, not just the translation from tongue to tongue, but the translation of a whole society that has ceased to exist and of a people not only gone, but butchered. The wonder of Singer's narrative power is that, despite all barriers, "to our surprise, we find that we are more like these vanished people than we had ever guessed; and that their lost world, being so fully human, is after all, contiguous with the one we already know."[89]

Ben Siegel's earliest essay on Singer, published in 1963, presented correctives to those who viewed Singer as a naive storyteller: "Singer is no primitive. Despite his exotic materials and idiomatic style, he is a sophisticated stylist with the easy fluency and craftsmanship attained by only the finest writers in any culture";[90] to those who found, in *The Family Moskat*, Singer's "astringent portrait" of Jews facing the Holocaust like the "flaying of a prophet,"[91] Siegel contended that "Singer omits none of their flaws—tragic or pathetic; on the other hand, he unfailingly endows his characters with compensatory flashes of generosity and courage. Failing to win our admiration, they evoke compassion and understanding. At their worst these embattled spirits contain those biological juices which nourished their ancestors down the dark centuries. No outraged prophet, Singer thus forces the reader to pass judgment."[92] Other essays in the early 1960s presented solid reviews of Singer's work or isolated important themes, discussing his affirmation of community (J. A. Eisenberg),[93] the maintenance of faith in a demonic world (J. S. Wolkenfeld),[94] and the use of folkore and the irrational (Michael Fixler).[95].

Singer was not without his detractors. Warren Miller complained that Singer was praised by those ignorant of Jewish life. M. Z. Frank wrote "Even at his best, he runs to the weird, the morbid and the perverse. His work has a surfeit of sex, often in the wrong places."[96] Frank included discussion of Singer's reception by Yiddishists, especially Chonon Ayalti and Leib Feinberg. Ayalti questioned the authority of any non-Yiddish reader to evaluate Yiddish writers. Feinberg suggested that, in Frank's words, "the goyim, Gentile and Jewish, like such stories precisely because in them the Jews are shown up to be even more vicious than the goyim."[97]

Jacob Glatstein continued the attack. He wrote that although Singer's stories have a Jewish facade, they actually read better in translation. In fact Singer's Yiddish lacks "artistic breath," so he is easily translated, there being no nuance or stylistic originality to worry about. The reading tradition of non-Jews has prepared them to be "thrilled" by superstition and horror stories, by dehumanized heroes, and by the "hoary old wives' tales, made alien by villainy, brutality, and cynicism."[98] Glatstein concluded that "it is little short of amazing that this autodidact who has so poorly digested the 'philosophies' he espouses in his memoirs should have gained stature as a world literary figure."[99] Such attacks, particularly from the Yiddish community, would continue throughout Singer's career. As Irving Howe put it, "It is hardly a secret that in the Yiddish literary world Singer is regarded with a certain suspicion."[100]

Jacob Sloan, who had translated *Satan in Goray*, responded to Jacob Glatstein's attack on Singer. He remembered "rejoicing in the felicities of style" in the novel, defended Singer's right to his own imaginative perceptions of *shtetl* life, and suggested that Singer would do well "not to dilute his strength with any more imitations of himself," but to focus on contemporary treatments of the modern world.[101] Irving Howe also defended Singer's Yiddish, a "prose with a verbal and rhythmic brilliance that, to my knowledge, can hardly be matched. . . . Behind the prose there is always a spoken voice, tense, ironic, complex in tonalities, leaping past connectives."[102]

In 1968 *Isaac Bashevis Singer and the Eternal Past*, the first book-length study of Singer, was published by Irving Buchen and included chapters on each of the novels plus a discussion of the short stories. Buchen maintained that to foreground either Singer's Yiddish traditions or his modernist connections is to distort the whole. Singer's fiction serves as "an historical crucible for the meeting of the living and the dead, the modern and the ancient."[103] Singer's demons had most often been discussed either as otherworldly barriers to empathetic responses to his characters whose inner lives are always distanced from the reader, or, conversely, as psychological manifestations of those inner lives. Linda Zatlin would make the division one between "soul drama" or "pysche drama."[104] Buchen, instead, suggested that "the unconscious and the cosmic are not alternatives but avenues to each other."[105]

In his study of contemporary Jewish-American writers, Max Schulz pointed out that "one of the central paradoxes of Singer's fictional world is that even as he pays loving tribute to the value system of a back-country Jewry—. . . firm in a simplistic faith in . . . 'a seeing universe, rather than a blind one'—Singer questions such a world picture with the narrative structures he composes for them."[106] Singer moves between belief and skepticism, denying the moral cohesion of the world. As Schulz makes clear, "the danger in this strategy is real, for the coherence of Singer's fictional world depends on his maintaining a perilous tension between irreconcilables. If he relaxes an instant, his story is threatened with fragmentation."[107] Reading Schulz helps to contextualize what had begun to be seen, in the wake of Ted Hughes, as Singer's existentialism. What looks like existentialism may more likely be the Jewish capacity for acceptance of the absurdity and incoherence of the world "without losing faith in the moral significance of human actions."[108]

The decade ended with the publication of two collections of essays and Ben Siegel's publication of an overview of Singer's work and reception for the Minnesota series of pamphlets on American writers.[109] Irving Malin's collection, *Critical Views of Isaac Bashevis Singer*, reprinted essays, reviews, and interviews published throughout the decade as well as several new pieces and a valuable bibliography. Marcia Allentuck's collection, *The Achievement of Isaac Bashevis Singer*, included studies of *The Family Moskat*, *Satan in Goray*, *The Magician of Lublin*, *The Manor*, and *The Slave*, as well as several short stories, including "Gimpel the Fool," and "The Spinoza of Market Street." Eli Katz brought a new perspective to bear on the assumption that Yiddishists disliked Singer because of his negative portrayals of Jews. He pointed out that a "study of Yiddish literature . . . reveals that the classical Yiddish literary tradition itself is not predominantly one of prettification; that the sores and boils which afflicted East European Jewish life were plainly evident to the older writers and were unabashedly treated in their literary works."[110] Katz saw Singer's deviation from the Yiddish literary tradition in his use of the irrational and in his portrayal of disintegrating, rather than socially cohesive, communities.

The decade of the seventies, which would culminate with Singer's winning the Nobel Prize, opened with an essay on the changing cultural metaphor of the mirror in which George Salamon compared Singer's short story "The Mirror" with E. T. A. Hoffmann's "The Story of the Lost Reflection," revealing how each posits a moral and metaphysical existence of "utter ambiguity."[111] Within the following two years, Ruth R. Wisse and Sanford Pinsker published books on the figure of the schlemiel, each with a chapter on "Gimpel the Fool," and Irving Malin wrote an introduction to Singer for Ungar's Modern Literature Monograph series.[112] Wisse discussed Gimpel as a rare post-holocaustal example of the believing fool. "Raised by Singer to his most exalted extreme, the schlemiel defies all rational distinctions and even the limits of life in his determination to remain fully human."[113]

Edwin Gittleman, who had written a brilliant analysis of *Satan in Goray*, did the same for the narrative voices in *A Friend of Kafka*, discussing how the process of telling is itself the primary reality of Singer's fiction:

> While the mode of narration increases the formal distance separating the reader-listener from the substance of the narrative, it nevertheless creates an intimacy between narrative voice and reader. Each is engaged in a reciprocal transaction which defines the other's role. But it is a dangerous intimacy. In effect, the narrative voice aggressively invades the consciousness of the reader and struggles to control it. An alien presence whose revelations resist being confirmed by the reader's own experience, the narrative voice nevertheless has succeeded in dramatizing and enacting the one basic experience which makes Singer's aural act of the short story possible: the reader, while reading, is— without understanding it at the time—possessed by a *dybbuk*.[114]

My essay, "The Hidden God of Isaac Bashevis Singer," provided an overview that placed Singer in the context of secular absurdists, but acknowledged that his was a more paradoxical vision: "Singer's doubt concerning the nature of eternity produces fiction which maintains an uneasy coalescence of dread and consolation."[115]

In *The Resonance of Dust*, Edward Alexander furthered Mary Ellmann's discussion of Singer's critique of social Darwinism:[116] "the main thrust of Singer's attack is directed against the evolutionist belief in perpetual and progressive motion, because, as historians have often argued, it is analogous to the Marxist belief in the infallibility of the historical process."[117] Within this critical framework, Alexander provided readings for *Satan in Goray*, *Enemies, A Love Story*, and *The Family Moskat*.

The study of Singer's elusive identity in American letters continued to engage critics in the seventies. Abraham Bezanker reiterated how Singer "straddles two worlds, the West European culture with its emphasis upon irony, detachment, and cynicism, and the Yiddish culture with its greater warmth, religiosity, and its Chassidic regard for the occult."[118] Josephine Knopp elaborated on the "duality in Singer's relationship to the Yiddish literary tradition,"[119] to contextualize her sensitive analyses of *Satan in Goray* and *The Magican of Lublin*, but neither critic went beyond what Goodheart and Katz had had to say on this issue. Ruth R. Wisse did. Her post-Nobel retrospective pushed forward discussions of Singer's "difference" by introducing into the debate concerning his place the fact of Singer's "curious detachment": "His position between the contending values of a traditional past and an ideologically-impelled future seems to have endowed Singer with a curious detachment, curious certainly within the mainstream of Jewish literature which took any number of directions but was invariably *engagé*. More onlooker than participant, Singer has seen the forces of opposing ideas canceling one another out . . . Singer has referred to himself as 'unsentimental.' He did not nurse ideals that could be shattered, or trust the human condition enough to believe in ultimate remedies."[120]

In this valuable essay on Singer's narrative technique, Wisse addressed the issue of the naive storyteller, a role that Singer, the public man, played for the amusement of his audiences. But Wisse demonstrated that Singer was not only a studied craftsman but an essayist who "has carefully considered the nature of his craft."[121] His early commitment to narrative realism, a commitment formed in opposition to literary expressionism, was followed by the use of historical chronicles and folk material "to explore those subjects and ideas that could not be treated with sufficient freedom in contemporary realistic settings."[122] Yet, by containing his folk material within a realistic form, Singer "undercuts the assumptions of materialism and natural reason on which literary realism rests."[123]

In attempting to locate a niche for Singer outside the Yiddish tradition, the early reviews and essays foregrounded his modernism. Singer had never been accepted in academic circles as a modernist, however. Ben Siegel's essay on *Enemies, A Love Story*, situated Singer "closer to the European tradition— Jewish and non-Jewish—than to the novels and tales of his contemporaries in America. . . . He avoids any trace of those 'advanced techniques' of collage and parody and quick shifts of consciousness now captivating so many fictionists. Nor does he allow language to dominate his events. Instead, he relies on the storyteller's conventional devices: suspense and humor, direct character depiction, and the lucid unfolding of action."[124]

In her essay, straightforwardly entitled "I. B. Singer's Misogyny," Evelyn Torton Beck, citing examples of Singer's derogatory stereotyping of women, introduced an important issue, which later, with the publication of "The Bond" in *The Image and Other Stories* would become more widely discussed.[125] Although acknowledging the cultural context of Singer's misogyny, Torton Beck insisted upon his responsibility in creating portraits damaging to women.

The eighties and early nineties brought an array of critical works on Singer. Books included introductions by Edward Alexander and Lawrence Friedman and my study of the Kabbalic subtexts of Singer's fiction, as well as a monograph by David Neal Miller, two collections of interviews, and a collection of essays.[126] In 1981, the inaugural issue of the new series of *Studies in American Jewish Literature* was devoted to Singer, and in 1985 and 1989 respectively, issues of *Yiddish* and *Prooftexts* were partially devoted to Singer. Thematic studies of individual novels and stories proliferated. Among the many notable examples were those of Bonnie Lyons and Judith Finde Sheridan, who looked at Singer's use of sexuality as a metaphor of cosmic redemption, its misuse as a metaphor of damnation.[127] Sarah Blacher Cohen treated the women in *Enemies, A Love Story*, and *Shosha* as forceful motivators of male protagonists.[128] Sam Girgus focused on the woman as demon, a dangerous outsider who "questions the validity of all aspects of a patriarchal society's assumptions."[129] Thomas Hennings delineated thematic and structural parallels between "Gimpel the Fool" and the Book of Hosea.[130] Joseph Sherman placed *Enemies, A Love Story*, in the context of Singer's major works, which, as Asa Heshel Bannet put it in *The Family Moskat*, deal with characters who "had lost God and had not won the world."[131] Anita Susan Grossman explored the problems of Singer's mixing of genres in his fictionalized autobiographies and in his autobiographical fiction,[132] a subject that Anita Norich would richly contextualize with discussions of the autobiographical writings of three Singer siblings.[133]

Singer's apolitical stance had been the subject of discussions in reviews by social critics. In academic writing the issue often emerged in thematic studies of messianism, such as Julian Rice's essay on "The Captive," a story that views Zionism as messianic heresy.[134] According to John Milfull's discussion of messianism in Benjamin, Singer, and Kafka, Walter Benjamin was able to balance elements of the sacred and of the profane—that is, to remain faithful to messianic beliefs while embracing Marxism—and perhaps to see in the fulfillment of Marxist ideals in human society a concomitant messianic fulfillment. Singer, on the other hand, conflates messianic dreams and social utopias and reveals their inevitable collapse into a renewed exile.[135]

In "Isaac Bashevis Singer; or, The American-ness of the American Jewish Writer," Leslie Fiedler pushed forward the discussion of Singer's place in American letters. While Singer's status as a "Jewish" writer is called into question by Yiddishists, his status as an "American" writer is implicitly questioned by American readers who see him only as ethnically defined. But Fiedler suggests that there are three writers called Isaac—Isaac Warshafsky, the journalist of the *Forward*; Isaac Bashevis, the writer of Yiddish books; and Isaac Bashevis Singer, the writer of novels and stories published in English—"American English, American."[136] Not only does Singer have an increasing body of fiction set in America, but "lostness" is the leitmotiv of this fiction. And it is this theme that "makes him seem finally one of us, one more Stranger in a Strange Land; which is to say, one more American."[137] Fiedler suggests that the "American version of his Polish hayloft" into which Herman Broder seems to lose himself at the end of *Enemies, A Love Story*, is "nothing more nor less than America itself: the Wilderness America of writers Singer has never read, like Melville and Twain, Hemingway and Faulkner, Mailer and Bellow—a mythic land as invisible to the other characters in Singer's novel as their world is to us, except in his pages where improbably our boundaries meet."[138]

Considerations of Singer from a postmodern perspective were central to several important essays. David Packman discussed Singer's first-person narrator, the "I" who "slides between worlds—fact and fiction; non-text and text . . . Having inscribed himself into a fictive world, the author becomes a textual fragment: paradoxically, less the text's creator than its creation. . . . Singer's ghostly existence in translation is a metaphor for the dissociation any writer may perceive between self and text . . ."[139] Eileen Bender provided a valuable treatment of Singer's work as it has been reinscribed in film and in so doing suggested another way of approaching the debate among Singer scholars regarding translation. She wrote: "He is consistently duplicitous. His writing is in the language of simultaneous translation: actually, his original copybook scripts are in Yiddish, for which there is a dwindling number of literate readers. Singer's English, which he continues to regard as a borrowed tongue, must be tested with 'translators': he joins his imagination to theirs. 'To me,' he tells us. 'the translation becomes as dear as the original.' Yet he seeks not a definitive version, but an intertextual simulation, alive to double possibilities, registering both reality and ghostly afterimage."[140]

Ken Frieden treated the monologues of demonic narrators as an analogue of Yiddish itself:

Yiddish lives on in scattered communities and in books; the demon, like a Yiddish writer, lives off the textual past. . . . the demonic narratives give voice to the Yiddish language itself, which calls to us from the ruins. But given the diversity of the modern world, we are overwhelmed by an apocalyptic din of—not monologue, but—polylogue. Beyond these conflicting voices we may sense the distant echo of a more familiar voice without sound. Straining to hear, we begin to grasp the intrinsic power of words. Language transcends the individuality of men and women, and continues to live on after their community is destroyed.[141]

Frieden celebrated the redemptive possibilities of a language that can transcend the destruction of the individual and the community.

My treatment of language in Singer foregrounded the Kabbalah's presumptions concerning the linguistic nature of reality,[142] and, in a later essay, linked Kabbalic allegory with postmodern linguistic theory: "Both linguistic theory and Kabbalic allegory posit meaning as dispersed. . . . For both, meaning is removed and indeterminate. . . . And for both, there is no ultimate foundation of meaning external to the linguistic process . . . meaning is always just a flicker away. Like Singer's crown of feathers, it falls apart just as we think we have grasped it."[143]

In a richly provocative essay, Marilyn Chandler isolated language from the world of experience and argued for the failure of the language of patriarchy to transmit traditions and culture and to make meaningful connections in a post-holocaustal world. From a perspective decidedly different from Fiedler's masculinist reading of *Enemies*, Chandler reread it as Singer's feminist novel. *Enemies* posits the "necessity of a radical new beginning, a return to the Adamic act of naming and a whole reorientation of language, this time through women and womanly experience."[144]

On other fronts, Chone Shmeruk discussed Singer's use of ethnic stereotypes, of parallel structures and of patterns of passage in the historical fiction, some of which has yet to appear in English. His essay introduced a systematic approach to the historical fiction, which, for the most part, has been neglected, and suggested interesting questions, such as the problem of historical veracity, which can be asked in tandem with Singer's autobiographical works. Shmeruk points to the direction in which much fruitful study of Singer remains to be undertaken.[145] He integrates his knowledge of both Yiddish and English texts in a way that avoids the battle over which are Singer's primary texts. Dan Miron's essay, "Passivity and Narration," deftly redefined issues of the apolitical nature of Singer's narrative, his relationship to Yiddish literature, and what has been identified as his existentialism: "In essence, the difference between Bashevis' work and the whole of the modern Yiddish literary corpus . . . reveals itself in one crucial aspect. Bashevis approached the act of literary creation with a base-experience of underlying awareness that falls under the sign of fatalism and nihilism."[146] Acknowledging that it is impossible not to be caught in the spell of Singer's storytelling, Miron calls for (and begins himself) a "substantial critique from a Jewish-Zionist vantage point [that] will have to struggle with Bashevis' work."[147]

The essays written expressly for this volume are rooted in the scholarship of the last thirty-five years, but each extends the existing, or opens new, critical avenues for Singer studies. David Hirsch discusses the American immigrant transformation of Old World piety into New World secularism and, in so doing, treats Singer within a distinctively American cultural context. Workng in the less well-studied arena of Singer's children's literature, Alida Allison has begun the crucial task of working with Singer's translations in manuscript, a project through which she offers insight into Singer's theory of language and into the process of translation itself. Nancy Berkowitz Bate and Joseph Sherman tackle controversial topics concerning gender and sexual orientation. Bate's discussion of Singer's women is a counterpoint to that begun by Evelyn Torton Beck, while Sherman reads Singer's homosexual stories from an Orthodox perspective. Each of these essays should stimulate debate on important issues in Singer scholarship.

Meanwhile, in a tug-of-war that has yet to cease, Yiddishists and American critics continue to engage in a long turf battle over Singer's works. Clearly some Yiddishists have been made uneasy by Singer's "modernism," his stress on sexuality and the irrational, his indifference to traditional Yiddish values, and his acceptance, by those who read him in translation, as a spokesman for a lost Yiddish world. As Joseph Landis pointed out in his eloquent discussion of Singer, "Is it any wonder that much of Isaac Bashevis Singer's Yiddish audience, a product of the Jewish Enlightenment, has read him with, at best grudging admiration, at worst, downright hostility: He so often leaves those readers puzzled. His world seems so familiar. His universe is so strange."[148] Other Yiddishists have denounced Singer even as they have attempted to clear the field of contending views by claiming that only those who can read him in Yiddish hold interpretive rights to his work.

But Singer exists in two, not one, *oeuvres*—one in Yiddish and one in English—or perhaps he exists in some ghostly space between. For most of his working life, when he was closely engaged in the translation process, translating became a revisionary act for him. He called them his second originals, yet his English texts, from which all other translations were authorized, might be considered his final drafts. The claim could be advanced. But to make a claim for definitive texts in either Yiddish or English is to lose sight of the fact that Singer produced texts in both languages. He was a writer and a rewriter, transforming and translating himself anew, embodying within his multiple texts mutable visions that can speak to us anew over time.[149]

That Singer can be read through existentialist eyes or filtered through lenses ground by postmodern linguistic theory does not indicate, as his detractors would have it, that he is a mere chameleon. It means that he is translatable across the changing contexts of twentieth-century thought. That he failed to replicate the Yiddish experience just as some would wish it replicated is of considerable interest, but it is not a useful measure by which to form ultimate judgments about him. The Nobel award citation notwithstanding, he was *not* the historian of a lost world. "Entirely absent from his work is any merely historical motive," wrote Susan Sontag, any "impulse to evoke this world and thereby to preserve it simply because it is both past and mercilessly destroyed."[150] Amid contentious critical voices— those that castigated him for distorting a shared heritage, those that lauded him for being modern and postmodern—Singer kept insisting that he was just telling stories. And so he was. With care, with intelligence, with a savvy awareness of his audience, he gave voice to a uniquely multivalent literature, true to neither one tradition nor another, but only to himself and to all those who, in hearing his voice, can recognize their own.

Notes

1.   In a series of bibliographies, David Neal Miller has undertaken the work of finding and dating all of Singer's work in Yiddish. See Miller, *Bibliography of Isaac Bashevis Singer* (New York: Peter Lang, 1983).

2.   Richard Plant, "Frustrated, Undying," *New York Times*, 22 October 1950, 34.

3.   Nathan Rothman, "Jews before 'The Wall,' " *Saturday Review*, 25 November 1950, 18.

4.   Joshua Kunitz, "Passion without Nobility," *New York Herald Tribune Book Review*, 19 November 1950, 24.

5.   For an exception to this perspective, see Eli Katz, "Isaac Bashevis Singer and the Classical Yiddish Tradition," in *The Achievement of Isaac Bashevis Singer*, ed. Marcia Allentuck (Carbondale: Southern Illinois University Press, 1969), 14–25; discussed below.

6.   Eugene Goodheart, "The Secrets of Satan," *Saturday Review*, 25 November 1961, 28.

7.   Dick Adler, "The Magician of 86th Street," *Book World*, 29 October 1967, 8.

8.   Dachine Rainer, "Goray and the Devil," *Saturday Review*, 17 December 1955, 36.

9.   Meyer Levin, "A False Messiah," *New York Times Book Review*, 13 November 1955, 14.

10.   Irving Howe, "In the Day of a False Messiah," *New Republic*, 31 October 1955, 20.

11.   Judd Teller, "Unhistorical Novels," *Commentary* 21 (April 1956): 393.

12.   *New York Times Book Review*, 29 December 1957, 4.

13.   Paul Lauter, "The Jewish Hero: Two Views," *New Republic*, 24 November 1958, 18. Stanley Edgar Hyman would echo Lauter's comparison with Hawthorne in his review of *The Slave* (*New Leader* [23 July 1962]), referring to Singer as "the Yiddish Hawthorne."

14.   Hyman, "The Yiddish Hawthorne," 21.

15.   Milton Hindus, "Isaac Bashevis Singer," *Jewish Heritage* 5 (Fall 1962): 50. Hindus's review in the *New York Times*, 26 June 1960, 26, states, "if upon rereading his book we are not convinced that he has altogether succeeded, it is clear that he is a writer of far greater than ordinary powers."

16.   Milton Rugoff, "The Odd Saga of Yasha Mazur, Magician," *New York Herald Tribune Book Review*, 28 August 1960, 7.

17.   Francis King, "Egypt's Exodus," *New Statesman*, 15 September 1961, 355–56.

18.   Irving Howe, "Demonic Fiction of a Yiddish Modernist," *Commentary* 30 (October 1960): 351.

19.   Ibid.

20.   Irving Howe, "Stories: New, Old, and Sometimes Good," *New Republic*, 13 November 1961, 19, 22.

21.   Goodheart, "Secrets of Satan," 28.

22.   Herbert Kupferberg, "Where Evil and Good Walk Side by Side," *New York Herald Tribune*, 19 November 1961, 7.

23.   David Lodge [Review of *The Spinoza of Market Street and Other Stories*], *Spectator*, 11 May 1962, 628.

24. Goodheart, "Secrets of Satan," 28.
25. Hindus, "Singer," 52.
26. Frieda Clark Hyman, "Jewish Themes in Recent Fiction," *Jewish Spectator*, October 1962, 24.
27. Jean Stafford, "The Works of God, the Ways of Man," *New Republic*, 18 June 1962, 21.
28. David Boroff, "The Sins of a Good and Pious Man," *Saturday Review*, 16 June 1962, 19.
29. Ted Hughes, "The Genius of Isaac Bashevis Singer," *New York Review of Books*, 22 April 1965, 9.
30. "Exotic but Not Remote," *Atlantic Monthly*, August 1963, 143.
31. Stanley Edgar Hyman, "The Yiddish Hawthorne," *New Leader*, 23 July 1962, 21.
32. Hughes, "Genius," 8.
33. Stanley Edgar Hyman, "Isaac Singer's Marvel's," *New Leader*, 21 December 1964, 17, 18.
34. Warren Miller, "The Last of the Line," *Nation*, 4 January 1965, 15–16.
35. Paddy Chayefsky, "Of Dybbuks and Devilkins," *Reporter*, 22 April 1965, 85.
36. Hughes, "Genuis," 10.
37. Jacob Glatstein, "The Fame of Bashevis Singer," *Congress Bi-Weekly*, 27 December 1965, 18.
38. Alfred Kazin, "His Son, the Storyteller," *New York Herald Tribune Book Week*, 24 April 1966, 10.
39. Ibid.
40. Albert H. Friedlander, "Rabbis, Angels, and Demons," *Saturday Review*, 7 May 1966, 91.
41. Jules Chametzky, "In the Shtetl of Bilgoray," *Nation*, 17 October 1966, 392.
42. Ibid., 393.
43. Jules Chametzky, "The Old Jew in New Times," *Nation*, 30 October 1967, 438.
44. L. E. Sissman, "Parallels," *New Yorker*, 7 February 1970, 99.
45. "A World of Their Own," *Times Literary Supplement*, 26 February 1970, 217.
46. Stanley Elkin, "A View from the Outside," *New York Times Book Review*, 20 October 1968, 4, 5.
47. Stefan Kanfer, "Sammler's Planetarians," *Time*, 21 September 1970, 101.
48. Sara Blackburn, "In the Jewish Ghetto and the Ghetto of the Mind," *New York Times Book Review*, 20 September 1970, 45.
49. Michael Woods, "Victims of Survival," *New York Review of Books*, 7 February 1974, 10–12.
50. Nero Condini, "Singer Skips to a Fiery Dance on the Edge of the Abyss," *Village Voice*, 2 February 1976, 49–50.
51. Charles E. Vernoff [Review of *Passions*], *America*, 22 May 1976, 462–63.
52. Roger Sale, "Isaac Bashevis Singer, Also Known As 'I'," *New York Times Book Review*, 2 November 1975, 7–8.
53. Michael Wilding, "The Slap," *London Review of Books*, 17 April 1986, 22–23.
54. Robert Alter, "Versions of Singer," *New York Times Book Review*, 28 October 1979, 1 ff.
55. Richard Burgin, "The Sly Modernism of Isaac Singer," *Chicago Review* 31, no. 4 (Spring 1980): 67, 65, 67. Leon Wieseltier earlier referred to Singer's "sly modernism"; see "The Revenge of I. B. Singer," *New York Review of Books*, 7 December 1978, 6.
56. Phoebe Adams [Review of *Enemies, A Love Story*], *Atlantic Monthly*, July 1972, 230.

57. "Polygamous Pressures," *Times Literary Supplement*, 17 November 1972, 1387.

58. Lore Dickstein, "Demons of Paranoia," *New York Times Book Review*, 25 June 1972, 5.

59. Thomas Edwards, "People in Trouble," *New York Review of Books*, 20 July 1972, 20–22.

60. Lis Harris, "Soul Expeditions," *New Yorker*, 20 November 1978, 225.

61. Wieseltier, "Revenge," 6.

62. Ibid.

63. Ibid., 8.

64. Alter, "Versions," 1.

65. Harold Bloom, "Isaac Bashevis Singer's Jeremiad," *New York Times Book Review*, 25 September 1983, 3.

66. Thomas Sutcliffe, "Making the Leap into Faith," *Times Literary Supplement*, 23 March 1984, 311.

67. Stefan Kanfer, "Brothers and Masters," *Time*, 17 October 1985, 95.

68. Bloom, "Jeremiad," 3.

69. *Kirkus Reviews*, 15 August 1988, 1189.

70. Jonathan Kirsch, "The Dybbuk Made Him Do It," *Los Angeles Times*, 14 April 1991, 11.

71. Bette Pesetsky, "Looking for Love on Krochmalna Street," *New York Times Book Review*, 24 March 1991, 7.

72. John Bayley, "Singer's Last Word," *London Review of Books*, 24 October 1991, 18.

73. Clive Sinclair, "Singer's Sweetened Poison," *Times Literary Supplement*, 4 October 1991, 25.

74. Ibid.

75. David Leavitt, "Slaves to Lust and Other Passions," *New York Times Book Review*, 30 June 1985, 23, 3.

76. Zachary Leader, "Listening to the Mad Hurricane," *Times Literary Supplement*, 4 April 1986, 356.

77. Wilding, "Slap," 23.

78. Leader, "Mad Hurricane," 356.

79. Janet Hadda [Review of *The Image and Other Stories*], *Los Angeles Times Book Review*, 25 August 1985, 1.

80. Bryan Cheyette, "Mistakes Made and Mended," *Times Literary Supplement*, 21 October 1988, 1180.

81. Jay Cantor [Review of *The Death of Methuselah and Other Stories*], *Los Angeles Times Book Review*, 1 May 1988, 12.

82. Lore Dickstein, "An Account Book Full of Humiliations," *New York Times Book Review*, 24 November 1992, 7.

83. Alfred Kazin, *Contemporaries* (Boston: Little, Brown & Co., 1962), 287.

84. "I recommend him, by the way, to the Swedes if they want to give any more prizes to the highest representatives of a culture which stems straight from the sacred books upon which we have all been brought up." Edmund Wilson, *Commentary* (December 1966): 32.

85. This characterization of Singer was also elaborated on shortly afterwards (October 1960) by Irving Howe who wrote "He is one of the few Yiddish writers whose relation to the Jewish past does not depend on that body of attitudes and values we call Yiddishism. He writes *in* Yiddish, but is often quite apart from the Yiddish tradition. He is, so to say, a writer of the pre-Enlightenment and post-Enlightenment; he would be equally at home with a congregation of medieval Jews and a gathering of modern intellectuals, perhaps more so than at a meeting of the Yiddish P. E. N. Club." "Yiddish Modernist," 352. This review

forms part of Howe's "Introduction," in *Selected Short Stories of Isaac Bashevis Singer* (New York: Modern Library, 1966), which was also published as "I. B. Singer," *Encounter* 26 (March 1966): 60–70.

86. Eugene Goodheart, "The Demonic Charm of Bashevis Singer," *Midstream* 6 (Summer 1960): 88–93.

87. Howe, "Yiddish Modernist," 351.

88. "Isaac Bashevis Singer." *Jewish Heritage* 5 (Fall 1962): 47. See also Irving Saposnik, "Translating *The Family Moskat*," *Yiddish* 1 (Fall 1973): 26–37.

89. Dan Jacobson, "The Problem of Isaac Bashevis Singer," *Commentary* 39 (February 1965): 50.

90. Ben Siegel, "Sacred and Profane: Isaac Bashevis Singer's Embattled Spirits," *Critique* 6 (Spring 1963): 24.

91. "Jews before 'The Wall,' " *Saturday Review*, 25 November 1950, 18.

92. Siegel, "Sacred and Profane," 27.

93. J. A. Eisenberg, "Isaac Bashevis Singer—Passionate Primitive or Pious Puritan?" *Judaism* 11 (Fall 1962): 345–56.

94. J. S. Wolkenfeld, "Isaac Bashevis Singer: The Faith of His Devils and Magicians," *Criticism* 5 (Fall 1963): 349–59.

95. Michael Fixler, "The Redeemers: Themes in the Fiction of Isaac Bashevis Singer," *Kenyon Review* 26 (Spring 1964): 371–86.

96. M. Z. Frank, "The Demon and the Earlock," *Conservative Judaism* (Fall 1965): 1.

97. Ibid., 5.

98. Glatstein, "Fame," 18.

99. Ibid.

100. Howe, "Introduction," xvi. See note 85 above.

101. Jacob Sloan, "I. B. Singer and His Yiddish Critics," *Congress Bi-Weekly*, March 7, 1966, 4–5.

102. Howe, "Introduction," vi.

103. Irving H. Buchen, *Isaac Bashevis Singer and the Eternal Past* (New York: New York University Press, 1968), 206.

104. Linda G. Zatlin, "The Themes of Isaac Bashevis Singer's Short Fiction," *Critique: Studies in Modern Fiction* 2, no. 2 (1969): 41.

105. Zatlin, "Themes," 207.

106. Max F. Schulz, *Radical Sophistication: Studies in Contemporary Jewish-American Novelists* (Athens: Ohio University Press, 1969), 14.

107. Ibid., 19.

108. Ibid., 22.

109. Ben Siegel, *Isaac Bashevis Singer* (Minneapolis: University of Minnesota Press, 1969), 6.

110. Eli Katz, "Isaac Bashevis Singer and the Classical Yiddish Tradition," in *The Achievement of Isaac Bashevis Singer*, ed. Marcia Allentuck (Carbondale: Southern Illinois University Press, 1969), 15.

111. George Salamon, "In a Glass Darkly: The Morality of the Mirror in E. T. A. Hoffmann and I. B. Singer," *Studies in Short Fiction* 7 (Fall 1970): 632.

112. Ruth R. Wisse, *The Schlemiel As Modern Hero* (Chicago: University of Chicago Press, 1971); Sanford Pinsker, *The Schlemiel As Metaphor* (Carbondale: Southern Illinois University Press, 1971; revised and enlarged, 1991); Irving Malin, *Isaac Bashevis Singer* (New York: Ungar Press, 1972).

113. Ruth R. Wisse, "Holocaust Survivor," in Wisse, *The Schlemiel*, 65.

114. Edwin Gittleman, "Dybbukianism: The Meaning of Method in Singer's Short

Stories," in *Contemporary American-Jewish Literature*, ed. Irving Malin (Bloomington: University of Indiana Press, 1973), 257–58.

115. Grace Farrell Lee, "The Hidden God of Isaac Bashevis Singer," *Hollins Critic* 10, no. 6 (December 1973): 2. (Since 1989, my work has been published under the name Grace Farrell.)

116. Mary Ellman, "The Piety of Things in *The Manor*," in *Achievement*, 124–44.

117. Edward Alexander, "The Destruction and Resurrection of the Jews in the Fiction of Isaac Bashevis Singer," *The Resonance of Dust* (Columbus: Ohio State University Press, 1979), 154, 155–56.

118. Abraham Bezanker, "I. B. Singer's Crises of Identity," *Critique* 14, no. 2 (1972): 85.

119. Josephine Knopp, *The Trial of Judaism in Contemporary Jewish Writing* (Urbana: University of Illinois Press, 1975): 33.

120. Ruth R. Wisse, "Singer's Paradoxical Progress," *Commentary* (February 1979): 35.

121. Ibid., 33.

122. Ibid., 35.

123. Ibid.

124. Ben Siegel, "The Jew As Underground Confidence Man: I. B. Singer's *Enemies, A Love Story*," *Studies in the Novel* 10, no. 4 (Winter 1978): 405.

125. For other discussions, see reviews by Leavitt and Wilding, above.

126. Edward Alexander, *Isaac Bashevis Singer* (Boston: Twayne, 1980), and *Isaac Bashevis Singer: A Study of the Short Fiction* (Boston: Twayne, 1990); Lawrence S. Friedman, *Understanding Isaac Bashevis Singer* (Columbia: University of South Carolina Press, 1988); Grace Farrell Lee, *From Exile to Redemption: The Fiction of Isaac Bashevis Singer* (Carbondale: Southern Illinois University Press, 1987); David Neal Miller, *Fear of Fiction: Narrative Strategies in the Work of I. B. Singer* (New York: New York University Press, 1985); Richard Burgin, *Conversations with Isaac Bashevis Singer* (New York: Doubleday, 1985); Grace Farrell, ed., *Isaac Bashevis Singer: Conversations* (Jackson: University Press of Mississippi, 1992); David Neal Miller, ed., *Recovering the Canon: Essays on Isaac Bashevis Singer* (Leiden: E. J. Brill, 1986).

127. Bonnie Lyons, "Sexual Love in I. B. Singer's Work," *Studies in American Jewish Literature* 1 (1981): 61–74; Judith Finde Sheridan, "Isaac Bashevis Singer: Sex as Cosmic Metaphor," *Midwest Quarterly: A Journal of Contemporary Thought* 23, no. 4 (Summer 1982): 365–79.

128. Sarah Blacher Cohen, "Hens to Roosters: Isaac Bashevis Singer's Female Species," *Studies in American Fiction* 10, no. 2 (Autumn 1982): 173–84.

129. Sam B. Girgus, "The Devil and the Demon Woman: Symbols of Freedom in I. B. Singer," *Letterature d'America: Rivista Trimestrale* 6, no. 27 (Spring 1985): 132.

130. Thomas Hennings, "Singer's 'Gimpel the Fool' and The Book of Hosea." *Journal of Narrative Technique* 13, no. 1 (Winter 1983): 11–19.

131. Joseph Sherman, " 'Can These Bones Live?': Destruction and Survival in Isaac Bashevis Singer's *Enemies, A Love Story*," *English Studies in Africa* 26, no. 2 (1983): 141–52.

132. Anita Susan Grossman, "The Hidden Isaac Bashevis Singer: Lost in America and the Problem of Veracity," *Twentieth Century Literature* 30, no. 2 (Spring 1984): 30–45.

133. Anita Norich, "The Family Singer and the Autobiographical Imagination," *Prooftexts* 10 (1990): 91–107.

134. Julian C. Rice, "I. B. Singer's 'The Captive': A False Messiah in the Promised Land," *Studies in American Fiction* 5 (1977): 269–75.

135. John Milfull, "The Messiah and the Direction of History: Walter Benjamin, Isaac Bashevis Singer, and Franz Kafka," in *Festschrift for E. W. Herd*, ed. August Obermayer (Dunedin: Otago German Studies, 1980), 180–87.

136. Leslie Fiedler, "Isaac Bashevis Singer; or the American-ness of the American Jewish Writer," *Studies in American Jewish Literature* 1 (1981): 125; reprinted in *Fiedler on the Roof: Essays on Literature and Jewish Identity* (Boston: David R. Godine, 1991).

137. Fiedler, "American-ness," 129.

138. Ibid., 131.

139. David Packman, "The Anecdotic Author in Isaac Bashevis Singer's 'The Captive,' " *Cross Currents* (1983): 299.

140. Eileen T. Bender, "Androgynous Scribes, Duplicitous Inscription: Isaac Bashevis Singer's Cinematic Dreamscapes," in *The Kingdom of Dreams in Literature and Film*, ed. Douglas Fowler (Tallahassee: Florida State University Press, 1986), 115.

141. Ken Frieden, "I. B. Singer's Monologues of Demons," *Prooftexts* 5, no. 3 (September 1985): 268.

142. Grace Farrell Lee, "Belief and Disbelief: The Kabbalic Basis of Singer's Secular Vision," *From Exile to Redemption* (Carbondale: Southern Illinois University Press, 1987), 12–24.

143. Grace Farrell, "Suspending Disbelief: Faith and Fiction in I. B. Singer," *Boulevard* 9, no. 3 (Fall 1994): 115–16.

144. Marilyn R. Chandler, "Death by the Word: Victims of Language in *Enemies, A Love Story*," *Studies in American Jewish Literature* 7, no. 1 (Spring 1988): 111, 116.

145. Chone Shmeruk, "Polish-Jewish Relations in the Historical Fiction of Isaac Bashevis Singer," *Polish Review* 32, no. 4 (1987): 401–13.

146. Dan Miron, "Passivity and Narration: The Spell of Bashevis Singer," *Judaism* 41, no. 1 (Winter 1992): 8.

147. Ibid., 17.

148. Joseph C. Landis, "I. B. Singer: Alone in the Forest," *Yiddish* 6, nos. 2–3 (Summer–Fall 1985): 20.

149. As poet Willis Barnstone writes, "With the fall of Babel, God dispersed the word, gave us tongues and the solitude of difference, and also the impossible but pleasurable duty to repair our separation. . . . With the deconstruction of Babel, God gave us not only tongues and their anxiety but a knowledge of mutability. After Babel nothing can be seen as fixed, for the eye has discovered that with each passing second every living thing transforms and is translated anew. Even those things inert, dead, are not fixed but are distorting, translating." Willis Barnstone, *The Poetics of Translation* (New Haven: Yale University Press, 1993), 3–4.

150. Susan Sontag, "Demons and Dreams," *Partisan Review* 29, no. 3 (1962): 461.

REVIEWS

♦

In the Day of a False Messiah

IRVING HOWE

In the mid-seventeenth century, the east European Jews were decimated by the rebellion-pogrom of the Cossack leader Chmielnicki. Many of the survivors were then caught up in a religious enthusiasm that derived, all too clearly, from their total desperation. They began to summon apocalyptic fantasies, to indulge in long-repressed religious emotions which, paradoxically, were stimulated by the pressures of Cabbalistic asceticism.

As if in response to their yearning, a messianic pretender named Sabbatai Zevi appeared in the Near East. Everything that rabbinical Judaism had confined or suppressed found release in Sabbatai's movement: the temptation of the doctrine that faith alone will save, the impulse to evade the limits of mundane life by forcing a religious transcendence, the union of erotic with mystical appetites, the lure of a demonism which the very hopelessness of the Jewish situation rendered plausible. In 1665–6 Sabbatianism reached an orgiastic climax, whole communities out of a conviction that the messiah was at hand, abandoning the Mosaic law and the inhibitions of exile.

Their hopes were soon smashed. Confronted with persecution by the Turkish Sultan, Sabbatai converted to Mohammedanism. Nonetheless, Sabbatianism survived for a time as a secret cult which celebrated Sabbatai as the apostate saviour, who had been required to descend to the depths of the world in order to emerge on the heights of salvation.

Satan in Goray, a short novel translated from the Yiddish, shows the Jews of a small Polish town abandoning themselves, in a transport of mass delusion, to the false messiah. It is a remarkable book, brilliant, enigmatic, and it deserves the attention of anyone interested in modern literature. The author, a younger brother of I. J. Singer, is one of the two or three most gifted living writers of Yiddish prose: his command of Yiddish idiom, his range of metaphor, his fierce short-breathed rhythms mark him as virtuoso. Though he has written an interesting longer novel, he is at his best in short forms, grotesque and lyrical outbursts.

Like most Yiddish fiction, *Satan in Goray* is focussed on the community, its main theme, as its main "character," being the collective destiny of the Jews in exile. The norm of communal life is so deeply ingrained in the

From *The New Republic* 133 (31 October 1955): 20. Reprinted by permission.

traditional Jewish imagination that any deviation will constitute a significant action for the Yiddish reader, one inherently possessing those potentialities for conflict and disaster that go to make up the idea of the dramatic. Goray, an obscure Jewish town in Poland, tries to reestablish its life after the Chmielnicki massacres, but people cannot go on as before, not even Jews trained in suffering and endurance. The Rabbi who warns against ecstasies born of mere desire is pushed aside. The town is overwhelmed by a millenial hysteria. First come the ascetics, who break down the sanctions of rabbinic law, and then the possessed and the depraved who experiment in sin and satanism with the justification that the dawn of the messianic age means the lapsing of the Commandments.

Singer has peopled his novel with a number of sharply etched figures: a self-mutilating ascetic who brings the Sabbatian word to Goray and then expires in anguish when his hope is betrayed, a corrupt and dionysian ritual slaughterer who rules Goray in its moment of abandonment, and a haunting epileptic girl who symbolizes the martyrdom of the community, being married first to the ascetic, then to the ritual slaughterer, and finally being entered by the spirit of a dead person.

The prose of *Satan in Goray* is both fast and rich. Singer piles up local detail after detail, partly as a means of authenticating a novel that runs the risk of abstractness and rhetoric because of its concentration on collective life, and partly because he has an enormous interest in everything that is strange and colorful. But for all its local richness, the over-all structure of the book is rigidly economical. Singer makes the boldest elisions in his narrative, cuts through the usual packing of the Yiddish novel, and drives toward his climax with a furious energy. His materials are thoroughly traditional, but he himself is a modern writer who has learned the lessons of Flaubert and Turgenev. Yet because he remains partly attached to the Yiddish literary tradition, he can bring surprising resources to his work. At the climax of the novel, when the epileptic girl is being exorcised of the *dybbuk* and the tension has become almost unbearable, Singer suddenly turns to the meandering archaic mode of the old Yiddish tale, and the result is not merely a fascinating *tour de force* but the achievement of perspective and a kind of serenity.

Partly his power derives from an ability to hold such contrary elements as the miraculous and the skeptical, the moral and the exotic in a delicate tension. At times the style of *Satan in Goray* seems almost *as if* it were the style of a man possessed, so thoroughly does he give himself to the subject; yet he also maintains a rigorous distance, one is always aware of the *conditional* nature of his absorption in the Sabbatian experience. He brings to play upon Jewish life a mind that delights in everything that is antique and curious yet is drenched with the assumptions of modern psychology, and the result is an exquisite balance between the impulse to surrender to his subject and the temptation to deny it.

The translation is extremely good, though it communicates more of the color than the pace of the original Yiddish. But I must quarrel with Mr. Sloan's introduction. He writes: "As Isaac Bashevis Singer . . . reminds us: once the core of faith is gone, Satan must triumph and the forces of evil overwhelm mankind." This gratuitous religiosity has nothing whatever to do with the novel, not even if one could bring a testimonial from the author proclaiming his piety. For the point of Singer's achievement is that it does not lend itself to any such obvious or pre-fabricated point: he accepts the Sabbatian episode as a human experience, tragic, and absurd in its own terms, and not requiring any contemporary tags in order to validate it.

Still more questionable is Mr. Sloan's effort to assimilate the Sabbatian collapse to twentieth century politics. "Like the people of Goray," he writes, "we too have found that . . . there are no simple and complete solutions to the tragic complications of being fallible human beings in an incomprehensible universe." This sentence, laden as it is with the overtones of our contemporary wisdom, indicates that Mr. Sloan has absorbed the message of Edmund Burke or, if one wants to get right up to date, of Russell Kirk; but it has nothing to do with *Satan in Goray*.

The events of our time are enacted by men who, whatever their disagreements, all accept in common the necessity for action *within* history. But the traditional Jewish judgment, which plays an implicit role in the development of Singer's novel, is that salvation cannot come through history. At the end of the archaic fable that climaxes *Satan in Goray*, the "moral"—toward which we may expect so sophisticated a writer as Singer to retain a certain ironic reserve—is stated: "Let none attempt to force the Lord: To end our pain within the world . . ." The heresy of false messianism is that in trying to force a premature apocalypse it enters not the realm of the sacred but the realm of the secular. Messianism is thus reduced to historical action, and historical action itself viewed largely as the province of the demonic. This, at least, is the working imaginative hypothesis of *Satan in Goray*, and regardless of whether Singer as a person fully agrees with it one thing should be clear: it has nothing in common with and should not be assimilated to, the problems of modern politics, all of which are rooted in the common assumption of secular historicity.

Satan in Goray stands in its own right, a work of the imagination which neither permits nor requires easy statements. It is a work that the readers of the *New Republic* should turn to—though one can't help reflecting that even if every *NR* reader did rush out to buy it, that would come to a small percentage of those now absorbed in the troubles of Marjorie Morningstar. But for anyone who wants to distinguish between the genuine possibilities of the Yiddish literary imagination and its debasement in American mass culture, the comparison between Singer and Wouk should be highly instructive—no less instructive than say, a comparison between Maimonides' *Guide to the Perplexed* and Rabbi Liebman's *Peace of Mind*.

Demons and Dreams

SUSAN SONTAG

The typical modern novel is "psychological" in that the world it presents is really a projection, a bodying forth of the self (or selves) whose analysis constitutes the subject of the novel. One feels the novelist does not really believe in the world in which he has ostensibly situated his characters, because we observe that his characters do not believe in it: the self-absorption of the characters in modern fiction devours both themselves and their world. The relations between self and world are variously but quite regularly defined as boredom, disgust, contempt, frustration, nostalgia. The world in such novels is not really "there" in the same sense that the characters are "there"; the arena of the novel has been preempted by the agony of disembodied emotional and intellectual struggles. The farthest reach of the post-classical novel in both its bias toward psychologizing and its verbal inventiveness is identical: it is an empty stage, an infinite enumeration, an indefinitely repeated gesture or cry. The purest form of the post-classical novel is the nightmare.

It is I think altogether to the credit of Isaac Bashevis Singer that his fiction provides modern taste with a generous ration of nightmare, in the form of demons, dreams, deformity, and disease—without sacrificing the centrality of plot or the substantiality of a world. In the age of post-classical fiction, Singer continues to practice the classical virtues. His rare gift for constructing inventive and compelling plots has been much remarked on by critics. What has not been sufficiently commended, however, is his extraordinary power of sensuous evocation. Every page of Singer's fiction is crowded with physical objects—phylacteries and prayer books, handkerchiefs and dogs, dunes and trees, chandeliers and fiddles, lemonade and knives, sleighs and garlic, beards and mice. These things are brought to life for the reader not by being described individually, but simply in their marvelous abundance and rightness of juxtaposition. They are neither accessories in a psychological drama, nor props to make credible a world. In most of his stories, objects are at the very center of the stage, actors in the dialectic between the material world and the spiritual forces, principally demonic,

"Demons and Dreams" by Susan Sontag first appeared in *Partisan Review*, Vol. 29, No. 3 (1962): 460–63. Reprinted by permission of *Partisan Review* and Susan Sontag.

which invade it. There is no need for Singer to describe: objects are there, charged, overcharged, with the tension between their employment as instruments of righteousness and as vessels of demonry.

Singer does not face the typical problem of the modern writer of having to improvise a milieu and make it credible to his readers, or of having to take a familiar (or potentially familiar) milieu and make it exotic to his readers. This is not because of anything inherently more plausible, or answerable to his readers' experience, in the world he presents; but simply because of the unfailing assurance and lack of apologetic distance with which he moves in it. It is an utterly bounded, though not a limited world: that of Eastern European, particularly Polish, Jewry, with its whole complex history from the seventeenth to the early twentieth century of Cabbalistic mysticism and magic, Cossack persecution and massacre, the Sabbatian heresy, Hassidism, and the translation under the pressure of the Enlightenment of the religious ideals of study and pious unworldliness into the secular ideal of the scholar-intellectual. On the face of this highly local and historically dense environment, Singer inscribes the universal conflicts of reason versus the flesh, and of creedal and ritual religion versus a free spirituality. Entirely absent from his work is any merely historical motive, the impulse to evoke this world and thereby to preserve it simply because it is both past and mercilessly destroyed. There is no nostalgia and no pathos, because there is no distance. Singer's fiction is intimate, meticulous, laconic, and unsentimental. At times he reminds one of Babel—except he is more spacious, less ambiguous and troubled in tone.

Singer's characters are typically beset by motives whose clarity and forcefulness confound the hesitations of our modern psychological sophistication. They are wholly conscious motives, that can be ranked on the traditional schedule of virtues and vices. Lust, envy, gluttony, pride, and avarice predominate among the vices; pity, simplicity, and humility among the virtues. (Singer's accounts of gluttony include some of the most stunning descriptions of the pleasures of eating since the *Iliad*.) He brilliantly executes this premodern account of motivation, which includes a self-understanding of character as a drama of contending supernatural forces. Of necessity, these are not characters in the modern, infinitely expandable, individual sense, but creatures of a vigorously collective psychology. Singer presents an image of Jewry not in terms of individuals struggling in an alien setting—the familiar image of the Jew from Shylock to Swann—but in terms of a rigorously bounded, sensuous community of physical things and almost palpable beliefs and avoidances. It is a world whose moving principle is appetite, whether the appetite for learning and salvation or for warm flesh and succulent foods and fine clothes and furnishings, and in this respect most deeply removed from the world of modern fiction, whose principal subject is the failure of appetite and passionate feeling.

In the treatment of his recurrent theme of the temptation of demonry, the strength of Singer's fiction lies in his exploration of the demonic not as a function of individual aberration but as the aberration of a community. The Jewry of which he writes is saturated with magical superstition, and convulsed by the inexplicable sorrows of persecution and the exaltations and hysterias of Messianic hope. It is an era magnetized by the mystery of transgression—enthralling as a subject of fiction and of great interest also as a crucial, but largely suppressed, chapter in Western religious history which reached its climax in the seventeenth century, the century in which Lurianic Cabbalism, with its indeterminate borderline between mysticism and magic, was the dominant spiritual influence throughout the Jewish Diaspora.

Usually in Singer's fiction, the devil has the last word, and his human characters do not survive the paradoxes of their humanity. However, in Singer's latest novel, *The Slave*, as the author himself is reported to have said, for a change God has the last word. The novel is again set in Poland, over a period of twenty years following the Chmielnicki massacres, and traces the fortunes of a virtuous man both desperately encumbered and supremely graced by his spiritual scruples, who struggles with physical bondage, prohibited love, the perverseness of oppression, and the coercions of his own oppressed community. Perhaps precisely because it is a study in goodness, *The Slave* differs from most of Singer's previous work in having a less hectic, less exotic atmosphere. The novel has a warmth, a wholesomeness which befits a work which dares to tell a passionate, exalted love story and to end with a large romantic gesture of reunion-in-death as tearfully satisfying and old-fashioned as the end of *Wuthering Heights*.

The demonic is more alien here, for the main representatives of superstition are the un-Christianized Polish peasants to whom the hero is sold as a slave, rather than the *shtetl* Jews. There is less dwelling on ethnic eccentricity, and more emphasis on the beauty and equanimity of nature. The tone also is more neutral, more classically "novelistic"—it is neither the chatty tone of the folk narrator of some of Singer's stories nor the ironic tone of the malicious spirit or demon who narrates others. The novel also has a greater inwardness of characterization, which follows on the fact that the two main characters are from the inception of the story separated off from their communities. The devout hero, Jacob, is twice alienated from the Jewish community from which he was torn by the Chmielnicki massacres: by solitude and the absence of his books during the period of his slavery, and by love for a Gentile woman, forbidden alike by Jewish and Polish law. The heroine, Wanda, is set apart from her brutish family and neighbors, first by her innate refinement and later by her love for Jacob, and then from the Jewish community in which she can live as Jacob's bride only by pretending to be mute. The novel recapitulates Singer's familiar themes—but at a certain remove, because the hero and heroine both transcend these conflicts. The way in which Jacob succumbs to but finally rejects the Sabbatian temptation, for instance, is only scantily described.

It cannot be denied that Singer has sacrificed a certain exotic intensity and sensuousness in the measured affirmations of *The Slave*. The sensuous charge of Singer's fiction does seem to have some inextricable connection with his vision of a universe in which the negative or demonic pole is the stronger. Let's assume, however, that the modern educated sensibility still has some appetite left for the climaxes of true love and noble death, alongside its appetite for the demonic and fantastic. This being the case, *The Slave* should not only renew our sense of the possibility of still writing good novels but also renew our capacities for emotional catharsis as distinct from the endless exacerbation of the emotions which most modern fiction provides.

Isaac Singer's Marvels

STANLEY EDGAR HYMAN

With the publication of Isaac Bashevis Singer's latest book, *Short Friday and Other Stories*, it becomes obvious that Singer is more than a writer; he is a literature. In a review of *The Slave* in these pages (July 23, 1962), observing that Singer writes moral fables and allegories rather than stories, and romances rather than novels, I called him "the Yiddish Hawthorne." So he is, but one would not know from that comparison how much coarse merriment there is in his work (the Yiddish Rabelais?), or that he can write a model modern short story when he is so inclined (the Yiddish Hemingway?).

Short Friday, with 16 stories translated by a variety of hands, is fuller and more ambitious than Singer's two earlier collections in English, *Gimpel the Fool* (1957) and *The Spinoza of Market Street* (1961): it better displays the breadth of Singer's range. His masterpiece, to my taste, remains "The Black Wedding" in the 1961 volume, but several stories in the new book invite comparison with it.

"Blood" begins with the chilling topic sentence: "The cabalists know that the passion for blood and the passion for flesh have the same origin, and this is the reason 'Thou shalt not kill' is followed by 'Thou shalt not commit adultery.' " "Blood" is about Risha, the young second wife of an elderly pious estate owner. She succumbs to a passion for Reuben the ritual slaughterer that conceals a deeper passion for slaughter itself. In a scene of perverse sensuality, she is excited and seduced by watching Reuben cut the throats of her fowl. Risha progresses inexorably from adultery to slaughtering animals herself and copulating with Reuben as the blood gurgles from severed throats, to selling horsemeat and pork to the Jews as kosher meat, to Christian baptism, to apotheosis as a werewolf eaten by dogs. The story is utterly convincing, not in the realm of the rational (the world does not divide so neatly into vegetarians and werewolves), but in a realm of the imagination where the reader as well as Risha is intoxicated and maddened by the hot gush of blood.

An equally marvelous story, "Yentl the Yeshiva Boy," is about a girl

Reprinted with permission of *The New Leader*, (21 December 1964): 17–18. Copyright © the American Labor Conference on International Affairs, Inc.

whose bedridden father secretly studies Torah and Talmud with her, making her unfit for the life of "the noodle board and the pudding dish." After his death Yentl disguises herself as a yeshiva student named Anshel. By the terrible momentum inherent in each first sin, in Singer's world (as in Hawthorne's), Yentl-Anshel finds herself in love with her friend and fellow student Avigdor, but married to Hadass, the girl Avigdor loves. The recognition scene, in which Yentl is able to convince Avigdor that she is a girl only by showing him the evidence, is as funny, pathetic, and beautiful as anything Singer has written. The mad triangle of the story is ultimately resolved by a symbolic union like that at the end of *The Slave*: Yentl flees, Avigdor marries Hadass, and they produce a son named Anshel.

A third story, almost as remarkable as those two, is "Zeidlus the Pope." It tells of a prodigy of Talmudic study, Zeidel Cohen, who is tempted by Satan (the narrator of the story) and falls. Zeidel's weakness is pride; Satan convinces him that he is "a pearl lost in sand" among the Jews, a petty and small-minded people who exalt mediocrity and are unworthy of their intellectuals (Singer must have enjoyed himself writing those speeches). Zeidel is persuaded to convert to Christianity, where his genius will be acknowledged by his prompt elevation to the throne as Pope Zeidlus the First. Instead, as a Christian Zeidel is the same learned misfit that he was as a Jew. He ends up as a blind beggar, and at his death the imps of Gehenna await him with boiling pitch, and *they* at last acclaim him Pope Zeidlus.

This world of the Jewish *shtetl* in Poland, with an earlock at every ear, and a demon tugging at every earlock, is made blindingly real, as I observed in 1962, at the price of making 20th century America seem phantasmagoric (as perhaps it is). Two stories in *Short Friday* deal with American life; so far as I know they are Singer's first such ventures. One, "Alone," is a fantasy about Miami Beach in the hurricane season. The narrator, alone in an empty hotel, pursued by a repulsive hunchbacked girl, meditates on the possibility that Substance with its Infinite Attributes lies behind the world of appearance. As he meditates, he is reassured by an advertising airplane that "They still served soup with kasha and kneidlach, knishes and stuffed derma at Margolies' restaurant." The teeth of a deep sea fish in a pier are "evidence of a wickedness as deep as the abyss." Which level is American Substance: the derma in the sky, the abyss in the sea, or the hump on the girl?

The other look at America, "A Wedding in Brownsville," is a realistic short story, and a magnificent one, but at its heart is the same unsubstantiality. A successful New York physician, Dr. Solomon Margolin, who was Schloime-Dovid, the son of the Talmud teacher in the Polish *shtetl* of Sencimin, has a transcendent experience at a wedding of Senciminers in Brownsville in Brooklyn. There he rediscovers his childhood sweetheart, Raizel, thought to have been killed by the Nazis. But perhaps she is an illusion, and Raizel was really killed; perhaps Dr. Margolin is an illusion and

Schloime-Dovid was slaughtered with the rest of his family; perhaps we are
in "a cosmic Brownsville, a cosmic Wedding?"

Everywhere in the book are marvels and delights. Thus, "Three Tales,"
an old-fashioned popcorn chain of supernatural narratives, has an irresistible
beginning: "There were three in the circle: Zalman the glazier, Meyer the
eunuch, and Isaac Amshinover. Their meeting place was the Radzyminer
study house where they visited daily to tell each other stories. Meyer was
only present two weeks out of every month; being one of those whom the
Talmud calls periodic madmen, he was out of his mind the other two.

A very few of the stories seem to me unsuccessful: "Big and Little,"
an anecdote; "Jachid and Jechidah," a heavy-handed demonstration of the
immortality of the soul; and "Short Friday," a pious fable. Even those are
written with so much vitality and style that their very failures are beguiling.

Many of the themes in *Short Friday* are familiar from Singer's other
books. The precipitous tumble from meat eating through sexual license to
apostasy and demonic crime, so economically charted in "Blood," is chroni-
cled at greater length in *Satan in Goray*. The protagonist of "Zeidlus the
Pope" is a Jewish Faust like Yasha Mazur in *The Magician of Lublin*, and a
more luckless one.

Sometimes in *Short Friday*, as in the earlier "The Black Wedding,"
Singer's demonology becomes a metaphor for repressed sexuality, so that
mythology and folklore function as a vocabulary of psychopathology. The
story says that what motivates Yentl in her transvestism is that "her soul
thirsted to study Torah," that Satan the Evil One drives her to propose to
Hadass and continue the imposture into marriage. But Singer knows Yentl
is a lesbian—in fact she tells Avigdor so, as best she can, with "I'm neither
one nor the other"—and Torah and Satan alike are here folk metaphors for
latent homosexuality. Similarly, "Blood" is a study of the sadistic erotic
personality, and the Jewish folklore in the story, from ritual slaughtering
to lycanthropy, serves primarily as external dramatization for an internal
motivation.

Two themes familiar in Singer come with a new urgency in *Short Friday*.
One is that the life for the *shtetl* in Eastern Europe is Jewish life; there is
no other. Tishevitz may be so small that the tenth member of its congregation
is a billy goat, but in Singer's view it is the entire Jewish universe. The
demon narrator of "The Last Demon," stranded in Tishevitz, is of course a
Jewish demon. "I've heard that there are Gentile demons," he says primly,
"but I don't know any, nor do I wish to know them." With "the destruction
of Tishevitz," the narrator tells us, "There are no more Jews, no more
demons." "We have also been annihilated," he explains, "I am the last
refugee." Through the reunions in "A Wedding in Brownsville" runs the
litany: "tortured, burned, gassed," "died, shot, burned."

The Nazis destroyed the Jews, but those who escaped will be as ruth-
lessly destroyed *as Jews* by America (or by Israel, or by any place). Jews in

America, deprived of their *shtetl* culture and language, become "grandmothers with dyed hair and rouged cheeks" at Miami Beach, or backslappers in rented tuxedos at Brownsville weddings.

If the Jews are just about extinct, then even in their ugliness and repulsive habits they must be treasured, like California condors. *Short Friday* displays a broad spectrum of sanctity: from the werewolf Risha and the drunken murderer Leib to the saintly rabbi of Tishevitz, martyred by the Nazis, and Shmul-Leibele and his wife Shoshe of the title story, so pious and good that after their marital exertions on Sabbath eve they are promptly gathered up to Paradise by an angel.

In Singer's world, werewolves and saints are of equal interest and value, along with Velvel the Barrelmaker and a hunchback peddling pickled herring. Yentl thinks that she is too important "for chattering with silly women," and Zeidel believes himself too brilliant to waste away in a little Jewish village. But Isaac Bashevis Singer, who believes himself to be an extinct writer using a dead tongue, preserves them impartially—Yentl and the women, Zeidel and the village—in the immortal amber of his art.

The Genius of Isaac Bashevis Singer

TED HUGHES

Isaac Bashevis Singer emigrated to the United States in 1935, which was the year of his first novel, *Satan in Goray*. Since then, he has written more or less exclusively about the Jewish world of pre-war Poland, or more exactly—it's a relevant qualification—about the Hasidic world of pre-war Poland, into which he was born, the son of a rabbi, in 1904. So not only does he write in Yiddish, but his chosen subject is even further confined in place, and culture, and now to the past. Nevertheless, his work has been lucky with its translators, and he has to be considered among the really great living writers, on several counts.

He's produced three more novels, that have been translated, and three volumes of short stories. Looking over his novels in their chronological order (the stories are written in and among, but they belong with the novels) the first apparent thing is the enormous and one might say successful development of his vision. Vision seems to be the right word for what Singer is conveying. The most important fact about him, that determines the basic strategy by which he deals with his subject, is that his imagination is poetic, and tends toward symbolic situations. Cool, analytical qualities are heavily present in everything he does, but organically subdued to a grasp that is finally visionary and redemptive. Without the genius, he might well have disintegrated as he evidently saw others disintegrate—between a nostalgic dream of ritual, Hasidic piety on the one hand and cosmic dead-end despair on the other. But his creative demon (again, demon seems to be the right word) works deeper than either of these two extremes. It is what involves him so vehemently with both. It involves him with both because this demon is ultimately the voice of his nature, which requires at all costs satisfaction in life, full inheritance of its natural joy. It is what suffers the impossible problem and dreams up the supernormal solution. It is what in most men stares dumbly through the bars. At bottom it is amoral, as interested in destruction as in creation, but being in Singer's case an intelligent spirit, it has gradually determined a calibration of degrees between good and evil, in discovering which activities embroil it in misery, pain, and emptiness,

Reprinted with permission from *The New York Review of Books*, vol. 4 (22 April 1965): 8–10. Copyright © 1965 Nyrev, Inc.

and conjure into itself cruel powers, and which ones concentrate it towards bliss, the fullest possession of its happiest energy. Singer's writings are the account of this demon's re-education through decades that have been—particularly for the Jews—a terrible school. They put the question: "How shall man live most truly as a human being?" from the center of gravity of human nature, not from any temporary civic center or speculative metaphysic or far-out neurotic bewilderment. And out of the pain and wisdom of Jewish history and tradition they answer it. His work is not discoursive, or even primarily documentary, but revelation—and we are forced to respect his findings because it so happens that he has the authority and power to force us to do so.

Up to 1945, this demon in Singer's work shows itself overpowered. *Satan in Goray* and *The Family Moskat* give the story of its defeat. In some way these two books belong together, though they are ten years apart. *Satan in Goray* seems to me his weakest book—important, and with a stunning finish, but for the most part confusingly organized. Perhaps we wouldn't notice this so much if we weren't comparing it with his later works, where the inspired rightness of his technical inventions are a study in themselves. *Satan in Goray* recounts the effects of the Sabbatai Zevi Messianic hysteria on a small Hasidic community in seventeenth-century Poland. Sabbatai Zevi's followers, who frequently appear in Singer's stories, effectually apotheosized the Evil One. They proclaimed salvation through a sort of ecstasy of sinning, as if there were something purifying in the sheer intensity with which they surrendered to the forbidden, to the supercharged otherworld of disruptive powers and supernaturals which the Law, in its wandering history, had collided with and put under and thereafter had to hold under—a terrific population accumulating under the Cabala and on the Holy Fringes of everything, several entire religious and erstwhile creators screwed down under dots, letters, and ritual gestures. This isn't altogether ancient history. Something of it has been dogmatized in modern psychology and avant-garde literature. One could argue that the whole of modern Western life is one vast scientifically programmed surrender to what was formerly unknown and forbidden, as if salvation lay that way. The Sabbatai Zevi psychic epidemic is an accurate metaphor for a cultural landslide that has destroyed all spiritual principles and dumped an entire age into a cynical materialism emptied of meaning. Which is why the sufferings of Netchele, the bride of the leader of the Sabbatai Zevi sect in Goray, in whose brain the general eruption of infernal license finally concentrates, belong to this century and not to the seventeenth. And why we can say her sufferings are perhaps an image of what Singer's own muse, representative of the Polish Jews, has undergone.

The key to Singer's works seems to be an experience of the collapse of the Hasidic way of life under the pressure of all that it had been developed to keep out. Something like this is a usual moral position among poets who come at some revolutionary moment, but who need to respect order. Singer comes at the moment when the profound, rich, intense Hasidic tradition, with the whole Jewish tradition behind it, debouches into the ideological chaos of the mid-twentieth century. Visited with all that the old Law excluded, such poets are burdened with the job of finding new Law. But when the hosts of liberated instinct and passion and intellectual adventure and powers of the air and revelations of physical truth are symbolized by Satan, as they must be for a Hasidic Jew, and the old, obsolete order is symbolized by the devotion and ritual that are a people's unique, spiritual strength and sole means of survival, the position must be a perilous one to manage. We can trace the workings of the whole conflict much more definitely—though without the symbolic impact of *Satan in Goray*—in Singer's next book, *The Family Moskat*.

Coming ten years later, *The Family Moskat* is radically different in style from the earlier book, cast in panoramic Tolstoyan mould, 600 pages long, covering the fates of the rich, patriarchal Moskat's large family and—in suggested parallel—of a whole people, from the beginning of this century up to the first Nazi bombs on Warsaw. The protagonist is one Asa Heshel, a young, precociously freethinking but, to begin with, outwardly orthodox Hasidic Jew, the son of a provincial rabbi, who arrives in Warsaw seeking life and the divine truths. He becomes entangled with Moskat's family. Thereafter, it is the story of the moral disintegration of the Polish Jews.

It is a monumental, seethingly real picture of Warsaw Jewish life, without a mistimed paragraph. In this city, the Jews are under the millstone of the west, and their inner coherence is breaking up. In the process, typical mutations appear. But the main current of the book flows through two men, Asa Heshel and Abram. Abram is a volcanic enjoyer of life. The gentile pressures have stripped him of all but the last nods towards orthodoxy, but they haven't frightened his energy: he keeps his Hasidic wholeness and joy. Though he lives more or less entirely in sin in every direction, collapsing finally on a tart's bed and dying in his mistress's, he remains "a true Hasid" and "biologically a Jew." But it is all at a last gasp, it is all headlong into the new gentile age, into death, on the precarious foundations of a damaged, over-passionate heart. He is full-pressure Jewishness, making the leap, naively. He calls Asa Heshel, his protegé, a coward, and by superficial contrast Asa Heshel's behavior is cowardly all right. But Asa Heshel has recoiled. He has made the leap early, without dying, bodily, into the wilderness of Darwin and the physicists, the ceaseless covert battleground of Western civilization, and he has recoiled. He has no illusion that life lies that way. Yet he has allowed the wind off it to deprive him of his traditional faith, the meaning of his life. And that first treachery to God spreads a faithlessness, a heartlessness, into all his actions and thoughts. His two marriages founder and struggle on in torture. His grand, intellectual ambitions fritter out in sterility and cynicism. He regards all the possibilities of life with frozen distrust. For him, God has died, yet he can't love anything else. The creation is a heap of atoms, a sterile promontory battered by blind appetites. His deep suspicion and perhaps hatred of women is equalled by his cold, desperate lust for their bodies. The great projected work of his youth, "The Laboratory of Happiness," accompanies his pointless wanderings, decaying, finally lost. All the moral and intellectual consequences of his people's loss of faith, and their pursuit of the new, chaotic world, seem to have concentrated in his brain. Behind his coldness, he is suffering the death Netchele suffered, in *Satan in Goray*, possessed and out of her mind, and perhaps this is the connection between the two books.

Adele, his second wife, on the point of leaving him to escape to Israel from the first rumors of Hitler, finds the words for Asa Heshel: "He was one of those who must serve God or die. He has forsaken God and because of that he was dead—a living body with a dead soul." It is from this situation of Asa Heshel's that the general moral implications of Singer's vision radiate. Asa Heshel, after all, is not only a Hasidic Jew. He is a typical modern hero. Remembering that Singer writes in Yiddish, for a primarily Jewish public, we can still see that he writes out of such essential imagination that he raises Jewishness to a symbolic quality, and is no longer writing specifically about Jews but about man in relationship to God. And his various novels and stories—with a few exceptions among the stories—describe the various phases and episodes of this relationship, though in concrete Jewish terms. This is pretty near to saying that, in Singer, the Jew becomes the representative modern man of suffering, and understanding, and exile from his Divine inheritance, which of course isn't altogether Singer's own invention.

Asa Heshel ends up, hurrying under the Nazi bombers with his latest woman, Jewish also, but a set Communist. He knows he has fallen the whole way. Communism is the ideological antithesis to the Holy Life, created by Jews living in defiance or denial of God, as Lucifer, fallen from praising in heaven, organized the abyss. In her company, Asa Heshel meets the philosopher, the bewildered genius, one-time hope of the gentilized Jewish intellectuals, who closes the book, among the falling bombs, with "The Messiah will come soon . . . Death is the Messiah. That's the real truth." This is the final logical point in Asa Heshel's progress, as death was the final point of Netchele's. The forsaking of God, the rejection of the life of Holy Disciplines, is a crime, as it turns out, without redemption, and, as history in this book seems to demonstrate, draws on itself the inevitable penalty: anonymous death—whether symbolic or actual hardly matters—in a meaningless wasteland of destruction and anguish.

Singer's vision arrived there, in despair in the absurd Universe, at a point where most comparable modern writers have remained, emotionally, despite their notable attempts to get beyond it. The Existential Choice, taken to its absolute limit of wholeheartedness, becomes inevitably a religion—because man is deeper and more complicated than merely rational controls can keep hold of. Then his beliefs, disciplines, and prohibitions have to be cultivated against the odds as in a world of poisons one chooses—sensibly after all—food that nourishes. Singer is at a point there, that is to say, where he has every sane and human reason to rebuild an appreciation of the Faith it was death for him to lose. So here again the Jewish Hasidic tradition takes on a Universal significance, as a paradigm of the truly effective Existential discipline, which perhaps it always has been. The core of the Jewish faith, unlike most larger persuasions, is one long, perpetually-renewed back-to-the-wall Choice, one might say in this context, to affirm a mode of survival against tremendous odds. It has kept the Jewish heart in one piece through three thousand years of such oppressions and temptations as dissolved other peoples in a few decades. So it is not surprising if Singer, in his books, gravitates back towards it as a way out of the modern impasse, salvaging at the same time the life of spirit and all the great human virtues.

The Family Moskat is the matrix from which Singer's subsequent work grows. His next two novels, The Magician of Lublin and The Slave are like dreams out of Asa Heshel's remorse. The Magician, Yasha Mazur, fallen from the Faith, is a kind of Satan, the opportunist of his own inspired ingenuity. But, unlike Asa Heshel's, his belief has not wholly died, it has (merely) been buried. It recovers him from the pit, and in a bricked-up cell in his yard he becomes an ascetic, a famous Holy man. In this, he has not rejected the world. He has accepted the only life that does not lead to misery for himself and for everybody he knows. The Slave goes a great step further in the same direction. Jacob—a slave of Polish peasants in the seventeenth century—is brutishly treated. He is stalled among the beasts. He is threatened with constant death yet he keeps his faith. He falls in love with the peasant daughter of his master, converts her, and returns with her to live in a Jewish settlement. It is a story of heroic dedication: no disappointment or persecution or obstacle can shake him—as Asa Heshel was so easily shaken—from the chosen way, and he becomes, again, a kind of Saint.

In this book, one of Singer's deep themes comes right to the surface. Singer implies—and seems to build his novels instinctively around the fact—that there is an occult equivalence between a man's relationship to the women in his life and his relationship to his own soul—and so to God. Netchele, in Satan in Goray, seems to bear a relationship to Singer himself. Hadassah, Adele, Barbara, and Asa Heshel's mother, precisely define the stages of Asa Heshel's fall. Esther, Masha and Emilia define the three Yasha Mazurs, in The Magician, Wanda and Sarah, two names of one woman, correspond to Jacob creating his soul out of chaos, and Jacob and the Saint. These correspondences are subtle and revealing. On the mythical or symbolic plane, these women are always at the core of everything Singer is saying about his hero. And it's on this plane that we can best see what an achievement The Slave is, and perhaps why it comes to be such a burningly radiant, intensely beautiful book. Singer is answering his age like a prophet, though what he is saying may seem perverse and untimely. If the world is Gehenna, it is also the only "Laboratory of Happiness," and in *The Slave* Jacob and Sarah achieve a kind of Alchemical Marriage, a costly, precarious condition, but the only truly happy one. So what are we to understand? The dynamics of man's resistance to demoralization and confusion, the techniques of "creating" God and Holy Joy where there seemed to be only emptiness, never change, but they demand a man's whole devotion. And they can be abandoned in a day, whereon the world becomes, once more, Gehenna.

His stories fill out these guiding themes, or exploit situations suggested by them, in dozens of different ways, but they give freer play to his invention than the novels. At their best, they must be among the most entertaining pieces extant. Each is a unique exercise in tone, focus, style, form, as well as an unforgettable re-creation of characters and life. A comic note, a sort of savage enjoyment that scarcely appears in the novels, more or less prevails, though it is weirdly blended with pathos, simplicity, idyllic piety, horror. There is some connection here, in the actual intensity of the performance, and the impartial joy in the face of everything, with traditional Hasidic fervor. In substance, these stories recapitulate the ideas and materials of Jewish tradition. Intellectually their roots run into the high, conservative wisdom of the old Jewish sages. Yet it is only a slight thing that prevents many of them from being folk-tales, or even old wives' tales, narrated by a virtuoso. They all have the swift, living voice of the oral style. Some of them are very near a bare, point-blank, life-size poetry that hardly exists in English. "The Black Wedding," in the volume titled *The Spinoza of Market Street*, is a more alive, more ferocious piece of poetic imagination than any living poet I can think of would be likely to get near. Likewise "The Fast," and "Blood," in *Short Friday*. The stories often turn on almost occult insights—as the connection between blood-lust and sexual lust, in "Blood." It is his intimacy with this dimension of things that carries Singer beyond any easy comparison. Stories that are deadpan jokes, like "Jachid and Jechidah," or fantasies, like "Shiddah and Kuziba," are not only brilliantly done, but are also moral/theological fables of great force, and direct outriders of Singer's main preoccupations. No psychological terminology or current literary method has succeeded in rendering such a profound, unified, and fully apprehended account of the Divine, the Infernal, and the suffering space of self-determination between, all so convincingly interconnected, and fascinatingly peopled. But, it is in the plain, realistic tales, like "Under the Knife" in *Short Friday*, that we can isolate his decisive virtue: whatever region his writing inhabits, it is blazing with life and actuality. His powerful, wise, deep, full-face paragraphs make almost every other modern fiction seem by comparison labored, shallow, overloaded with alien and undigested junk, too fancy, fuddled, not quite squared up to life.

The Sly Modernism of Isaac Singer

RICHARD BURGIN

Without being a literary theoretician, or ever wishing to, Isaac Bashevis Singer has found himself embroiled in various controversies concerning the aims of fiction. He is, for instance, aesthetically at odds with those fictionists who feel the urge to impart an "important" social, political, or philosophical message in their work. As he has said, "The moment something becomes an '-ism' it is already false."

More importantly, perhaps, his commitment to character, plot, clarity, to, as Henry Miller said, "returning literature to life," has informed all his fiction from *Satan in Goray* and his first major novel *The Family Moskat*, to his recent collection of stories *Old Love*, and dramatizes one of contemporary fiction's central debates which is being rather furiously waged in universities and journals across the country. Summed up briefly, we have those writers (and the critics sympathetic to them) who constitute the so-called avant-garde and essentially conceive of fiction as a great chain of being (or, in a sense, as a branch of science) in which the writer believes that fiction is a constantly evolving entity and that if one is not contributing to its evolution then that seriously undermines the validity of the writer's work. There are, of course, writers who are ambivalent about this issue or consider it a pseudo-issue, but increasingly one feels a sense of polarization between the experimentalists and those writers who continue to work with plots, character development, and a strong sense of the mechanisms and operations of society.

Curiously one of the principal literary and spiritual progenitors of the experimentalists, Jorge Luis Borges, could scarcely be more conservative in his literary tastes. Not only has he read none of today's avant-gardists (his very poor eyesight may have something to do with this) but he considers Joyce and Beckett not of the first rank, and Kafka much inferior to Henry James. A list of his favorite "modern" authors would certainly include De Quincey, Robert Louis Stevenson, Chesterton, Emerson, and Frost (see my book *Conversations with Jorge Luis Borges*). More importantly he feels that since we live in a world of infinite or at least indeterminate Time, the concept of an avant-garde is illusory, a misnomer based on a misunderstanding of man's relation to Time. Though one can scarcely imagine a more different

From *Chicago Review* 31 (Spring 1980): 61–67. Reprinted by permission of *Chicago Review*.

writer, Singer's metaphysics are quite close to Borges's and are crucial to understanding his work and its sly modernism.

Sartre noted in an essay on Faulkner that every writer's style reveals his metaphysics, and in a less than obvious way this is also true of Singer. Consider his prefatory note to *Passions* (1975) in which Singer precisely and simply states his aesthetics:

> While obscurity in content and style may now be the fashion, clarity remains the ambition of this writer. This is especially important since I deal with unique characters in unique circumstances, a group of people who are still a riddle to the world and often to themselves—the Jews of Eastern Europe, specifically the Yiddish-speaking Jews who perished in Poland and those who emigrated to the U.S.A. The longer I live with them and write about them the more I am baffled by the richness of their individuality and (since I am one of them) by my own whims and passions.

In Singer's case we are dealing with a writer who adheres religiously to the goals of clarity and specificity, writing about only what he knows through some form of direct experience. This is a seminal reason why there is some degree of confusion on the question of his modernity or his contemporary relevance. For Singer is a writer, in an age of cultivated ambiguity, who *wants* us to perceive the epiphanies, doubts, and ambivalence of his characters. The other key term in his brief statement of aesthetics is "riddle"—for that is finally what the universe is for Singer. What he wants us to understand about his characters are their attempts to comprehend the structure and *modus operandi* of a universe that resists understanding. It is one of his special strengths that his characters are not disembodied creations who merely represent metaphysical problems, or their author's obsessions, but are invariably imbued with exceptional vitality and credibility. One could say without exaggeration that Singer feels and is able to dramatize characters in the same natural way that Kant saw the World in Ideas. The apparent contradiction, then, is of a writer who composes lucid, direct sentences about people and situations he knows, but whose metaphysics like Kafka's and Borges's are rooted and have never escaped from the interminable riddles of the modern world. It is clarity, then, in the service of illuminating our essential riddle of existence. Let us not forget that Kafka and Borges employ very similar techniques.

One other reason why Singer has adopted many of the stylistic features of nineteenth century fiction is that he feels the work of that period is vastly superior to that of the twentieth. He therefore adopted as his masters Tolstoy, Dostoyevsky, and Flaubert, who expressed their social, psychological, and philosophical conceits in a "natural" way through their characters' relations to each other, and their particular situations in a concrete social milieu. Yet Singer's sensibility is more "modern" than these writers', to whom he is frequently compared.

To understand this more fully we must return to the notion of social structure, which the avant-garde often treats negatively or else with the assumption that there simply isn't any structure to be negative about. For these writers, the family, society's first structure, is generally fractured and uncommunicative at best, and more often a procession of horrors; a never-to-be-reconciled nightmare. But in *Old Love*, as in many of his stories, novels, or memoirs, Singer is always returning to 10 Krochmalna Street in Warsaw where he grew up. In the celebrated memoir of his childhood, *In My Father's Court*, the entire book is set in his neighborhood. Despite the tensions that existed in his family, especially the conflicts between his father's unwavering devotion to Judaism and the more worldly interests of his children, the overpowering feeling that emerges in grand dimensions from *In My Father's Court* is the essential goodness of his parents. Certainly Singer's stories in *Old Love* (as in all of his fiction), demonstrate an acute awareness of man's capacity for weakness and simple cruelty. What distinguishes his fiction from the work of many experimentalists is that man is always seen in a definite context of family and society that even world war (and Singer has written about both of them) does not destroy. This sense of continuity ultimately forms a basis for the deeper mystery of human character that clarity always provides.

When Singer moves from the family, or from man in society, and considers our cosmic structure, his contradictory attitudes are even more difficult to unravel. Though he has characterized our knowledge of the universe as "a little island in an ocean of non-knowledge," Singer nonetheless affirms his belief in God (here he may differ slightly from Borges for whom this question, like infinity itself, is beyond our attempts at description). But Singer has nonetheless described his God as, "a silent God . . . perhaps a petty God, an amnesiac, perhaps a cruel God." In the last analysis he is certain only that we have too little information to know or even to criticize this God who speaks in a language of incomprehensible deeds.

In *Old Love* Singer pursues these concerns while broadening his thematic range, dealing explicitly for the first time with homosexuality and bi-sexuality in "Two," with sado-masochism in "Not for the Sabbath," even with incest in "The Bus." Despite his emphasis in *Old Love* on the sexually aberrational aspects of his characters, as well as the exotic locations of his stories (Spain, Brazil, Israel, Miami), we are firmly rooted in Singer's fictive world populated by demons and imps, resonating with the author's fascination for detail liable to deliquesce in a moment into other worldly visions.

The darker side of sexuality has always been one of Singer's preoccupations; thus, this current collection is more of an extension of an ongoing investigation than an exploration of completely new terrain. Most importantly, not only are Singer's style and point of view consistent with his life's work, so are his aesthetics. A closer look, for example, at "The Bus," the last, longest, and most fully developed story in *Old Love*, may help us understand the sly modernism of Singer I mentioned earlier.

The story begins (as Tolstoy recommended fiction should) in the middle; that is we are immediately in a crisis the narrator finds inexplicable:

> Why I undertook that particular tour in 1956 is something I haven't figured out to this day—dragging around in a bus through Spain for twelve days with a group of tourists. We left from Geneva. I got on a bus around three in the afternoon and found the seats nearly all taken. The driver collected my ticket and pointed out a place next to a woman who was wearing a conspicuous black cross on her breast. Her hair was dyed red, her face was thickly rouged, the lids of her brown eyes were smeared with blue eyeshadow, and from beneath all this dye and paint emerged deep wrinkles. She had a hooked nose, lips as red as a cinder, and yellowish teeth.
>
> She began speaking to me in French, but I told her I didn't understand the language and she switched over to German. It struck me that her German wasn't that of a real German or even a Swiss.

In these opening lines the reader is confronted with what we might call two fields of tension: the continuity of concrete detail and the world of deception, ambiguity, and misconception. The concrete information given the reader includes chronological time, around three in the afternoon in 1956; a definite place, Spain, and a vivid description of Madame Weyerhofer, one of the story's protagonists. But every time information is given it is immediately undermined. The narrator knows he is on a bus, but does not know why. He is pointed to a seat next to a woman flaunting an ominous sign (the black cross) and everything about this woman's appearance seems elusive, at best, or perhaps completely meretricious (dyed hair, rouged face, a use of German that seems suspect).

Though she wears a cross, Celina Weyerhofer soon discloses that she is Jewish, in fact a former inmate of a concentration camp. Her husband, a Swiss bank director who is sitting across from her, compelled her to convert to Christianity because, as she explains, "He hates me."

Since the rules of the bus require passengers to exchange seats daily, he soon gets to know her husband whom his wife has characterized as a pathological liar and latent homosexual. He, in turn, describes his wife's pathology to the narrator.

As the tale grows more dense, it also becomes more bizarre. We soon realize that "The Bus" is not going to be a study of the Weyerhofers, for the narrator meets a Mrs. Metalon from Istanbul whose adolescent son Mark, a genius who could do logarithms at the age of five, is scheming to get her married again, this time to the narrator. With a minimal degree of structural complication, Singer artlessly increases the complexity of his story without sacrificing any of its narrative thrust.

When the bus arrives in Spain the narrator is assigned a hotel room without a bath and Mark invites him to use his mother's. By accident, while looking for the Metalon's room, he knocks on the wrong door and ends up in Mrs. Weyerhofer's room. She tells him that the bath is merely a pretext for Mrs. Metalon to seduce him. Later, on the bus, after she has once again delayed the trip with one of her shopping excursions, she goes even further to discredit Mrs. Metalon.

> ". . . By the way, I want you to know that this boy, Mark, who wants so desperately for you to sit next to that Turkish concubine, is not her son."
> "Then who is he?"
> "He is her lover, not her son. She sleeps with him."
> "Were you there and saw it?"
> "A chambermaid in Madrid told me. She made a mistake and opened the door to their room in the morning and found them in bed together . . ."

The narrator ponders the possibility.

> "Who knows what she told me might have been the truth.
> Sexual perversion is the answer to many mysteries . . ."

What the narrator is dealing with is a set of truths or realities represented by the Weyerhofers and the Metalons, each of whom denies the other's credibility and assures the narrator that his or her truth is the one in which to believe. This is a recurring, indeed, almost archetypal situation in contemporary fiction from the masters of undermined or contradicted truth—Conrad, Faulkner, Kafka, Borges, Beckett, Calvino—to their numerous disciples. What makes this theme unique in "The Bus" is that Singer has built it unpretentiously through the personalities and detailed situations of each of the characters. Like Kafka, the more he elaborates, the more clearly he writes; and the more mysterious his situations become. Even the narrator's own motives and passions are unknown to him. He yearns for Mrs. Metalon one moment, but when he has a chance to sleep with her his passion cools. Effortlessly the bus begins to assume symbolic dimensions, but like Kafka's castle it's a multiple symbol or, one might say, an overdetermined one. The bus is at once a symbol of human desire, consciousness, a search for reality, and also an escape from it. Of course, these categories are hardly mutually exclusive; indeed, a central theme of the story is their interrelationship. Consciousness must always desire and when that fails (one recalls James Agee's line, "Desire fails, everything's a prayer") one begins the inevitable progression of self-doubt, of looking for solace in faith, one becomes in effect like Beckett's Watt who relentlessly tries to rationalize the inexplicable. In just this way Singer's narrator in "The Bus" confronts man's essential dilemma here discreetly raised to metaphysical proportions: the problem of not knowing.

As Beckett's characters wait for Godot uncertain if he will ever arrive, Singer's characters, like Kafka's land surveyor in search of the Castle, are always moving. In the case of "The Bus" there is a clear destination for the narrator's trip, as there is for the land surveyor, but it is a place Singer treats with far less importance or mystification than Kafka does his Castle. It is, in fact, completely demystified, simply a place one can find on a map. Nevertheless, the narrator never reaches it, for, unable to unravel his own tangled motives, he ultimately gets off the bus and takes a train to Biarritz. In the train's diner, incredibly, he encounters Mrs. Weyerhofer who has finally left her husband after denouncing him in front of the other bus passengers as a "Nazi, homosexual, sadist."

During their brief, acerbic conversation on the train the narrator asks her, "Why did you keep the bus waiting in every city?"

". . . I don't know," she said at last. "I don't know myself. Demons were after me. They mislead me with their tricks."

The narrator looks out the window meditatively.

A nocturnal gloom hovered above the landscape, an eternity that was weary of being eternal. Good God, my father and my grandfather were right to avoid looking at women! Every encounter between a man and a woman leads to sin, disappointment, humiliation.

Shortly after this reflection the narrator announces, "I'm finished, gastronomically and otherwise."

But the last word of the story is left for Madame Weyerhofer. "Don't rush," she said. "Unlike the driver of our ill-starred bus, the forces that drive us mad have all the time in the world."

Singer's bus, then, is another "little island in an ocean of nonknowledge." In fact it is far too elusive to constitute even a tiny island, and accordingly the narrator vacates it. Both the theme and its treatment reveal Singer to be spiritually akin to Borges, Kafka, Beckett, and Nabokov, for whom the problem of knowledge itself replaces the essential concerns of Tolstoy, Dostoyevsky, and Flaubert. This theme and its particular kind of modernism, or, if you will, post-modernism, are not unique to "The Bus." We find it in the novels *Enemies, A Love Story*, Singer's most recent novel *Shosha*, and to a substantial degree in *The Magician of Lublin*. Moreover, we find it in many of his stories from "Gimpel the Fool" to much of *Old Love*. Indeed the problem of knowledge, which I believe to be a crucial one for contemporary or avant-garde writers, is literally spelled out in the last sentence of the title story of *A Crown of Feathers* (1970): ". . . If there is such a thing as truth it is as intricate and hidden as a crown of feathers."

This writer is somewhat baffled by those critics who relentlessly stress

Singer's devotion to traditional literary and "moral" values while ignoring the meanings that are apparent behind the surface simplicity of his style, and his natural storyteller's gift. (Remember Joyce and Faulkner, Kafka, Borges, and Nabokov are all good, almost obsessive, storytellers.) "The Bus," then, like most of the fiction in *Old Love*, reveals a writer who manages to dramatize eternal paradoxes in a wholly contemporary fashion without making us overly aware of it. To my knowledge few fictionists have this gift and have demonstrated it so often.

Singer's Last Word

JOHN BAYLEY

A story no doubt originating in Norway goes over the ground about persons of different nationality required to write an essay on elephants. The Englishman of course writes about hunting them, the French about their love-life, the Swede about elephantine manners and etiquette, the Dane about the ivory business. The Norwegian produces an essay on Norway and Norwegians. A laborious jest with many permutations, but it serves to show that a people likes to think that while other countries have their own characteristics they have what really matters—themselves. And for a people to write about itself can be both inspiration and good business.

It certainly was for Isaac Bashevis Singer. His incomparable sense of Polish Jewry, the Yiddishness in which he was brought up, renders itself to the reader as if in the palpable form of experience: the words seem to sit us down and bring us beer and brandy with a side order of jellied calves feet cooked in garlic. How is it done? By the author hugely enjoying being himself, his past, his culture? Singer says that with Yiddish you get vitamins you don't get in other languages, and we can well believe it. But would the fascination be so strong if the world he described still existed? That's another question. The story, the place, depend on the past as much as they do in that other great wizard, Walter Scott, whose powers were as great as Singer's and of the same kind. But beyond the tavern door where the calves feet and chopped liver are eaten and the stories told, the terrible present is about to happen. In an interview in *Encounter* in 1979 Singer said that though the Jews of Poland had died in the Holocaust, "something—call it spirit or whatever—is still somewhere in the universe. This is a mystical kind of feeling but I feel there is truth in it." It is the same quasi-mystical connection that Scott felt with his country's past. What Singer did not exploit was the connection between a vanished way of life and the manner of its death— but the implication is there. In the shadow of arrest and execution under Stalin another Jewish writer, Babel, ironically referred to his new art of silence, and everything in Singer's extraordinarily vivid world throws the shadow of the same oncoming silence.

Bayley, John. "Singer's Last Word." First published in the "London Review of Books," volume 13, no. 20 (October 24, 1991): 17–18.

As the Norwegian story suggests, to be condemned to a consciousness of oneself as Norwegian, Irish, Jewish, English or Scottish can also be an intolerable bore and a burden. That it was never one for Singer would be because his whole provenance had become his art, the art he so richly produced. His story "A Friend of Kafka" wonderfully suggests that genius's love-hate relationship with his background, the superlative ways he found to escape in his writing from what was inescapable. But Kafka was writing in German—and very much his own German—not in Yiddish. Bruno Schulz, killed in the Jewish quarter of his home town by a Gestapo officer in 1941, wrote a Polish of such delicacy and exquisite animation that his *nouvelles* were praised by native writers for being some of the finest stylistically in their language. But could one say that neither Schulz nor Kafka are as much themselves in their writing as Singer seems to be in his Yiddish, which he could himself translate into an English that still retains something of its demotic succulence? In one sense, certainly, the language and the life he wrote of may still be alive, in New York and in other places: but the kind of Jewishness—incarnate in speech and spirit, in herring and onion roll—where Singer's characters reside seems a long way either from modern America or from modern Israel, or from the problems authors like Amos Oz write about in their contemporary Hebrew.

Singer's memoir of his early years, *Love and Exile*, may be, as he says, "basically autobiographical," but names and dates and the course of events have been changed, in some cases both for family reasons and "because the true story of a person's life can never be written." *Love and Exile* is as much an evocation, the summoning-up of a corporate and social being and way of life, as are the tales and the novels. His elder brother and sister are writers and translators with whom he co-operated, both in Poland and later in the USA. His father was a rabbi first in a Polish village and then in the town of Radzymin. His mother, whose name was Bathsheba, could scarcely believe late in life that her son had possessed such a memory for places they had lived in and people they had known before he was three or four years old. He convinced her with names and dates, and she said: "What a memory! May no evil eye befall you."

Nor did it, on the whole. When he went to Warsaw as a young man Singer promised his father "that I would conduct myself as a Jew." He took a mistress, admittedly a Jewish one, twice as old as himself, and adopted all sorts of goy ways. Polish girls were amused by him and admired his red hair and blue eyes. Even the army sergeants were fairly good-natured when he had to present himself as a conscript, and remarked: "Woe to the Polish nation if this has to be her defender." He was granted a deferment, which grew tacitly into exemption, even though Jewish boys were expected to serve in the Polish Army and Hitler would soon be coming to power. Indeed he knew a Jewish girl whose fiancé had become an officer during his period of service and won acclaim for his horse-riding and his feats of military daring.

In spite of his happy family background, Singer thought of himself as a split personality (a phrase he found in a book) and felt that "some kind of enemy roosted within me, or a dybbuk who spited me in every way and played cat and mouse with me." He lived hand-to-mouth in a bohemia peopled by communists and *Volksdeutsch*, Jewish editors for whom he did proof-reading and young Jews scheming to get to Palestine. A temporary marriage was the accepted way to secure official permission, and Stefa, the officer's fiancée, interviewed young Singer with a view to this arrangement, intending to move on afterwards to America. Nothing came of it, but Singer detached himself in part from his elderly mistress, who had become a fanatical believer in spiritualism, and got a room with a respectable retired Jewish couple, where he seduced the Polish maid, or she him. His landlord was a friend of Dr. Zamenhof, the inventor of Esperanto, a language in all respects the opposite of Yiddish.

One dwells on the hallucinatory vividness of Singer's recollections in *Love and Exile* because they form the basis of the last novel he wrote before his death a few months ago. *Scum* concerns a middle-aged man called Max Barabander, who has made a respectable fortune in the Argentine and is married to an assimilated woman with a Spanish background. His young son has died. Finding himself virtually impotent at the age of 47, he travels back via Paris and Berlin to his old roots in Warsaw. The time is 1906. The currency is the rouble, for Poland is part of the Russian empire, recently disturbed by war with Japan and an abortive revolution. But the Russians are still the ruling class, and Max Barabander's experiences merge naturally into those of Singer in *Love and Exile*, who used to wander endlessly with his moribund mistress (she was dying of TB) through the Russian cemetery, so much grander than the Jewish and Polish ones, where yellowing photographs of whiskered officials and high-bosomed women in crinolines were fixed to every tomb.

The date is significant. Singer was born in 1904, and claimed to remember what happened to him at the age of two. Max is his alter ego, and Max finds himself drawn to Krochmalna Street, a dubious quarter of the ghetto and the name of the street in which Singer and his family had lived when his father came to Warsaw as a rabbi. Max is staying at the Bristol Hotel, but it is in Krochmalna street that he at once feels at home—or does he? The wife of the local fixer, met in the pub, fancies him, but when it comes to the point he can do nothing. He is divided between intense pleasure and relief at being in his own place, joking in Yiddish (when a rabbi gently asks him why no beard, he automatically wisecracks: "better a Jew without a beard than a beard without a Jew"), and a sense of suicidal emptiness, as if even the gusto of being Yiddish again cannot help him possess or retain his own private ego. He is nothing but a voice. "He relied completely on his tongue, which was his ruler and destiny." The youthful Isaac of *Love and Exile* had instinctively rejected "leftism," the fashionable creed of his young acquaintance, whether Jewish or Polish, because it "wanted to abolish privacy, and to institute a perpetual public domain." Max yearns for the domain of Yiddishness, but it too deprives him of himself—or perhaps he has never had a self? Only the rabbis who were both Max's and Singer's father and grandfathers possessed that, when they immersed themselves in the Torah. Singer's father said to him: "The Torah is bottomless. No matter how much one studies one can never grasp all of it. Without the Torah the world would not exist." The only world that exists for Singer and for Max is the world of their voices, the world they rediscover with the tongue.

The extraordinary vividness of Singer writings has this poignancy at its bottom: he is conscious of having no other way of being himself. He knows, gently but emphatically, that he is not himself a very interesting man. He cannot, like Kafka or like Bruno Schulz, invent and inhabit a world of his own. It is this that gives his last novel something of the touching inwardness of *The Tempest*. He resigns his magic, but has no home of his own to go to: so that, as in the case of the downward-drifting Max, every third thought must be his grave. But let us not be sad about it, for Singer himself is certainly not. Humour, and not savage humour, is what survives of us. *Scum* is not a felicitous title, but it probably inadequately renders some genially forceful Yiddish word or expression—*Psia Krew* perhaps, "dogs' blood"—expletising the doings and denizens of Krochmalna Street. Unlike Singer in *Love and Exile*, Max does not meet any of those passionately secularised Jews who had transferred all their powers of belief and being to Zionism or to the Communist Party. Although they existed in 1906, they were still comparatively rare birds.

Max's chief concern in the world to which he has returned is not to find his roots—he has a brother and sister in the south in Roszkow, as Singer himself no doubt still has kin in Radzymin—but to rediscover his virility. A thieves' quarter in Warsaw in which all is familiar but in which he is not known, is indeed an exotic stranger, should be perfect for the purpose. In no time he is engaging himself to the rabbi's young daughter Tsirele, concealing the existence of his own wife back in the Argentine and promising her father to perform all the rites and learn all the texts to fit him for an orthodox marriage. Tsirele, fascinated by the stranger, comes to see him at the Bristol Hotel but will not let him make love to her. More indulgent female acquaintances fail to restore his manhood, just because they are more indulgent, as Max gloomily diagnoses. But he keeps on trying. He hatches a scheme to ship young women out to the Argentine, on a purely voluntary basis, of course, and again finds the first candidate all too fatally willing. He contemplates suicide or flight or both, when a gratuitous accident solves his problems by putting him in the hands of the police. He has come home in all senses, and fulfilled a destiny which in more terrible form awaits the next generation.

This is Singer's most autobiographical story, and his last. All the old animation is there, and the joy in belonging heart and soul to this great and vital race, but there is melancholy too: the sense of limitation, the recognition of his impotence—his powerlessness to be an original artist and a man outside his race. Like Keats, however incongruous the comparison may seem, Singer lives in a perpetual recall of sensuousness, in a kind of chamber of maiden thought, out of which his art cannot break, however much he himself may wish to do so. And yet how funny he is! In rabbinical terminology the penis is called the *yesod*, "the sign of the holy covenant"; and in his relations to the rest of the world the youthful Singer seemed to have all the time "a kind of negative erection, if one may use an expression like this . . . sex, like art, cannot be made to order—at least not in my case." A positive erection has to find its old family womb. So he remained a divided man. As he wrote in *Love and Exile* about his early days in America, "I was still a Yiddish writer who hadn't made it, estranged from everything and everybody. I could live neither with God nor without him." The words of Ecclesiastes were always in his mind: "Of laughter I said it is madness and of mirth what doth it?"

ESSAYS

◆

The Saint As Schlemiel

ALFRED KAZIN

When I first read "Gimpel the Fool" (in the quick and pungent English of Saul Bellow) I felt not only that I was reading an extraordinarily beautiful and witty story, but that I was moving through as many historical levels as an archaeologist at work. This is an experience one often gets from the best Jewish writers of our time—Babel, Kafka, Bellow have assimilated, even conquered, the whole tradition of modern literature while reminding us of the unmistakable historic core of the Jewish experience. Equally, a contemporary Yiddish writer like Isaac Bashevis Singer uses all the old Jewish capital of folklore, popular speech and legendry, yet from within this tradition itself is able to duplicate a good deal of the conscious absurdity, the sauciness, the abandon of modern art—without for a moment losing his obvious personal commitment to the immemorial Jewish vision of the world.

Perhaps it is the ability to incarnate all the different periods that Jews have lived through that makes such writers indefinably fascinating to me. They wear whole epochs on their back; they alone record widely separated centuries in dialogue with each other. Yet all these different periods of history, these many *histories*, represent, if not a single point of view, a common historic character. It is the sympathy with which they are translated and transmuted into contemporary terms, that makes the balance that is art.

Gimpel himself is an example of a legendary Jewish type—the saint as *schlemiel*. The mocked, persecuted and wretched people, who nevertheless are the chosen—chosen to bear a certain knowledge through a hostile world—are portrayed again in the town fool, a baker who is married off to a frightful slut without knowing what everyone in town knows, that she will bear a child in four months. Gimpel is *the* fool of the Jews: a fool because he is endlessly naive, a fool because, even when he does learn that he has been had, he ignores his own dignity for the sake of others. His wife's unfaithfulness, her shrewishness—these are not the bourgeois conceal-ment, the "cheating" on one's spouse that it would be in another culture, but a massive, hysterical persecution. The child she already has she passes

From "The Saint as Schlemiel" in *Contemporaries* (Boston: Little Brown & Co., 1962), 283–88. Reprinted by permission of Alfred Kazin. First published in 1958.

off as her "brother": Gimpel believes her. When she gives birth to a child four months after the wedding, Gimpel pays for the circumcision honors and rituals, and names the boy after his own father. When he cries out that his wife has deceived him, she deliberately confuses him, as usual, and persuades him that the child is "premature":

> I said, "Isn't he a little too premature?" She said that she had a grandmother who carried just as short a time and she resembled this grandmother of hers as one drop of water does another. She swore to it with such oaths that you would have believed a peasant at the fair if he had used them. To tell the plain truth, I didn't believe her; but when I talked it over the next day with the schoolmaster he told me that the very same thing had happened to Adam and Eve. Two they went up to bed, and four they descended.

The humor of this is always very real, for these people are rough old-fashioned village types who know their own. The town boys are always playing tricks on Gimpel, setting him on false trails; he is mocked at his own wedding—some young men carry in a crib as a present. His wife, Elka, is a living nightmare, a shrew of monumental proportions, a Shakespearean harridan. Yet in Gimpel's obstinate attachment to her we recognize, as in his customary meekness, the perfection of a type: what to the great world is folly, in itself may be wisdom; what the world thinks insane may, under the aspect of eternity, be the only sanity:

> She swore at me and cursed, and I couldn't get enough of her. What strength she had! One of her looks could rob you of the power of speech. And her orations! Pitch and sulphur, that's what they were full of, and yet somehow also full of charm. I adored her every word. She gave me bloody wounds, though.

One night, Gimpel comes home unexpectedly and finds another man in bed with Elka; this time he has had enough, and he separates from her. But the town mischiefs take her side and persecute him, while Gimpel worries whether he *did* see the man:

> Hallucinations do happen. You see a figure or manikin or something, but when you come up closer it's nothing, there's not a thing there. And if that's so, I'm doing her an injustice. And when I got so far in my thoughts I started to weep. I sobbed so that I wet the floor where I lay. In the morning I went to the rabbi and told him that I had made a mistake.

Elka has another child and "all Frampol refreshed its spirits because of my trouble and grief. However, I resolved that I would always believe what I was told. What's the good of not believing? Today it's your wife you don't believe in, tomorrow it's God Himself you won't take stock in.''

Even his superstitions—Singer uses local demons and spirits as dramatic motifs—become symbols of his innocent respect for the world. One night, after covering the dough to let it rise, he takes his share of bread and a little sack of flour and starts homeward:

> The moon was full and the stars were glistening, something to terrify the soul. I hurried onward, and before me darted a long shadow. It was winter, and a fresh snow had fallen. I had a mind to sing, but it was growing late and I didn't want to wake the householders. Then I felt like whistling, but I remembered that you don't whistle at night because it brings the demons out. So I was silent and walked as fast as I could.

He returns home to find his wife in bed with the apprentice. Characteristically, he suffers rather than storms; characteristically, "the moon went out all at once. It was utterly black, and I trembled"; characteristically, he obeys his wife when she sends him out of the house to see if the goat is well; characteristically, he identifies himself tenderly with the goat, and when he returns home, the apprentice having fled, the wife denies everything, tells him he has been seeing visions, shrieks prodigious curses. Her "brother" beats him with a stick. And Gimpel: "I felt that something about me was deeply wrong, and I said, 'Don't make a scandal. All that's needed now is that people should accuse me of raising spooks and '*dybbuks*.' "

So he makes peace with her, and they live together for twenty years. "All kinds of things happened, but I neither saw nor heard." When his wife dies, she tells him that none of their children is his, and the look on her dead face seems to say to him—"I deceived Gimpel. That was the meaning of my brief life."

Now Gimpel is tempted by the Spirit of Evil himself, who then tells him that it is all nothing. " 'What,' I said, 'is there, then?' 'A thick mire.' " And, succumbing to the devil, Gimpel urinates into the risen dough. His dead wife comes to him in a dream—and, when he weeps in shame at his act, "It's all your fault," she cries—"You fool! You fool! Because I was false, is everything false, too?"

When the mourning period for his wife ends, he gives up everything to tramp through the world, often telling stories to children—"about devils, magicians, windmills, and the like." He dreams constantly of his wife, asks when he will be with her; in his dreams, she kisses him and promises him that they will be together soon. "When I awaken I feel her lips and taste the salt of her tears."

The last paragraph of the story, Gimpel's serene meditation before death, is of great beauty. It sums up everything that Jews have ever felt about the divinity that hedges human destiny, and it is indeed one of the most touching avowals of faith that I have ever seen. Yet it is all done with lightness, with wit, with a charming reserve—so that it might almost be read as a tribute to human faithfulness itself. "No doubt the world is entirely an imaginary world, but it is only once removed from the true world. . . . Another *schnorrer* is waiting to inherit my bed of straw. When the time comes I will go joyfully. Whatever may be there, it will be real, without complication, without ridicule, without deception. God be praised: There even Gimpel cannot be deceived."

Singer's story naturally suggests a comparison with I. J. Peretz's famous "Bontsha the Silent," who was offered everything in heaven, and meekly asked for a hot roll with fresh butter every morning for breakfast. One thinks also of Sholem Aleichem's Tevye the dairyman, who recited his prayers even as he ran after his runaway horse. But in his technique of ambiguity Singer speaks for our generation far more usefully than the old ritualistic praise of Jewish goodness.

While Bontsha and Tevye are entirely folk images, cherished symbols of a tradition, Gimpel—though he and his wife are no less symbols— significantly has to win back his faith, and he wins it in visions, in dreams, that give a background of playfulness and irony to this marvelous subtle story.

This concern with the dream, this everlasting ambiguity in our relations with the divine—this is a condition that our generation has learned to respect, after rejecting the dogmas first of orthodoxy and then of scientific materialism. This delicacy of conception unites Singer to the rest of imaginative humanity today: Man believes even though he knows his belief to be absurd, but what he believes represents a level of imaginative insight which shades off at one end into art, at the other into Gimpel's occasional self-doubt, the thought that he may be "mad."

It is the integrity of the human imagination that Singer conveys so beautifully. He reveals the advantage that an artist can find in his own orthodox training—unlike so many Jews who in the past became mere copyists and mumblers of the holy word. Singer's work *does* stem from the Jewish village, the Jewish seminary, the compact (not closed) Jewish society of Eastern Europe. He does not use the symbols which so many modern writers pass on to each other. For Singer it is not only his materials that are "Jewish"; the world is so. Yet within this world he has found emancipation and universality—through his faith in imagination.

His case is very much like that of Nathaniel Hawthorne, who also grew up in an orthodoxy against which one had in some sense to rebel in order to become a writer at all. Only a Jewish writer in the twentieth century could make one think of Hawthorne, who said that although his ancestors would have been shocked to see him become a writer of storybooks, his values would not have surprised them. Singer illustrates the extraordinary ubiquity of the Jewish writer in time: the demons, the spirits, even the fools belong to the woodland past, the dark mythological background of modern life. At least one of his stories, "From the Diary of One Not Born," could have come out of Hawthorne's stories, for Singer is concerned with the same theme of temptation that led Hawthorne to fill up New England woods with witches. But the positive way in which Singer makes one feel that he has a conviction (very different from Hawthorne and, indeed, from most Jewish writers today) shows the burden of spiritual responsibility that his work carries. The Jews have been so long kept from art that it is interesting to see, at least in Singer, how much respect there is for orthodoxy. For him, at least, it nourished the secret of art—the revelation of the truth that lies in imagination.

Introduction to *Radical Sophistication*

MAX F. SCHULZ

THE "JEWISH-AMERICAN SCHOOL" OF NOVELISTS

There was no Lake school of English poets in 1810, although the *Edinburgh Review* crowd liked to maintain such a fiction. Similarly there is no Jewish school of novelists now. There are only Jewish-American writers practicing their craft. The number currently active is legion. To name them all would be to outdistance in length and in dullness the Homeric roll call of the captains of Agamemnon's army. In ambition they range from the noble infirmity of those bidding for the future to the pragmatism of those dazzled by the glittering present. Their styles encompass the historical romance and black humor; their subjects, the Jewish experience and the human ordeal. What they have in common are a place and a time (America of the 1950's and 1960's) and a set of manners (urban Jewish-American).

How does one explain the emergence in American letters of so many Jewish writers? Irving Howe, in commenting on I. J. Singer's *Yoshe Kalb*, reminds us of the mimetic uses to which the novel puts a set of manners or code of beliefs. The novelist, he remarks, has to be "tightly locked within the premises of his culture" for his work to have validity.[1] The imaginative re-creation of nineteenth-century East European Jewry by the Singer brothers certainly would support this claim—as would the imaginative achievement of the southern writers of several decades ago. In America no ethnic or regional group presently enjoys more coherent and conscious identification with an older cultural tradition than the American Jew. Yet the literary milieu of the current Jewish-American writers is American rather than Jewish. Few write, as does Isaac Bashevis Singer even after living more than thirty years in this country, about the unique Jewish experience. Furthermore, a Jewish literary tradition has been around for a long time. Why then did the Jewish writers of the thirties fail to produce a viable literature that reached a large American reading public, while the Jewish writers of the sixties succeed beyond belief? A culture which the writer accepts as part of the

From the introduction to *Radical Sophistication: Studies in Contemporary Jewish-American Novelists* (Athens, Ohio: Ohio University Press, 1969): 3–6, 13–22. Reprinted by permission of Max F. Schulz. Some notes have been renumbered from the original.

pulse of his being and which he uses as a point of view for broaching experience may be a requisite, but it is obviously not a necessary catalyst for producing great literature.

Special historical forces must account, if only in part, for the periodicity of art. In 1948 in a symposium on the state of American writing, John Crowe Ransom opined that the condition of great artistic creation is a "kind of exuberance of animal spirits."[2] In saying this he merely alluded to what is itself an effect, not an ultimate cause. Why does the condition for great writing wax and wane in the history of a nation? More than simple exuberance calls writers into being. And why exuberance at one time and not at another? Behind such massive affirmation of life as the Elizabethan's or the Romantic's usually can be found a tension reflecting the merger of social and intellectual forces, which simultaneously brings an old order to an end and a new one into being. For the artist at such moments, life becomes both nostalgically retrospective (or defiantly reactive) and optimistically affirmative. Caught between past and future, he inevitably experiences the conflict of contrary loyalties, of antithetical responses. Out of the resultant tension and the desire to resolve it into meaningful order comes occasionally great art. One thinks of the outburst of poetry and drama in the England of Elizabeth's reign when medieval thought and organization of society were breaking up before the new humanism; and of the poetry in the England of George III's rule when the Augustan world picture of a fixed benevolent nature was giving way to the modern concept of an organic world in perpetual flux. In our time, surely the southern writers of the 1930's and 1940's came in response to the disintegration of the southern agrarian myth under the onslaught of industrialization, with the consequent need to define their minority position as a subculture in relation to the dominant urban Yankee society. In like fashion, historical forces seem to have been at work since the end of World War II to account for the concerted appearance of so many first-rate Jewish-American writers. First, the viability of Israel after the holocaust of Europe in the 1940's has renewed the Jew's pride in his Jewishness, so that he no longer hides it apart in exclusively Jewish enclaves but lives openly, if still self-consciously, with it in Gentile neighborhoods. Secondly, Leslie Fiedler cannot be entirely wrong when he claims even that the urban American Jew "is in the process of being mythicized into the representative American."[3] *Commentary* and *Midstream* as well as Jewish Centers from the East River to the Los Angeles River are lamenting the assimilation of the American Jew—his sense not only of his racial but also of his cultural apartness—into the gray sameness of middle-class America. The tension between the old and new generation, between ghetto and suburb, bar mitzvah and little league baseball, synagogue and college, gabardine and Ivy-League suit, has spurred the Jewish writer to an evaluation of his heritage as Jew, American, and modern man.

Less concerned than the Jewish writer of the thirties specifically with the experience of the Jew in America, the best of the contemporary Jewish-American novelists explore the larger theme of the man of heart in a mass-produced civilization. The characters and manners of his stories are usually Jewish simply because they are what he knows best; hence only inferentially as part of the larger issue of the existential posture of modern man does he touch upon the plight of the marginal Jew. The themes of a lost past (as much a part of the curdled American dream as of the Jewish Diaspora) and of the human capacity to feel and through that feeling to triumph over the computerized blankness of twentieth-century existence recur in the works of these men. . . .

The Jewish-American writer is admittedly bitten with the twentieth-century neurosis which regards the mass of people as blind to the real problems of life; hence, in a general way he accepts the idea that the growth of the individual must be achieved, not socially as the Declaration of Independence heralds, but existentially. Yet as a Jew and as an American he never forgets the effect that the private act has on the community. Thus, in his novels the pressure is always toward affiliation of man-alone once again traditionally with the group. The ambivalence of this view is characterized by the ambiguity of the endings of these novels. Their special ambience, which derives from the unresolved tension of such conflicting modes of thought, is strikingly revealed in the writings of Isaac Bashevis Singer, who grew to maturity as the son of a rabbi in the ghettos of Eastern Europe but who has lived the past thirty years in America.

ISAAC BASHEVIS SINGER

Singer's is a twentieth-century sensibility attempting an imaginative re-creation of the social and religious milieu of Polish Jewry of the previous three centuries. The unique—and now vanished—circumstances of this society confront Singer's historical consciousness with special irrefrangibility. Tolstoy could revert in *War and Peace* to the time of the Napoleonic invasions without risking intellectual dislocation, for his society still assented essentially to the assumptions of his grandfather. Tension of a profound philosophical order, however, affects the moral pattern of Singer's stories as a result of the radically different *Zeitgeists* of the author and of his dramatis personae. One of the central paradoxes of Singer's fictional world is that even as he pays loving tribute to the value system of a back-country Jewry—dirty, ignorant, but firm in a simplistic faith in what Dr. Yaretsky in "The Shadow of a Crib" calls "a seeing universe, rather than a blind one,"[4]—Singer questions such a world picture with the narrative structures he composes for them. His rabbis and pious matrons may think and act in unquestioning accord with a Jewish cosmic vision, but their lives present the absurd pattern familiar to the modern sensibility. It is not without significance that in three of Singer's five novels now translated into English the historical setting is that of a catastrophe wrought upon the Jews by external circumstances, and that his protagonists are caught between rival claims of the Jewish and non-Jewish worlds. As in a Greek tragedy, impersonal fate and individual responsibility merge ambiguously in his stories.

The symbolic overtones implied in the title *The Slave* underscore this ambiguity. Jacob is carried off into slavery in the aftermath of the Chmiel-nicki pogroms of the second half of the seventeenth century. Yet even as he struggles—in captivity among the Polish peasants to whom he is sold—to retain his Yiddish tongue, to observe his religion, and to recreate in effect the Law, he falls in love with Wanda, the daughter of his master. Rescued after many years by elders of his village, he is driven by his love to return furtively for Wanda and against both the laws of the Jews and the Poles to introduce her into the village, or *shtetl*, as a true daughter of Israel. Thus Jacob is enslaved by man, society, religious law, spiritual fervor, human desires, and earthly passions. Who can discriminate between Jacob the indi-vidual who is personally accountable for his actions, and Jacob the victim who is determined by historical, social, and biological forces? Or between the Jacob who observes the historic role of the Jews by bringing Wanda to God and who fulfills in his life the return to Palestine, and the Jacob who is profoundly alienated from village and synagogue because of these deeds?

Similarly the enlightened and richly human integration of Yasha Mazur, *The Magician of Lublin*, into the freethinking, mobile, habitat of Warsaw contrasts inexplicably with the escalation of his conscience, the lapse of his skill at lock-picking and gymnastics, and the reversion of his beliefs to the Jewish faith of his forefathers. Three underlying patterns of theme and image provide an ironic commentary on the narrative of Yasha's progress from Pole to Jew. (1) The higher Yasha soars as profane tumbler, the deeper he plunges as sinful man into "the bottomless pit [pt. VI, ch. 9]." Only after his body has fallen from the balcony of the house he has tried to rob, spraining an ankle and arresting subsequent flight, can his soul begin to levitate. The controlling metaphor here is that of Icarus, with Yasha's rise and fall treated dualistically as both grace and damnation. (2) The more freely he roams from mistress to mistress, the more he feels his body to be imprisoned within Poland and his soul within the embraces of women. Only after he quits both roaming and wenching can he hope to be free. The controlling metaphor is that of a prison and of a spider spinning its web to entrap. (3) The more he dissembles, the more he is threatened by disclosure. Only when he renounces deception of his loved ones can he dare to be honest and open with all men. The controlling metaphor is that of a magician or master dissembler.

All three patterns underwrite the change in Yasha as one of religious casuistry. Despite the skill with which they are used, however, Singer is too responsible an artist and too economical a storyteller to indulge in such hackneyed paradigms humorlessly. They reflect rather the skeptical half of his response to his story, supplying us with an ironic measure of Yasha's transformation into a saintly person celebrated (as Emilia's letter is meant to corroborate) all over Catholic Poland. Yasha may have turned his back on his former amoral circus life for the Jewish religious ethos of the *shtetl*, but the mode and consequence of his gesture hardly reassure us of its efficacy. His unJewish antisocial adoption of the monastic ideal, walling himself off from the world as a way of serving both God and society, gives no greater moral illumination or meaningful pattern of his life than had his previous consorting with the thieves of Piask and his roaming of Poland as a performer. The temptations from within and from without—of evil talk, slander, wrath, and false flattery in the form of supplicants who look upon him as a holy man—continue to assail him and to interrupt his meditations. He remains in body and spirit, earthbound, imprisoned, reserved, and secretive; radically alienated from his pious wife and friends, his former associates, and the *shtetl* community; a sainted man holding daily audience to "entertain" the people as the magician in him had done in happier days.

Singer is seriously concerned with the complicated moral and ethical relationships of man to his God and to his society—with the degree to which human conduct describes a moral pattern affecting that of the community and with the extent to which man's actions form pointless arabesques under the indifferent push and pull of historical and psychobiological forces. In *The Family Moskat*, for example, Asa Heshel Bannett and the Warsaw Jews are portrayed as bringing about their own dissolution. Reb Meshulam at the age of eighty lecherously marries for the third time, introducing into the Chasidic community a Galician widow with modernized western habits. With devastating vividness the deterioration of the old pious solidarity of the Warsaw ghetto is depicted in the drunken cynicism, lust, and avarice of the Chanukah Ball, an auspicious place for Asa Heshel, ex-Yeshiva student, to meet his next mistress, the atheistic Communist Barbara. "More sex and fewer children. The bedroom is the key to all social and individual problems [pt. IX, ch. 4]," he tells Barbara. And in its marriage of Spinoza and Malthus, and its aimless, fruitless wanderings, his life passes moral judgment on himself and the Warsaw Jews as a society bent on self-destruction. In the concluding scene of the book he waits resignedly for the Nazi to fulfill his wish to die. He refuses to accompany Barbara, who elects to "keep on fighting for a while," and stands with Hertz Yanovar, religious scholar turned table-tipping occultist, the two quoting to each other in Polish rather than Hebrew the "real truth" of the Bible that "Death is the Messiah [pt. X, ch. 12]." Yet the advent of the Nazi is a jarring note, for in no moral or historical sense can the Warsaw Jews be held responsible for World War II and the Nazi pogrom. The same can be said of the historical phenomenon of the Enlightenment, which claims as victims Asa Heshel, sundry members of the Meshulam family, and Eastern European Jewry in general, diverting them from the paths of righteousness and tradition into the dead end of alienated self-seeking. And there is a sense in which the many chance turns of Asa Heshel's life—for example, his introduction to the libertine Abram Shapiro at the Chasidic synagogue where he had gone fresh from a country *shtetl* for guidance in attending a university—makes him as much a victim of cosmic irony as any of Hardy's characters. This positivist rendering of Asa Heshel's comings and goings on earth denies the contrary structure of meaning in the novel; that is, that there was a moral pattern to his life. With the insistence that there was possibly no coherent relation between him and the world, his life is robbed of moral significance, its events reduced to incoherent moments of sensation.

Clearly, Singer does not find it easy to fix the blame for personal catastrophe, as an older Judaic dispensation would have—and as Reb Abraham Hirsh in I. J. Singer's *The Brothers Ashkenazi* does when he is replaced as general agent of the Huntze factory by his son Simcha Meyer. Reb Abraham consoles himself with the words of King Solomon: "there is a time to plant and a time to pluck up that which is planted, a time to build up and a time to break down. Nothing happens . . . without the will of God, not even the breaking of a little finger [ch.24]." No such easy comfort is available to Isaac Bashevis Singer, despite the tender sympathy that he on occasion expresses for unaffected Jewish ritual and piety, as in the Jewish *Cotter's-Saturday-Night* story, "Short Friday." But even in this story there is the inexplicable twist of fate, which prompts the pious couple to copulate after the Sabbath meal, and then lets them suffocate in their sleep because of a defective stove. I suspect that it is this divorce of his religious sensibility from precise theological tenets, this drift of his thought away from the ethical certainties of the Judaic Law, which allows Americans to read Singer with an understanding and sympathy unavailable to the great Hebrew writer of this century S. Y. Agnon, and such great Yiddish writers as Sholem Aleichem and I. L. Peretz. Such stories as "A Tale of Two Liars," "The Destruction of Kreshev," "Shiddah and Kuziba," and "The Shadow of a Crib" dramatize the ambiguous hold on Singer's mind of belief and skepticism. In them believable *shtetl* types jostle with a wide assortment of supernatural spirits—with the line dividing the two very thin at times.[5] The use of an Arch-Devil narrator simultaneously demonstrates the notion of a seeing will, purpose, and plan in the everyday affairs of the *shtetl*, while underscoring the capriciousness of the forces manipulating human actions. At other times, in even more explicit fashion, Singer often parallels, as in "The Black Wedding" and in some of the stories just mentioned, a pious account of the protagonist's actions with a psychological or naturalistic explanation which denies the moral cohesion of that world. In the story "Cunegunde," for example, he explains the strange nocturnal torments of abused, demented

Cunegunde in her hovel from the viewpoint of her demon-obsessed mind and from that of naturalistic fact: "At night imps came to her bed, mocking her, wetting her sheet, calling her names, poking and biting her, braiding her hair. Mice dung and vermin remained after they had gone."[6]

The danger in this strategy is real, for the coherence of Singer's fictional world depends on his maintaining a perilous tension between irreconcilables. If he relaxes an instant, his story is threatened with fragmentation. The endings of *The Slave* and *The Magician of Lublin* are painful instances of such falls into disunity. Miraculously, to transform Wanda the Polish peasant into a Jewish Sarah and Jacob into a righteous man, or to metamorphose Yasha Mazur from circus prestidigitator to holy *Zaddik*, is to sentimentalize their lives under the intolerable pressure to give some kind of meaningful construct to them.

Singer's mind rejoices in dichotomies. In his autobiographical account of his boyhood he refers to his home as a "stronghold of Jewish puritanism, where the body was looked upon as a mere appendage to the soul." One day, visiting his older brother's atelier, he discovered the artist's healthy respect for the flesh. "This was quite a change from my father's court," he remarks, "but it seems to me that this pattern has become inherent to me. Even in my stories it is just one step from the study house to sexuality and back again. Both phases of human existence have continued to interest me."[7] The ambivalence of this intellectual position is pervasive in much that Singer writes. Thus he pays loving tribute to his brother as a "modern man" with the "high morality . . . of our pious ancestors."[8] Like the tightrope walker Yasha Mazur, Singer balances between these contrary modes of thought, his *modus operandi* at once archaic and modern, preoccupied with angels and demons and with Freud and Spinoza. He is drawn to the simple piety of his ancestors who never doubted the moral importance of life. He is also a man of the twentieth century, an uprooted European transplanted to America, seized by the contemporary vision of an absurd world—and his artistic integrity will not let the comfortable climate of divine reward and punishment remain intact. In the tension between moral cause and effect which his divided mind creates, his protagonists act out the unwitting drama of their lives. That these stories do not fragment into their unresolved elements attests to the remarkable narrative skill of Singer. That Singer has persisted despite the absence of an answer in posing again and again the question of the moral meaning of human experience attests to the radical sophistication of his vision.[9]

RADICAL SOPHISTICATION AND THE JEWISH-AMERICAN NOVEL

It is fashionable these days to see the Jew as the perfect symbol of the Camusian man. Although not as viable a fact in the fifties and sixties as in earlier periods, the Jew's lot of perpetual exile lends itself as a convenient symbol of alienation and hence of what one segment of contemporary thought conceives of as the essential consciousness of being man. Yet only in a highly qualified sense can what I have called the radical sophistication of Singer's vision be considered existential. As a Jew he appeals, however hesitantly, to a construct of beliefs that makes sense of the human experience. Nor does he, like the Christian, reject earth because of the expulsion from paradise. The Jew has historically been God-intoxicated and man-centered. His relationship with the world reveals itself simultaneously as *eros* and as *agapé*. "Mazeltov," Shifrah Tammar greets her daughter the morning after her wedding in Singer's "The Destruction of Kreshev"; " 'You are now a woman and share with us all the curse of Eve.' And weeping, she threw her arms about Lise's neck and kissed her."[10] Like the holy men of Chasidism bent on the hallowing of each day, she acknowledges the edict that love of man is a prerequisite to adoration of Jehovah. In short, the Jew pursues not the Christian pilgrimage from this world to the next, but performs the miracle of merger of the other world with this one.

During more than two thousand years of Diaspora the Jews have learned to breathe amidst the incertitude that is the daily air of a persecuted minority. A tenuous equipoise of irreconcilables is the best they could hope for; and it pervades their world picture. One could hardly expect otherwise with a people who have persisted for several milleniums in the belief that they are chosen, with a divine mission, when the contrary has been the fact of their daily lives. Out of this knowledge has grown a philosophy—anchored at one end by the teachings of Isaiah and at the other by the realities of this century—which conceives of the Jew as redeemer of the world through his acceptance of God's servitude.[11] But the encumbrance of evil—even when put to the service of God—is an uncertain business, never quite relieving the mind of inquietude. Christianity has stumbled over this legacy of sin since its inception. The Age of Enlightenment could only palely affirm with Alexander Pope that "Whatever is, is right," and "All partial evil, universal good."[12] Among Western men, the Jew has accepted most completely the ambience of this mixed blessing, this gift of the gods to man. The wisdom of the Jew's tragic passiveness is underscored by Singer in stories of what happens to a town when its people covenant with the Arch-Fiend in the interests of God, for example, in "The Destruction of Kreshev" and *Satan in Goray*. Grounded in the harsh realities of this life, the Jew retains unshakable conviction of man's spiritual destiny.

This capacity for belief in the face of "uncertainties, mysteries, doubts" is a radical sophistication that the Jew, with a culture historically of long standing, is currently giving to a century convinced in its existentialist isolation of the incoherence of existence. Today's intellectual, like the Coleridge that Keats characterized as "incapable of remaining content with half-knowledge," clutches at any "fine isolated verisimilitude caught from the Penetralium of mystery."[13] To him the contemporary Jewish novel has much to say. It is a commonplace among Jews that Judaism is not in the habit of disowning its great heretics completely. Rather it accommodates with worldly wisdom what is worthwhile in Spinoza, Maimonides, Freud, and Kafka. This willingness to accept the world on its own terms—disorderly, incoherent, absurd—"without any irritable reaching after fact and reason," and yet without losing faith in the moral significance of human actions, underlies the confrontation of experience in the best of the contemporary Jewish-American novels. . . .

Notes

1.   Irving Howe, "The Other Singer," *Commentary*, XLI (1966), 81.
2.   John Crowe Ransom, "The State of American Writing, 1948: A Symposium," *Partisan Review*, XV (1948), 879.
3.   Leslie Fiedler, "Saul Bellow," *Prairie Schooner*, XXXI (1957), 105. Fiedler characteristically, however, overstates the case in subsequent essays; cf. "Jewish-Americans, Go Home!" and "Zion as Main Street," *Waiting for the End* (New York: Stein and Day, 1964), pp. 65–103.
4.   Isaac Bashevis Singer, *The Spinoza of Market Street* (New York: Farrar, Straus and Giroux, 1958), p. 80.
5.   J. A. Eisenberg, "Isaac Bashevis Singer—Passionate Primitive or Pious Puritan," *Judaism*, II (1962), 346.
6.   Isaac Bashevis Singer, *Short Friday* (New York: Farrar, Straus and Giroux, 1964), p. 220.
7.   Isaac Bashevis Singer, *In My Father's Court* (New York: Farrar, Straus and Giroux, 1966), "The Purim Gift," p. 68; and "The Studio," p. 240.
8.   In the dedication of the English translation of Isaac Bashevis Singer, *The Family Moskat* (New York: Noonday Press, 1950).
9.   In many unseen and subconscious ways my point of view in this section has been influenced by Irving Howe's suggestive article, "Demonic Fiction of a Yiddish 'Modernist,' " *Commentary*, XXX (1960), 350–353.
10.   Isaac Bashevis Singer, *The Spinoza of Market Street* (New York: Farrar, Straus and Giroux, 1958), p. 182.
11.   Cf. Michael Fixler, "The Redeemers: Themes in the Fiction of Isaac Bashevis Singer," *Kenyon Review*, XXVI (1964), 380.
12.   Alexander Pope, *Essay on Man*, I, 292 and 294.
13.   Letter to George and Thomas Keats, 21 December 1817.

The Hidden God of Isaac Bashevis Singer

GRACE FARRELL

Isaac Bashevis Singer is a master story teller, a Yiddish Poe, impish narrator of things supernatural. His concerns are essentially religious: in large measure Jewish mysticism and folklore structure his vision and determine his style. However, his appeal transcends the parochial, for as his characters incessantly search out their elusive God, Singer evokes a universe akin to those of secular absurdists, a place where man appears alienated from any source of meaning and where the phenomenal world forever disintegrates about him. But while the vision of the absurdist is a recognition of nothingness and a justification for despair, Singer's is a more paradoxical sighting. He celebrates the impenetrable mysteries of creation, but, because those mysteries may conceal, not the splendor of Jehovah, but the face of evil, the celebration forever gives way to an apparition of eternal torment in worlds as yet unknown. Singer's doubt concerning the nature of eternity produces fiction which maintains an uneasy coalescence of dread and consolation. That same doubt prevents his tales from becoming moral allegories or exempla, for rarely is Singer so arrogant as to proffer an answer to the dilemma of human existence. Yet doubt never precludes the possibility that answers do exist, so always, Job-like, he gropes towards illumination.

In his search Singer creates labyrinths of illusion by layering dream upon dream, until, as a Nabokovian character once said, you feel ". . . as if you were rising up from stratum to stratum but never reaching the surface, never emerging into reality. . . . Yet who knows? Is this reality, *the* final reality or just a new deceptive dream?" As testament to both Singer's doubt and to his faith Gimpel the Fool speculates, "Perhaps the world is entirely an imaginary world, but it is only once removed from the true world." In one manner or another all of Singer's fiction is a reaching out for the "true world," that final reality where revelation will be more than a faint glimmer in a darkened universe.

However, Singer's faith in the possibility of attaining that other world, where "God be praised . . . even Gimpel cannot be deceived," is tempered by a scepticism made comic in tales like "The Warehouse," which transports

From the *Hollins Critic* 10 (December 1973). Copyright © the *Hollins Critic*. Reprinted by permission of the *Hollins Critic*.

the reader to the first sphere of heaven. There angels scratch buttocks with wings, and naked souls stand around in queues "waiting for the issuance of their new bodies." But if this is the "true world" of heaven, then God is conspicuously absent. As one agnostic soul stacked up in the warehouse puts it, "He is supposed to dwell in the seventh heaven, which is an infinity away. One thing we can be sure of, He's not here." Singer's scepticism, directed upward towards infinity where the Divine perpetually recedes from man's grasp, can reverse doubly upon itself. Thus an eerie perspective on his own incredulity is produced in "Jachid and Jechidah." There atheistic souls disbelieve in Earth. World sinks into illusory world, and only doubt survives.

As Isaiah (59:9–10) spoke of the Children of Israel, Singer might speak of mankind: "we wait for light, but behold obscurity; for brightness, but we walk in darkness. We grope for the wall like the blind, and we grope as if we had no eyes: we stumble at noon day as in the night, we are in desolate places as dead men." Those desolate places, Godless, are demon filled. A diaphanous net "as soft as a cobweb and as full of holes" is the only partition separating nature from supernature, labyrinth from labyrinth. And within that net hides a host of evil beings. Whatever its guise, whether devils and dybbuks ever lurking on the periphery of the unseen world or satanic specters of the Nazi Holocaust, the existence of evil is the one sure fact in the otherwise illusory material world of Singer's fiction. Cunning, murmurous voices of demonic narrators permeate the folktale worlds of the short stories. And even in the novels and tales set in Warsaw, New York, or Miami, far from the superstitions of the *shtetl*, ordinary reality continually dissolves into nightmare as devils are conjured up out of shadow and light. Man, it seems, abandoned by a distant God, is impotent victim of consummate jokesters who, like the wanton boys and the gods of *Lear*, tempt him to destruction. As the imp of "The Mirror" explains it, "When a demon wearies of chasing after yesterdays or of going round in circles on a windmill, he can instill himself inside a mirror. There he waits like a spider in its web, and the fly is certain to be caught."

II

The forces of evil infiltrate Singer's fictional worlds, disrupting the traditions of order, the laws and ancient rituals which define the relationships between man and man and between man and God. Dietary laws are not observed, ritual baths are not attended, prohibitions against the mingling of men and women are ignored, and in particular the rules surrounding marriage are disregarded. The regulations of faith preserve the order of the community. For Singer community has mystical significance as a continuation of God's creation. As Yahweh, victorious over the forces of the abyss, brought light out of the darkness, forming order from chaos, so man, by adhering to the Law of the Torah and by performing religious ritual, creates a communal order which stays the forces of evil and mystically unites the man of faith with the Divine. This process of creation, begun by God and continued by man, is an eternally ongoing struggle, with chaos forever a potential annihilator of order.

The forces of disorder penetrate inward, pervading every aspect of social and psychological order, and are reflected outwardly in storm: "The waves were barking at the Creator like packs of hounds. . . . Something in me cried out: *Shaddai*, destroy Satan. Meanwhile, the thunder crashed, the seas roared and broke with watery laughter." In *Satan in Goray*, a novel of messianic heresy set in seventeenth century Europe, storm becomes malicious, striking down Rabbi Benish, who attempts to stop an unsanctioned ball, a profanation of the law:

"... all at once a great hoarse wind rushed upon him, thrusting him back several steps, and began to drive him downhill from behind. . . . He rolled down the hill and all at once disappeared entirely, as though carried off. Casting a terrified glance over his shoulder, Rabbi Benish realized that evil was abroad and tried to return to his house. But at that moment his eyes were filled with sand. . . . the storm seized him, bore him aloft for a short distance, as on wings, and then cast him down with such violence that in the turmoil he could hear his bones shatter."

In the order of creation "the Lord on high is mightier far than the noise of great waters, mightier than the breakers of the sea" (Ps. 93:4), but here in Singer's world storm, the power of chaos, is resurgent throughout the landscape. It is not the whirlwind out of which God speaks, nor a divine force of nature like the Great Flood of Noah, which punished and admonished man for his transgressions against the Almighty. Rather, it is a cosmic force of evil infusing nature with vicious, chthonic vitality, "barking at the Creator," and obstructing His rabbi from restoring order in the community. While in Genesis God separated the land from the sea and calmed the watery abyss, storm, in a riot of uncreation, "overflows the shores and floats the land away."

Always the demonism in Singer's universe imitates in inverse the sacred. In *Satan in Goray* the hysteria and frenzy surrounding the appearance of a false Messiah culminates in the Satanic nightmare of the prophetess Rechele: "The Thing swept her over steep rooftops, gutters, and chimneys, huge and mildewy: there was no escape. It was stifling and the Thing pressed her to him, leaned against her. . . . the dark house was crowded with evil things, insane beings running hither and thither, hopping as on hot coals, quivery and swaying, as though they were all kneading a great trough of dough."

Throughout his works Singer subverts Christian images, using them as icons of messianic delusion. Here the birth at Bethlehem is transmuted into a macabre eruption of evil. Mary's vision, which revealed that she would become the mother of the Messiah by the Holy Spirit, becomes a dream of rape by a fiendish monster. In a malefic inversion of the conception and birth of Christ, "Satan enters into the body of a daughter of the Jews," and amid an account which parodies the language of the New Testament, a dybbuk, instead of a Messiah, is born.

Singer's devils invade the world, and with a power co-extensive with that of the Creator of order they recreate the cosmos in their own diabolical image and likeness. In one of his most successful tales, "The Gentleman From Cracow," the village of Frampol, which lay "amid thick forests and deep swamps, on the slope of a hill, level at the summit" is transfigured by Ketev Mriri, Chief of the Devils, into a Boschian landscape of Hell:

> Never before had Frampol seen such a sunset. Like rivers of burning sulphur, fiery clouds streamed across the heavens, assuming the shapes of elephants, lions, snakes, and monsters. They seemed to be waging a battle in the sky, devouring one another, spitting, breathing fire. It almost seemed to be the River of Fire they watched, where demons tortured the evil-doers amidst flowing coals and heaps of ashes. The moon swelled, became vast, blood-red, spotted, scarred, and gave off little light. The evening grew very dark, dissolving even the stars. The young men fetched torches, and a barrel of burning pitch was prepared. Shadows danced back and forth as though attending a ball of their own.

The sunset of Frampol embodies the chaotic forces of evil, which infuse violent movement into the shapes and colors of the sky, recreating the primordial battle of the heavens. Hellish phantoms introduce both a darkness and a fire so intense that even the stars dissolve. The young men, who are involved with an unauthorized ball, a transgression against the law, seek, in a symbolic re-enactment of the first creation, to rekindle light, but, enmeshed as they are in the forces of evil, succeed only in creating still more malefic beings in the shadows which play upon the walls, mimicking and mocking the dance.

The gentleman from Cracow, Ketev Mriri in disguise, is a false Messiah who ingratiates himself into the poor community of Frampol, spreading wealth and slowly undermining the rituals of faith. Finally he proposes one day that every girl of the village must marry before midnight, without the seven-day waiting period and the prescribed ablutions. The townspeople acquiesce, and in a pandemonium of movement and music the mismatched marriages take place. "Fiddles screeched, drums pounded, trumpets blared. The uproar was deafening. Twelve-year-old boys were mated with 'spinsters' of nineteen. The sons of substantial citizens took the daughters of paupers as brides; midgets were coupled with giants, beauties with cripples." Not only are the scared prohibitions regarding marriage ignored, but the people, in frenzy and hysteria, imitate the storm created by the powers of evil. As a result, in an apocalyptic fire every edifice of the law is annihilated.

> Now, as though the powers of darkness had been summoned, the rain and hail began to fall; flashes of lightning were accompanied by mighty thunder-claps. But, heedless of the storm, pious men and women embraced without shame, dancing and shouting as though possessed. Even the old were affected. In the furor, dresses were ripped, shoes shaken off, hats, wigs and skullcaps trampled in the mud. Sashes, slipping to the ground, twisted there like snakes. Suddenly there was a terrific crash. A huge bolt of lightning had simultaneously struck the synagogue, the study house, and the ritual bath. The whole town was on fire.

The re-enactment of the primal battle between God and Satan, Order and Chaos, is again portrayed as the waters, once separated from the firmament by Divine act, are fused back into the land. The people of Frampol, tempted and subjugated by the demonic, are sucked into the resulting sludge:

> There was nothing but one great swamp, full of mud, slime, and ashes. Floundering in mud up to their waists, a crowd of naked people went through the movements of dance. At first, the rabbi mistook the weirdly moving figures for devils, and was about to recite the chapter, "Let there be contentment," and other passages dealing with exorcism, when he recognized the men of his town. Only then did he remember the doctor from Cracow, and the rabbi cried out bitterly, "Jews, for the sake of God, save your souls! You are in the hands of Satan! . . ."
> But everything had turned to mud; the town of Frampol, stripped and ruined, had become a swamp. Its inhabitants were mud-splashed, denuded, monstrous. For a moment, forgetting their grief, they laughed at each other. The hair of the girls had turned into elflocks, and bats were entangled there. The young men had grown gray and wrinkled; the old were yellow as corpses.

Frampol is destroyed, and in the holocaust her children are slaughtered. But as man was created from the dust of the earth, so out of the slime of Frampol a new generation is born, a new town is built, and a new order is created. The people of Frampol were so tempted by greed that they blinded themselves to the reality of evil. They transgressed the rituals of faith and thereby let loose the powers of the abyss. Only by maintaining the law can the order established by the creative act of God be sustained within the community.

III

While messianic delusions invented by demons rob whole communities of their faith, destroying their religious institutions and casting them into the abyss, individuals, alienated from their ancient bonds, confused and melancholic, wander blindly, beset on every side by demons, unable to sustain any form of community in a world devoid of Divine presence.

Many of Singer's critics refuse to accept the reality of his demons. They insist that devils are no more than metaphors of psychological processes. The modern day demon is a function of the id, which, if not properly sublimated by the superego, can destroy the order upon which the ego, that cohesive sense of self, depends for all of its stability. However, it is important to remember Singer's statement that he believes in devils "not only symbolically but substantively . . . I truly believe that there are forces and spirits in this world, about which we know very little, which influence our lives." In a recent story from A Crown of Feathers Singer mischievously answers his suspicious critics: " ' . . . hidden powers that no one can explain exist everywhere . . . But how long do [the newspapers] write about anything? Here in America, if the Heavens would part and the angel Gabriel were to fly down with his six fiery wings and take a walk on Broadway, they would not write about it for more than a day or two.' " For Singer angels and demons do exist, but for the most part they go unnoticed. It is this belief in the substantive reality of supernatural forces which gives even those stories with contemporary, urban settings their aura of a folk tradition. Singer's demons are forces of the irrational in that they operate beyond the limits of reason. But this is not to say that they are manifestations solely of the psyche. They are supernatural beings, and, although they often function thematically as reflections of mental confusion, they always retain their autonomy as agents of Chaos.

For example, the short story "Alone," which is typical of Singer's realistic fiction in characterization, setting and theme, cannot be fully realized if the action is understood as functioning simply in the mind of the narrator. Only because the demons of his mind have counterparts in the Cosmos does his final renunciation of a she-devil acquire significance. Amid the noise and confusion of a Miami Beach Hotel, the narrator of "Alone" decides, as he has done many times before, that he would like to be alone. An imp must have overheard his wish, because his hotel suddenly closes down and he is forced to find another, one which turns out to be his alone. So he receives his wish, but "in such a topsy-turvy way that it appeared the Hidden Powers were trying to show me I didn't understand my own needs." Indeed, the misconception of his needs is the theme of the story. The solitude of the narrator proves to be burdensome, "Here before me, drenched in sunlight, was a summer melancholy. . . . Mankind, it seemed, had perished in some catastrophe, and I was left, like Noah—but in an empty ark, without sons, without a wife, without any animals." He wearies of his fulfilled wish in very little time, for "who can play games in an empty world?" And he decides that he was mistaken in his desires; what he needed all along was not total solitude, but a woman:

> Like all forms of life, I, too, wanted to be fruitful, wanted to multiply—or at least to go through the motions. I was prepared to forget any moral or aesthetic demands. I was ready to cover my guilt with a sheet and to give way wholly, like a blind man, to the sense of touch. At the same time the eternal questions tapped in my brain: Who is behind the world of appearance? Is it Substance with its Infinite Attributes? Is it the Monad of all Monads? Is it the Absolute, Blind Will, the Unconscious? Some kind of superior being has to be hidden in back of all these illusions.

By expressing his new desire in terms of the command of the Deity to Adam to increase and multiply, the narrator humorously creates the counterpoint between physical desire and spiritual longing which is at the heart of most of Singer's fiction. The juxtaposition of the narrator's musings upon lovemaking with the series of "eternal questions" reveals his confusion as to the nature of his needs. Like other characters he ponders the illusions of the world, but does not question the misapprehensions which are so obviously his own. But by declaring that he will forsake all moral and aesthetic laws, images of order which hold back the tides of chaos, the narrator invites the imps, ever ready for such an opportunity, to put him to the test, and in the process they unwittingly force him to clarify his relationship with God.

The pattern of temptation functions both on the cosmic level, as it does in "The Gentleman From Cracow" and many other of Singer's stories, and in the befuddled interior of the narrator's mind. Singer creates a series of illusions which question the substance of every aspect of the external world, while reflecting the chaotic state of the narrator's soul.

Confidence in the "reality" of the Miami Beach world is undermined as the large, bustling hotel in which the narrator has been living suddenly closes down, and he, reminiscing of his long since passed bachelor days, easily finds another, smaller, but empty one. Not only does this new world, so conveniently created just for him, seem to be a projection of his own mind, but the narrator's existence within the old world is suspect: "I was on Collins Avenue in Miami Beach, but I felt like a ghost, cut off from everything. I went into the library and asked a question—and the librarian grew frightened. I was like a man who had died, whose space had already been filled."

The demonic forces conjured up by the narrator's lack of faith in God and by his inability to understand his own motivations, infiltrate his solitary, illusory domain. "I saw houses eaten up by termites and a pond of brackish water in which the descendants of the primeval snake crawled and slithered."

They come in storm. "One gush and I was drenched as if by a huge wave. A fiery rod lit up the sky . . . The top of a palm tree sheathed in sackcloth, bent to the wind, ready to kneel." The chaos created by the storm permeates the narrator's mind. He moves through the hurricane as through a dream or an Alice-in-Wonderland delusion:

> In my confusion I kept on running. Sinking into puddles so deep I almost drowned. I rushed forward with the lightness of boyhood. The danger had made me daring, and I screamed and sang, shouting to the storm in its own key. By this time all traffic had stopped, even the automobiles had been abandoned. But I ran on, determined to escape such madness or else go under. I had to get that special delivery letter, which no one had written and I never received.

Throughout the story confidence in the outside world has been continuously undermined. Here the existence of his only concrete connection with an independent reality, the letter, "my only link with the outside world," is threatened. And the substance of the narrator himself begins to disintegrate. He becomes as one with the storm, screaming in its own key, drowning in its puddles. When he finds his hotel, in a mirror his "half-dissolved image reflected itself like a figure in a cubist painting." He is himself a figment of his own doubt, transmuted by the powers of the storm, whether within or outside of himself. He is ready for the test, set by forces of evil and by his own confused questioning. Thus, into his room enters the woman for whom he wished and for whom he had said he would forsake any moral or aesthetic demands. She is the Cuban hunchback who manages his empty hotel:

> I rested my head on the pillow and lay still with the eerie feeling that the mocking imp was fulfilling my last wish. I had wanted a hotel to myself—and I had it. I had dreamed of a woman coming, like Ruth to Boaz, to my room—a woman had come. She stared at me intently, as silent as a witch casting a spell. . . . I wanted to pronounce an incantation against the evil eye and pray to the spirits who have the final word not to let this hag overpower me. . . . In the hellish glare the Cuban witch crouched low like an animal ready to seize its prey—mouth open, showing rotted teeth; matted hair, black on her arms and legs: and feet covered with carbuncles and bunions. Her nightgown had slipped down, and her wrinkled breasts sagged weightlessly. Only the snout and tail were missing.

The narrator is tempted by the Cuban demon as Zirel, who also lacked knowledge of herself, was tempted by the imp of "The Mirror." Zirel, blinded by boredom and vanity, is overcome by the forces of evil, but the narrator acknowledges God and is saved. When the Cuban hunchback says, "Who cares what you do? No one see, [sic]" she is not only tempting him, she is confronting him with the eternal questions, which he had not been able to answer. His reply, "God sees," clarifies his relationship with the Transcendent and devitalizes the power of the demonic forces over him. He sleeps, and when he awakens the storm has ceased, his hotel is closed, and "the Cuban woman looked at me crookedly—a witch who had failed in her witchcraft, a silent partner of the demons surrounding me and of their cunning tricks."

Obviously Singer makes attempts to locate the demons of "Alone" in the narrator's psyche. The story is told by the hero. Through his eyes both the familiar world of Miami Beach and his image of himself disintegrate, the storm menaces him, the Cuban hunchback, "pale, thin, with her hair drawn back, and a glint in her black eyes . . . [wearing] an old-fashioned blouse edged with yellowed lace," becomes an infernal witch. Her temptation of him occurs between a dream and a period of sleep. And the letter, which seems to be the only object of substance in an otherwise dissolving world, never materializes. The reply to his question at the conclusion of the story, "Isn't there a letter for me?" is "No letter."

But to make of the narrator's temptation only a psychological situation in which the demonic elements of the id surface momentarily, is to diminish somewhat the impact of the story. The narrator had stated that he would forget any aesthetic or moral demands if only he were granted a "hot-eyed woman," and the accommodating imp provides him with the Cuban "with black piercing eyes." If her ugliness causes him to reject her then his affirmation of God is merely a ruse, and the temptation lacks significance. On the other hand, if his conscience, that socio-religious structure of his superego, causes him to reject her and sublimate his desires, because not to do so would be adulterous, then again the story fails, for never does Singer imply that the narrator's moral dilemma lies in that sphere. To do so at the very end of the story would be not only anti-climactic, but even priggish. It is true that the narrator discovers that he cannot renounce his aesthetic and moral scruples; he finds the Cuban ugly, and he remembers that he has a wife. But these demands are not in and of themselves important. Rather, they serve as additional indications of his self-deception and as metaphors of structures which must be maintained against disorder. When he declares that he is capable of renouncing them, and when he is unable to make a clear commitment to the Creator of order, the forces of evil, external to him, infiltrate his world and put him to the test. His temptation, therefore, is more than a mental construct. The Cuban is indeed a demon, not only a woman and not merely an hallucination. The psychological and the illusory are metaphors of his cosmic dilemma, rather than, as many critics would have it, the other way around. And the narrator's disorientation amid the polyphony of illusion created by the imps is a metaphor not only of a befuddled psyche, but of a collapsed cosmos.

IV

The forces of evil infiltrate the realistic worlds of Singer's novels much as they do his folktales. Demons still weave in and out of dreams, but they are most evident in the material world which crumbles under the weight of its own iniquity. The Hell which incessantly intrudes upon the *shtetl*, triumphs over the course of modern history: " 'evil spirits are playing with us. We came out of Gehenna, but Gehenna followed us to America. Hitler has run after us.' "

The Manor and its sequel *The Estate* celebrate the last knights of faith in the modern world. In these novels Singer delineates the gradual decomposition of the Jewish community from the Polish uprisings of 1863 to the last years of the nineteenth century. In the midst of political, philosophical and technological upheavals of monumental import, a few pious men fervently cleave to the all but shattered faith of their forebears. *The Manor* ends as Calman Jacoby, aware of the dissolution of the world about him and of the hedonism and atheism of his own son, retreats into his homemade synagogue where he chants the first Mishnah:

> Calman did not even remember when he had learned the chant in which he prayed and studied. It had come down to him through generations of ancestors. . . . The Hebrew letters were steeped in holiness, in eternity. They seemed to unite him with the patriarchs . . . Among these shelves of sacred books, Calman felt protected. Over each volume hovered the soul of its author. In this place God watched over him.

In a subcelestial world Calman's faith, hidden in his synagogue, no longer has the efficacy to create a community or to bind a family together. The murmur of his chant, that sound of God's holy word, diffuses into silence at the conclusion of *The Estate*. There the Rabbi of Marshinov prays for the truth as he dies, and like Rabbi Bainish in "Joy," he finally discovers his hidden God:

> The rabbi thought about darkness. It was nothing but the lack of light, the concealment of His face. . . . Suddenly something fluttered. . . . the rabbi saw a great light . . . [he] closed his eyes, but the light was still there: a radiance that shone neither outside him nor within him, but filled all space, penetrated all being. It was everything together: revelation, surcease from all earthy turmoil, the profoundest joy. . . . He had only one wish left: to let those who had sunk into doubt and suffering know what he had seen. He stretched out his hand to knock on the wall, but his hand made no sound.
> He lingered in this state until sunrise.

Here faith, although solitary rather than communal, does exist, and revelations of eternal splendor, although ineluctably yoked with silence, are at least possible. But in *The Family Moskat*, which spans three generations of a Jewish dynasty and concludes as the Nazis occupy Warsaw, evil is so pervasive that all traces of faith vanish into a holocaustal wasteland. The final words of the novel pronounce its revelation. " 'Death is the Messiah. That's the real truth.' "

With *Enemies, A Love Story* Singer pushes forward to a time past the Nazi Holocaust. " 'Everything has already happened,' Herman thought. 'The creation, the flood, Sodom, the giving of the Torah, the Hitler holocaust.' Like the lean cows of Pharaoh's dream, the present had swallowed eternity, leaving no trace." Herman Broder, New York polygamist, Polish survivor of the Holocaust, finds only evil in the hidden face of God: " 'Wasn't it possible that a Hitler presided on high and inflicted suffering on imprisoned souls?' " Left in a world where redemption and transcendence are devoid of all meaning, Herman is, in the end, overwhelmingly insignificant. "The sun was racing off somewhere with its planets in tow. The Milky Way turned on its axis. In the midst of these cosmic adventures, Herman stood with his handful of reality, with his ridiculous little troubles." Like his nineteenth century prototype Yasha in *The Magician of Lublin*, Herman is self-exiled from humanity, alone in a populous world. Unable to form any permanent relationships, incapable of understanding themselves or of making any decisions, they hide. Yasha walls himself up in a womb-like penitent cell with one small opening through which all the evil he had sought to evade swarms in one hundred-fold. Herman disappears, probably to conceal himself in the perpetual hideaway from which he never really escaped, "an American version of his Polish hayloft." To hide seems to be the only means of survival in a demonic universe. In a recent interview Singer admitted that, "the best thing you can do is run away from evil, not fight it. Because the moment you begin to fight evil, you become part of evil yourself." "The Magazine," a story from his newly released collection *A Crown of Feathers*, puts it this way:

> "There are still honest people. The trouble is that the wicked make all the noise and the just sleep."
> "They'll always sleep," I said.
> "They can be woken up."
> "If they're woken up, they'll become wicked."

V

It would seem impossible in a toppled universe suffused with demons and evil of every kind to proffer hope that man might find redemption in the traditions of his religion. The laws and rituals which purport to protect him from evil and to lead him into mystical union with a benevolent God, seem in their multiplicity to suffocate the very spirit they pretend to free. But in one lovely story, "Short Friday," Singer again reaches out for the "true world" of which Gimpel the Fool spoke. Shmul-Leibele, "half tailor, half furrier, and complete pauper," and his wife Shoshe attain perfect fulfillment through faith in the law. The plethora of ritual which they piously enact imbues them with a richness of pleasure and love unknown to any other characters. Never do they doubt, and not one demon dares intrude upon their world. When they die, asphyxiated by the fumes of their Sabbath stove, they awaken together in the grave like Poe's Monos and Una. But while "The Colloquy of Monos and Una" delineates the process of decay and ends once dust has returned to dust, the conversation of Shoshe and Shmul-Leibele ends only as their eternal life begins:

> Yes, the brief years of turmoil and temptation had come to an end. Schmul-Leibele and Shoshe had reached the true world. Man and wife grew silent. In the stillness they heard the flapping of wings, a quiet singing. An angel of God had come to guide Schmul-Leibele the tailor and his wife, Shoshe, into Paradise.

In the midst of tales of devils and destruction "Short Friday" might seem to be a sentimental fantasy, a bit of wishful thinking in a world where God conceals His face, and where, for the most part, man too, made in His image and likeness, hides. But in Singer's world the improbable is commonplace and anything is possible, even salvation.

The Destruction and Resurrection of the Jews in the Fiction of Isaac Bashevis Singer

EDWARD ALEXANDER

The best-known utterance about the Holocaust in the writings of Isaac Bashevis Singer is the concluding statement of the English version of *The Family Moskat*: "Death is the Messiah. That's the real truth." The setting is Warsaw at the time of the Nazi bombardment and invasion in 1939; the speaker is Hertz Yanovar (a Jew who has substituted psychic research for religion). The statement gains its tremendous force less from the events within the novel than from the reader's knowledge of what will befall the Jews after the novel ends, not only in Poland but everywhere in Europe. But it is also intended to pass adverse judgment upon the Jewish impatience for redemption, an impatience that expresses itself still to some extent in the religious longing of the traditional Jew but primarily in the developmental superstitions of the modern secular Jew. The novel shows how the Russian Revolution of 1905, which had accelerated the break-up of the Jewish world, had, paradoxically, quickened the messianic expectations both of the Chassidim who deplored this disintegration and of the *maskilim* (enlighteners) and leftists who welcomed it.

The Family Moskat is a study of the prospective victims of the Holocaust and of the reasons for their victimization. That Singer should, both in this novel and elsewhere, assume that the Holocaust is to be understood, insofar as it *can* be understood, primarily as an event in Jewish history, represents both an advantage and a shortcoming of his method. Singer never accepts the implications of the old joke told by liberals about the antisemite who claims that the Jews had caused World War I and gets the reply: Yes, the Jews and the bicyclists. Why the bicyclists? asks the antisemite. Why the Jews? asks the other. On the contrary, Singer sees the major catastrophes of Jewish history in the Diaspora as so many announcements of the Holocaust, of which they are the prototypes. Nowhere in his fiction does Singer assume that the Jews were the accidental victims of the Holocaust, or that the disaster might just as well have befallen another people. When Reb Dan

From *Judaism* 25, no. 1 (Winter 1976): 98–106. Reprinted by permission, copyright 1976 the American Jewish Congress.

Katzenellenbogen ponders the relationship between the pacific ethos of the Jews and the orgiastic violence of the gentiles, and asks of the latter: "What were they seeking? What would be the outcome of their endless wars?" we know what the answer is: the destruction of the Jews. A Europe for which the prospect of murdering Jews had become, in the late nineteenth century, a primary principle of social unity, cannot be said to have stumbled accidentally upon the Jews as victims. But if Singer avoids the pitfalls of the approach which assumes the perfect innocence of the Jews and the accidental nature of their victimization, he may be said to go to the other extreme in that he tends to view the Nazis as only the latest in the long succession of those murderous outsiders who have obtruded themselves upon Jewish history again and again. "Yes," sighs the narrator of *Family Moskat*, "every generation had its Pharaohs and Hamans and Chmielnickis. Now it was Hitler."

In *The Slave*, a novel ostensibly dealing with the plight of Jews in seventeenth-century Poland in the aftermath of the fearful massacres perpetrated upon the body of the Jewish people by the Polish peasant-revolutionary Chmielnicki, Singer is clearly writing about the Holocaust. Virtually all the questions that Singer's explicit Holocaust literature characteristically asks are posed in this novel. " 'Why did this happen to us?' " one of the men asked. " 'Josefov was a home of Torah.' " " 'It was God's will,' " a second answered. " 'But why? What sins did the small children commit? They were buried alive.' " How, the novel's hero asks, can the mind grasp such a quantity of horrors? "There was a limit to what the human mind could accept. It was beyond the power of any man to contemplate all these atrocities and mourn them adequately." What was the role of God in all this? Could so much evil really be explained as a test of man's faith, of his free will? "Did the Creator require the assistance of Cossacks to reveal His nature?" Could Chmielnicki really be a part of the godhead or was it perhaps true that this massacre of the Jews revealed the existence of a radical evil in the universe, a devil who had no celestial origins? *The Slave* also shows us Jews who are forced to dig their own graves before they are executed, berates the Jewish community for its shameful failure to offer forceful resistance to the murders, and preaches the scared duty of remembering forever those who were slaughtered. "Through forgetfulness," Jacob says of himself, "he had also been guilty of murder." In its dwelling upon the physical obscenities of the mass murders, *The Slave* may even be said to deal more concretely with the Holocaust than those novels and stories that approach it frontally.

Our reaction to Singer's tendency to generalize the Holocaust in this way will depend in part on whether we view antisemitism as a phenomenon deeply embedded in Western culture or as a movement quite distinct from religious Jew hatred, a movement that grew up only in the nineteenth century. Since a novelist ordinarily writes about what he knows, which in Singer's case is the Jews and the Christians of Poland, we can hardly expect him to give us a portrayal of the German murderers of Polish Jewry. Yet we might reasonably expect that a writer who in treating the Holocaust recognizes the centrality of the question "Why the Jews?" should at least not preclude us from asking the question, although he cannot ask it himself, "Why the Germans?" That Singer should implicitly short-circuit this question is the more disturbing in view of the fact that he cannot finally convince us or himself that the Holocaust is no different in kind from the long series of disasters that have befallen the Jews since the seventeenth century. *The Slave* celebrates survival and recovery; the characters of *Enemies* who have survived the camps never recover and cannot return to life.

Singer is not only not discriminating in his treatment of the murderers of the Jews; he at times comes close to viewing them as merely a function of the Jews' failure to be true to themselves and to their best traditions. The difficult and painful question of the Jews' co-responsibility for the disaster that was to engulf them is raised often in *The Family Moskat*, both by Jews and gentiles. At a political discussion early in the book, one of those overheated conspiratorial gatherings of Jews that Singer loves to recall, a man named Lapidus upbraids his leftist friends with this classic utterance: " 'We dance at everybody's wedding but our own.' " Leftist Jews, ready, even eager, to spill their ink and their blood lavishly for the liberation of every other oppressed group, have called into question the very existence of the Jews as a people. The Bialodrevna rabbi, for his part, charges that the enlightened Jews are "lead[ing] their own children to the slaughterhouse," a remark that gains in impact from the later description, filled with Singer's vegetarian zeal, of the actual slaughterhouse that Asa Heshel and Hadassah visit. A Polish inspector adds his sinister voice to this chorus of accusers when he tells Hertz Yanovar, who has been arrested (mistakenly) on charges of Communist activity, that the massive Jewish involvement in Bolshevism exacerbates antisemitism and "puts the very existence of the Jewish race in danger."

If we suspect Singer of stacking the evidence against his left-leaning Jewish characters, we should remember that his accusation of self-destructive zealousness can be amply confirmed by external sources, and particularly by the testimony of two of the most astute Jewish leaders of the early part of this century. Chaim Weizmann said that hundreds of thousands of young Jews in early twentieth-century Russia were convinced revolutionaries "offering themselves for sacrifice as though seized by a fever." Yitzchok Leibush Peretz wrote of the 1905 Revolution, which roused the hopes of so many leftist Jews, that the pogroms that accompanied it demonstrated a painful truth that the Jews would ignore at their peril: "In the hands of the Jew, the reddest of all flags has been placed forcibly and he has been told: 'Go, go on and on, with all liberators, with all fighters for a better tomorrow, with all destroyers of Sodoms. But never may you rest with them. The earth will burn under your feet. Pay everywhere the bloodiest costs of the process of liberation, but be unnamed in all emancipation proclamations, . . . You are the weakest and the least of the nations and you will be the last for redemption.' "[1]

Although it has been frequently and correctly observed, sometimes by Singer himself,[2] that his literary roots lie outside the Yiddish tradition, although within the Jewish tradition, there is one important respect in which he is a continuator of Abramovitch, Sholom Aleichem, and Peretz. Like them, he looks upon the Jews, with a rare exception here and there (usually, in Singer, a Zionist exception), as political imbeciles, incapable of recognizing not just political actualities, but the most fundamental political and human necessity—that of self-preservation. It is therefore hardly surprising that the verdict of his fiction should go clearly against those Jews who undermined first their right to exist as a people and then, inevitably, their right to exist at all by embracing the Socialist distinction between the Jews as a people—a particularly reactionary and obscurantist people—and individual Jews who enlisted in the party of humanity. The running argument in Singer's novels of modern life, over whether the hatred of Jews is increased by those Jews who retain their Yiddish and their caftan and their sidelocks or by those who assimilate themselves to the host culture by speaking Polish and shortening their jackets and their hair and their memory, was settled by history itself, for the plan to eliminate Jews from the face of the earth originated in a country where Jews aped the manners and the culture and often the religion of their prospective murderers. (To be sure, the German grandchildren, or at least great-grandchildren, of those Jews who had repudiated their faith would not have been among the murdered of Auschwitz; but they might have been among the murderers. " 'If we don't want to become like the Nazis,' " says Herman Broder in *Enemies*, " 'we must be Jews.' ")

But this application of the wisdom of hindsight (which, we should add, is better than the stupidity of hindsight) is not the core of Singer's analysis of the Jews' coresponsibility for the terrible fate that befell them. The hero of *Enemies*, looking back upon the destruction of his people, believes that the Holocaust will have had one (and only one) salutary effect if it has discredited the delusion of progress: "Phrases like a 'better world' and a 'brighter tomorrow' seemed to him a blasphemy on the ashes of the tormented." It was precisely the belief in progress, whether defined by Darwin or by Marx, that implicated Jewish *maskilim* and Jewish socialists in the deluge that eventually overwhelmed them and their brethren. First, it was this belief that sanctioned the elimination of biologically inferior species and socially backward classes; second, it intensified secular messianism and so prepared the arrival of the latest in the long line of false messiahs who have been a curse upon the history of the Jews.

In her brilliant essay on *The Manor*,[3] Mary Ellmann has shown how pervasive is the influence of Darwinian evolutionism on that novel's "emancipated" characters. According to her, Singer's critique of Darwinism dwells upon its tendency to blur distinctions between man and animal, Jew and gentile, piety and impiety. My own view is that the main thrust of Singer's attack is directed against the evolutionist belief in perpetual and progressive motion because, as historians have often argued, it is analogous to the Marxist belief in the infallibility of the historical process:

> The conversation turned to religion. Zipkin said straight out that he was an atheist. . . . Man, as Darwin had proved, was descended from the apes. He was just another animal: *homo sapiens*. Zipkin began discussing the doctrines of Marx, Lassalle, and Lavrov. The Polish Jew, he said, had once had a real place in society. Before the liberation of the serfs, he had acted as an intermediary between the landowners and the peasantry. He had outlived his role and become little more than a parasite. He wasn't productive, didn't speak the language of the country in which he lived, and sent his children to cheders. How long was the Jew going to wash himself in ritual baths and walk around in tzizis?

Darwin's Nature and Marx's History, hypostatized, speak with one voice on the Jewish people: *they* are the chief impediment to the removal of inferior races and backward classes that biology and history demand. When Ezriel Babad asks Zipkin whether all the Jews, including their own parents, must be destroyed because they are not peasants, his sister screams: " 'Leave our parents and the Jews out of it. . . . A parasite is a parasite, even if he's your father.' "

In *The Estate*, which continues the story of *The Manor*, the most articulate exponent of the view that both history and nature use mankind merely as raw material for the fulfillment of their high purposes is Zadok, the wayward son of the Chassid Jochanan. Zadok believes the moral laws of the Jews are confuted by the laws of biology that sanction, and indeed require, the Malthusian struggle for existence and catastrophic wars. " 'It's the same to nature who kills whom. For thousands of years bulls have been slaughtered and nature has kept quiet. . . . Why should a human life be so dear to Nature?' "

Zadok's reference to the slaughter of bulls as a model for the slaughter of men serves to remind us that Singer's vegetarianism, which he has called his only dogma,[4] however embarrassing it may be to some of his admirers, is crucial to his understanding of the Holocaust. For Herman Broder, "what the Nazis had done to the Jews, man was doing to animals." Singer believes that acceptance in any form whatever of the theory that might makes right must eventually victimize the Jews. Hence, in the dreams of Yoineh Meir, the slaughterer who in the story of that name forsakes his calling because he comes to believe that injustice to dumb beasts retards messianic redemption, "cows assumed human shape, with beards and side locks, and skullcaps over their horns." Singer's saints, like Jochanan, whose son will welcome the killing of bulls and of men, are not only troubled by the slaughter of animals but express tenderness over flies and bugs, as if they could feel that it was to be but a short step from the metaphorical depiction of Jews as parasites to their literal extermination as bugs.

But Darwinist-Marxist historicism is for Singer something more than just a modern expression of the doctrine that might makes right. It inspires in him a special revulsion because it joins to this doctrine the principle that morality is a consideration not of the present but only of the long run, and that the evil of the moment may be justified as working for the good of the developmental process. This principle, too, is a modern version of what is for Singer an ancient evil, which has spectacularly manifested itself in Jewish history in the form of apocalyptic messianism. *Satan in Goray* is Singer's most elaborate portrait of the type of the false Messiah, or rather of the atmosphere from which he is engendered. In this novel, and also in the story of "The Destruction of Kreshev," Singer shows that in the messianic frenzy that existed during the lifetime of Sabbatai Zevi in the seventeenth century and even long after his apostasy and death, many Jews, convinced of the Talmudic precept that the Messiah will come when one generation is either wholly innocent or wholly guilty, plausibly decided that the way to hasten redemption and the coming of the Messiah was to plunge deeper and deeper into evil and degradation. This seemed a shorter, less winding path, than that of plodding virtue. In "Destruction of Kreshev" Shloimele, a secret follower of the false Messiah, goes so far as to say: " 'I love fire! I love a holocaust . . . I would like the whole world to burn and Asmodeus to take over the rule.' " The moral of all such stories of impatient attempts to hasten the coming of the Messiah is enunciated by the old-fashioned narrator of the last two chapters of *Satan in Goray* at the end of that book: "LET NONE ATTEMPT TO FORCE THE LORD: TO END OUR PAIN WITHIN THE WORLD: THE MESSIAH WILL COME IN GOD'S OWN TIME. . . ."

When Singer moves to a modern setting, apocalyptic messianism becomes historicist activism that expresses itself through the by now familiar motto: "Worse is better." Precisely by exacerbating the evils, anomalies, and hatred within the existing social system, one is preparing the liberation from some mysterious region of the impulse that will remove anomaly, injustice, and hatred altogether. Ironically, however, it is now the religious characters or those who retain nostalgic sympathy for the Jewish religion who become the exponents of patience and the critics of messianic urgency. In the nineteenth century, the Jews who altogether repudiate their religious faith adopt a secular faith, whereas it is Ezriel Babad, vacillating between the enlightenment of Western Europe and the obscurantism of Chassidism, who passes judgment on his sister's belief in redemption, redemption through violent revolution: "She wanted to free the peasants and the proletariat. Like their father [the rabbi], she campaigned against the company of Satan. But what would come after victory? Not redemption, not saints who benefited from the splendor of the Divine glory, but lots of newspapers, magazines, theaters, cabarets. More railroads, more machines. . . ." Ezriel's own daughter, Zina, becomes a kind of schlemiel-revolutionary who masquerades as a pregnant woman and experiences the birth pangs not of the Messiah but of a revolutionary arms smuggler whose cartridges burst from under her dress in a trolley car. Appalled by the results of all these secular attempts to realize the millennium, Ezriel resolves that even his own pacific ideal of cultural pluralism "could not be brought about forcibly, nor could the Messiah be compelled to arrive." If Ezriel had survived to experience the Holocaust, he would, like his creator Singer, have viewed Hitler as a creation of Jewish as much as of German history. "The belief in false Messiahs," Singer has said, "is very old and very young. What was Stalin if not a false Messiah? And what was Hitler if not a false Messiah?"[5]

What Ezriel opposes to the future-oriented visions of the Darwinists and Marxists who wish to accelerate the movement of natural and social history is the wisdom of standing still or even moving in reverse that is embodied by the Chassidim. "When one gazes at the Talmudic scholars, one actually sees eternity. . . . How wonderfully they have isolated themselves amidst all this madness! They do not even know that they are at the end of the 'Magnificent' and bloody nineteenth century. In their Houses of Worship, it is always the beginning." For Ezriel, the stationariness of the Chassidim, their entire indifference to the messianic hopes of the Darwinians and revolutionists, their contempt for the alleged decrees of Nature and History that declare them parasitical and obsolete and reactionary, represent a splendid affirmation of human freedom and afford a glimpse of eternity itself.

For survivors of the Holocaust, however, the Chassidim are no longer distinctly available as a living embodiment of resistance to historical inevitabilities, or supposed inevitabilities. The characters in *Enemies*, many of them, live with the fear that the Holocaust really did show that the nineteenth-century ideologues who claimed that the voices of Nature and History were the voices of God were right after all. " 'Slaughtering Jews,' " says Masha, " 'is part of nature. Jews must be slaughtered—that's what God wants.' " One can no longer see eternity in the Chassidim because they and eternity itself have been consumed by the Holocaust. " 'Everything has already happened,' Herman thought. 'The creation, the flood, Sodom, the giving of the Torah, the Hitler holocaust. Like the lean cows of Pharaoh's dream, the present had swallowed eternity, leaving no trace.' " *Enemies* does not (like Bellow's *Mr. Sammler's Planet*, for example) explore the possibility of recovery from the trauma for those Jews who have survived the Holocaust, but assumes that for the Jews generally the Holocaust was the end of the world. For Herman, the only future lies in the past, as it exists not in living anachronisms like the Chassidim but in what he calls "Jewish books." For Herman, and by implication thousands like him, there is no community or homeland to which to return. "These writings were home. On these pages dwelt his parents, his grandparents, all his ancestors."

But what of the homeland that did in fact arise after the death of European Jewry? To put the question another way, does Singer ever countenance a Jewish defiance of history that expresses itself as a living social reality rather than through nostalgia and literature? For many Jews, especially young people in the D. P. camps after the war, Zionism was precisely that spiritual impulse which alone could both overcome the degradation and defy the absurdity of the Holocaust. Singer's treatment of Zionism, although at a considerable remove from the center of his imaginative world, nevertheless conveys his sense of how far the Jews can resist the sentence of death that modern historical "laws" appear to have decreed for them by themselves taking action within history.

Singer's most ambitious Holocaust novel, *The Family Moskat*, is also his most Zionist one. The book offers a series of parallel scenes intended to demonstrate that neither believers nor skeptics are capable of fathoming the enormity of Jewish suffering. When, at the outbreak of World War I, the Jews are expelled from Tereshpol Minor, Rabbi Dan Katzenellenbogen, as he guides the exodus of his people, is assailed with the all-expressive "*Nu?*" by the town freethinker and apostle of Western enlightenment, Jekuthiel the watchmaker:

> "*Nu*, rabbi?" he said.
> It was clear that what he meant was: Where is your Lord of the Universe now? Where are His miracles? Where is your faith in Torah and prayer?
> "*Nu*, Jekuthiel," the rabbi answered. What he was saying was: Where are your worldly remedies? Where is your trust in the gentiles? What have you accomplished by aping Esau?

To Jekuthiel it is inescapably clear that the Jewish God has been far less faithful to His people than they to Him; and to Rabbi Dan it is just as clear that if God cannot help the Jews, nothing can, for what salvation can come from imitating the ways of the oppressor? Both are right in what they deny, but unsupported in what they affirm. In either case, as Rabbi Dan says to himself: "The old riddle remained: the pure in heart suffered and the wicked flourished; the people chosen of God were still ground in the dust. . . ."

A similar parallelism aligns Rabbi Dan with his grandson Asa Heshel. Both labor during a lifetime over manuscripts grappling with the ultimate questions. The grandfather had produced three sackfuls of manuscripts, and "there had been a time when he had entertained the idea of publishing some of his commentaries." But a few days after the outbreak of World War I, "he crammed his manuscripts into the mouth of the stove and then watched them burn. 'The world will survive without them,' he remarked." Asa Heshel, a few days after the outbreak of World War II, repeats Jekuthiel's question, asking Barbara, " 'What do you think of God now, tell me.' " But he acknowledges the futility of his own hedonistic solution: "In the drawer of his desk lay an old version of 'The Laboratory of Happiness,' written in Switzerland. Asa Heshel unscrewed the door of the stove and thrust it inside."

If the mystery of Jewish suffering cannot be fathomed by the intellectual efforts of either the believers or the skeptics, perhaps the best response would be an existential one, in which action would cut through the knot that intellect has not been able to untie. "Get thee out of thy country" is an injunction with deep roots in Jewish consciousness, and one that sounds in the ears of several characters in *The Family Moskat*, including Asa Heshel himself, who after his first brush with antisemitism in Warsaw says to himself: " 'Yes, Abram is right. I've got to get out of Poland. If not to Palestine, then to some other country where there's no law against Jews going to college.' "

Since Abram Shapiro, who is something of a Chassid but more of a lecher, is the most prominent spokesman for Zionism among the novel's major characters, the book can hardly be said to be a Zionist tract. Nevertheless, Zionism is distinctly set apart from socialism, communism, and other left-wing movements that arouse the wrath of the orthodox, for the very good reason that only Zionism grasped the dimensions of modern antisemitism and understood its implications for the future of the Jewish people.

Abram rails against the Jewish intellectuals who gain their university credentials by loudly proclaiming that Jews are a religion, not a nation, and that the backward, dirty Jews from the east pollute the Western European atmosphere. He insists that the Exile alone has made of the Jews the " 'cripples, *schlemiels*, lunatics' " who inhabit Warsaw: " 'Just let us be a nation in our own land and we'll show what we can do. Ah, the geniuses'll tumble out of their mothers' bellies six at a time—like in Egypt.' " Abram's claims for Zionism are expressed with the hyperbole that characterizes all his utterances. Yet he sees with lucidity what is concealed, by vanity or self-interest or even good will, from the eyes of the modernizing, worldly assimilationists, who (like Adele Landau) seek to become indistinguishable from the gentiles: " 'And I suppose if we all put on Polish hats and twist our mustaches into points, then they'll love us,' Abram rejoined, and twisted at his own mustache. 'Let the young lady read the newspapers here. They squeal that the modern Jew is worse than the caftaned kind. Who do you think the Jew-haters are aiming for? The modern Jew, that's who.' " All the subsequent events of the novel will bear out what Abram says.

Apart from the Orthodox Jews, the most active opponents of Zionism in the novel are the socialist and communist revolutionaries, whose devotion to "humanity" slackens only when the Jews come into view. *The Family Moskat* is the first major work by Singer in which the intensity of his dislike of leftist political movements makes itself felt. There can be no doubt but that Singer views socialism and communism as antithetical, first to the interests of the Jews, then to the interests of society, and ultimately to those of humanity itself. It is significant that Singer endows an anti-leftist character named Lapidus with some of the memorable utterances of the novel even though he appears in but a single scene and has no role whatever in the action. Lapidus disturbs the smug humanitarianism of the circle of Jewish leftists gathered at Gina Genendel's by pointing out that they weep bitter tears over every Ivan, every Slav, every oppressed nation of the world, except the Jews. He recounts an experience he had in Siberia that epitomized the self-deceptive masquerade of Jews who seek a secular substitute for the religion they have deserted: " ' . . . I saw a bunch of Jews, with scrawny beards, black eyes—just like mine. At first I thought it was a *minyan* for prayers. But when I heard them babbling in Russian and spouting about the revolution—the S. R.'s, the S. D.'s, Plekhanov, Bogdanov, bombs, assassinations—I started to howl.' "

Lapidus lashes these Jews who, in strict accordance with socialist doctrine, deny the existence of the Jews as a people. Some deep-seated impulse of treachery leads worldly Jews to deny only to the people from whom they have sprung those human rights that are indivisible from national rights. Bernard Lazare once wrote of emancipated French Jews: "It isn't enough for them to reject any solidarity with their foreign-born brethren; they have also to go charging them with all the evils which their own cowardice engenders. . . . Like all emancipated Jews everywhere, they have also of their own volition broken all ties of solidarity."[6] Lapidus, for his part, is, like Abram, a Zionist who sees no solution to the anomaly of Jewish existence in an increasingly antisemitic Europe except " 'a corner of the world for our own.' "

Lapidus and Abram insistently ask the socialists why Jews should relinquish their nationality in order to assimilate with "humanity." In fact, they argue, if assimilation were successful, it would merge the Jewish people not with all humanity but only with the Polish people (or the German or the Hungarian), so that the division and strife of nations would continue just as before, but the People Israel would disappear from the earth. The Holocaust was to prove that assimilation was impossible in any case. For it was just as Hosea had long before predicted of the faithless of Israel: "She shall run after her lovers, but she shall not overtake them" (Hosea 2:9).

For the mature characters in *The Family Moskat*, Zionism is, as Theodor Herzl once said, "a return to the Jewish people even before it is a return to the Jewish homeland." It is not accidental that Asa's first Zionist utterances in the novel come on the occasion of his return from Switzerland to Tereshpol Minor. Upon entering the synagogue, Asa is overcome by "a heavy odor that seemed . . . to be compounded of candle wax, fast days, and eternity. He stood silent. Here in the dimness everything he had experienced in alien places seemed to be without meaning. Time had flown like an illusion. This was his true home, this was where he belonged. Here was where he would come for refuge when everything else failed." This joy in homecoming seems to depend on religion, yet when Asa tries to explain his feelings to his grandfather, what he says is that Jews are a people like every other people, and are now "demanding that the nations of the world return the Holy Land to them." The conjunction of the two passages is striking. Very soon there will be no Tereshpol Minor synagogue in which to seek refuge and home when all else fails—as it does—and the Zionist contention that the Jews of Europe are building on sand will be borne out.

It remains for the generation of Asa's children and their friends to translate the desire for a return to the Jewish people into "practical" Zionism. Young Shosha Berman marries an authentic Zionist pioneer named Simon Bendel, who clearly represents the most vital element of the youngest generation of Polish Jews in the novel. Singer's desire to single out Zionism from among the myriad political movements that contend with each other for the loyalties of Polish Jews disaffected from traditional religion is evident in his treatment of Simon and his beleaguered group of Hebrew-speaking agriculturists: "Everyone was against them—the orthodox Jews, the Socialist Bundists, the Communists. But they were not the kind to be frightened off. If the Messiah had not come riding on his ass by now, then it was time to take one's destiny into one's own hands."

It is precisely this desire of Zionism to preempt the tasks reserved for Messiah that provokes the wrath of the orthodox: " 'What's bothering you, rabbi? We are building a Jewish home.' " " 'Except the Lord build the house, they labor in vain that build it.' " This is not a debate, such as may be found in *Satan in Goray*, over the desirability of hastening the arrival of the Messiah by aggravating the evil situation of humanity so that deliverance will come to a generation steeped in degradation. Everybody, apart from the communists, recognizes that in a world dominated by Hitler, this would be a labor of supererogation. Rather, the Zionists take upon themselves the task reserved by religious tradition for the Messiah because they sense that modern antisemitism is not just another form of religious Jew-hatred but the instrument of a scheme to destroy the Jewish people forever.

The entire novel is animated by a tremendous pressure toward some kind of apocalyptic resolution of the worsening condition of the Jews of Europe. Early in the book, before either of the World Wars has taken place, it seems to the orthodox that things cannot get worse than they are:

> Speakers were thundering that Jews should not wait for Messiah to come, but build the Jewish homeland with their own hands. . . . The truth was that the Jews were being persecuted more and more. Day by day it became harder to earn a living. What would be the end of it all? There was only one hope left—for Messiah to come, to come quickly while there were still a few pious Jews left.

During World War I it seems even more certain to the orthodox that the cup must at last be full. What can be the meaning of the endless suffering of the Jews but that redemption is at hand? " 'Enough! It is time! High time for the Messiah!' " Even the fabric of daily life is interwoven with messianic expectation, so that Adele's delivery pains provoke the remark "Everything is attended by suffering . . . birth . . . Messiah. . . ." With the approach of Hitler, even many of the pious go off to Palestine, complaining about their elders and their God: " 'The old generation knows only one thing: Messiah will come. God knows, he's taking his time.' "

The culminating event of the novel would seem to be precisely the occasion on which Singer, if he wished, could demonstrate the convergence of catastrophe with redemption, Holocaust with rebirth in the homeland. It is the last Passover to be celebrated by the Jews of Warsaw before they and their civilization are buried in universal darkness. The celebration looks backward to the great holiday occasions earlier in the novel, when the spiritually dispersed members of what had formerly been the community of Israel are briefly united with their people and with their best selves; and it also looks forward to the yawning emptiness of the Jewish future in Europe. So insistent is Singer on the irresistibility of Jewish fate that for this Passover celebration he goes to the trouble of recalling, from Palestine as well as America, those characters who have already emigrated, despite the fact that all the Jews still resident in Poland "were possessed of the same thought: to be helped to get out of Poland while there was still time."

The Passover, described in great, loving detail by Singer, is the novel's most beautiful and most terrible occasion. Not only does it summon up and reenforce the memory of past holidays; it is a holiday on which the original redemption of the Jews from bondage and deliverance to their promised land is commemorated and the hope of their imminent salvation and return to the ancestral homeland is more immediate than at any other time of the year. In a voice broken with weeping, Pinnie Moskat recites: " 'And it is this same promise which has been the support of our ancestors and of us, for in every generation our enemies have arisen to annihilate us, but the Most Holy, blessed be He, has delivered us out of their hands. . . . ' " From the point of view of Jewish religion, Hitler is only the latest repetition of the Amaleks who have plagued the Jews throughout their existence. Yet many at the seder table wonder to themselves: "Would a miracle happen this time too? In a year from now would Jews be able again to sit down and observe the Passover? Or, God forbid, would the new Haman finish them off?"

The Passover service traditionally concludes with the exclamation "Next Year in Jerusalem!" If Singer wished to see in the qualified triumph of Zionism a kind of redemption for which the Holocaust had been a horrible price, or in the State of Israel a realization of the messianic expectations of so many of his Holocaust victims, here exactly would be the point for him to reveal his conviction. But he does nothing of the kind. Instead, he pointedly omits any mention of "Next Year in Jerusalem!" in his description of the seder and concludes with Pinnie's question: " 'These unleavened cakes, why do we eat them?' " Even though the novel treats Zionism sympathetically, and in this very chapter we are told that Asa's son David is observing the holiday in Palestine with his fellow pioneers, Singer will not endorse historicist views of the Holocaust as the labor pains of national rebirth or religious views of it as the price of redemption. Rather, he wants above all to convey the sense that for the Jews of Europe the end was at hand, and in a more absolute sense than any that could have been conceived by either orthodox or nationalist Jews. When Abram the Zionist tries to console the gloomy Asa by remarking that " 'the end of the world hasn't come yet,' " Asa replies that " 'the end of our world *has* come.' " The final scene of the English version of the novel[7] allows no hint of apocalypse in this disaster, no glimpse of a redemption beyond the catastrophe.

In the deepest sense, then, the Zionists of *The Family Moskat* who flee to Palestine are as homeless, as desperate for refuge, as Herman Broder of *Enemies* in the United States. For Singer, the ultimate refuge is in the instruments of Jewish spirituality. For him, "the two thousand years of exile have not been a dark passage into nowhere but a grand experiment in upholding a people only on spiritual values. Even though we have attained the land we longed for . . . this experiment is far from being concluded."[8] At the end of *The Manor*, Calman Jacoby finds a refuge from the acrid dissolvents of Polish Jewry not in the land but in the spirit of his ancestors, as embodied in his shelves of sacred books that reunite him with past generations. "The Hebrew letters were steeped in holiness, in eternity. They seemed to unite him with the patriarchs, with Joshua, Gamaliel, Eliezer, and with Hillel the Ancient. . . . Among these shelves of sacred books, Calman felt protected." Calman understands, though he cannot conceptualize, the truth that all those secularizing and reformist movements within the Jewish community that sought to confer upon the Jews emancipation and human rights had in fact deprived them of their freedom and their humanity. To be human was to stand where one's ancestors had stood, rooted in the language and laws and customs that were a permanent affront to evolutionism and progressivism.

For the survivors of the Holocaust, Jewish books become not only the means of remaining human by returning into the buried life of one's ancestors; they become the instrument for the resurrection of the dead. As another character, Herman Gombiner in the story called "The Letter Writer," says: "The spirit cannot be burned, gassed, hanged, shot. Six million souls must exist somewhere." Gombiner, during an illness, goes in search of his lost relatives, and his quest leads him, via Canal Street in New York City, into an underworld charnel-house, where he meets a gravedigger tending the bones. " 'How,' " asks Herman, " 'can anyone live here?' " " 'Who would want such a livelihood?' " The answer, of course, is that this is where Singer has chosen to live.

We can see this very clearly in one of his supernatural tales called "The Last Demon." Of the many stories in which Singer uses a first-person narrator who bears marked resemblances to the author, none comes so close to representing the author's inner relationship to his own work as this one. The narrator of the tale tells of his plight as the last remaining demon, whose occupation is gone because man himself has become a demon: to proselytize for evil in these times would be carrying coals to Newcastle. Like Singer himself, the last demon has been deprived of his subject, the Jews of Eastern Europe. "I've seen it all," he says, "the destruction of Tishevitz, the destruction of Poland. There are no more Jews, no more demons. . . . The community was slaughtered, the holy books burned, the cemetery desecrated." Like Singer, the last demon attempts to speak as if history had *not* destroyed his subject and as if he could defy time: "I speak in the present tense as for me time stands still." Like Singer, the last demon knows, or thinks he knows, that there is no judge and no judgment, and that to the generation that has indeed succeeded in becoming wholly guilty the only Messiah that will come is death: "The generation is already guilty seven times over, but Messiah does not come. To whom should he come? Messiah did not come for the Jews, so the Jews went to Messiah." Like Singer, finally, the demon must sustain himself on dust and ashes and Yiddish books. "I found a Yiddish storybook between two broken barrels in the house which once belonged to Velvel the Barrelmaker. I sit there, the last of the demons. I eat dust. . . . The style of the book is . . . Sabbath pudding cooked in pig's fat: blasphemy rolled in piety. The moral of the book is: neither judge, nor judgment. But nevertheless the letters are Jewish. . . . I suck on the letters and feed myself. . . . Yes, as long as a single volume remains, I have something to sustain me."

The attempt to resurrect the shattered remnant of Jewish life in Israel, one of the most extraordinary instances of national rebirth in history, one of the outstanding examples of Jewish defiance of history, ultimately plays but a minor part in the great body of Singer's fiction. Rather, he chooses to make of literature itself the instrument for preserving the memory, and resurrecting the souls, of the dead. The literature upon which this massive responsibility devolves is no longer a sacred one, nor is it written in Hebrew, the traditional sacred tongue but also a language that, in Singer's view, is now "becoming more and more worldly."[9] Yet, through an ironic reversal of the traditional relationship between Hebrew and Yiddish, the language of the majority of the victims of the Holocaust becomes for Singer the *loshen khoydesh*, the holy tongue of the Jewish people. "The deader the language," Singer has said, "the more alive is the ghost. Ghosts love Yiddish, and, as far as I know, they all speak it. . . . I not only believe in ghosts but also in resurrection. I am sure that millions of Yiddish-speaking corpses will rise from their graves one day, and their first question will be: Is there any new book in Yiddish to read? For them Yiddish will not be dead." And, we are implicitly invited to add, because of Yiddish they will not be dead. In his literary character, which is to say in his subject and language, Singer has made himself into a splendid anachronism whose flourishing existence defies the death-sentence imposed upon the Jewish people in the nineteenth century and nearly carried out in the twentieth.

Notes

1. *Peretz*, trans. and ed. Sol Liptzin (New York: YIVO, 1947), p. 18.

2. I. B. Singer and Irving Howe, "Yiddish Tradition vs. Jewish Tradition: A Dialogue," *Midstream* 19 (June/July 1973): 34.

3. Mary Ellmann, "The Piety of Things in *The Manor*," in *The Achievement of Isaac Bashevis Singer*, ed. Marcia Allentuck (Carbondale: Southern Illinois University Press, 1969).

4. Marshall Breger and Bob Barnhart, "A Conversation with Isaac Bashevis Singer," in *Critical Views of Isaac Bashevis Singer*, ed. Irving Malin (New York: New York University Press, 1969), p. 42.

5. David M. Andersen, "Isaac Bashevis Singer: Conversation in California," *Modern Fiction Studies* 16 (Winter 1970–71): 430.

6. Bernard Lazare, *Job's Dungheap* (New York, 1948), p. 97.

7. Irving Saposnik, in a vigorous and intelligent (although, in my view, ultimately mistaken) article entitled "Translating *The Family Moskat*," *Yiddish* 1 (Fall 1973): 26–37, has compared the differing implications of the English and Yiddish endings of the novel. He attaches great importance to the fact that the closing pages of the original, Yiddish version depict a group of Zionists escaping from Warsaw.

8. "Yiddish, The Language of Exile," *Judaica Book News*, Spring/Summer 1976, p. 27.

9. Ibid.

Singer's Paradoxical Progress

RUTH R. WISSE

The award to Isaac Bashevis Singer of the Nobel Prize for Literature brings to a climax the most fortunate career in modern Yiddish letters. With deference to Singer's demons, it would be only proper to spit three times upon such provocation, and to dispel their impish envy with the formula, may no evil eye behold him. But the occasion should be marked for rejoicing, especially since the decline of the language in which Singer writes, the destruction of his community, and the thwarted fate of many of his fellow Yiddish writers have so often required the compassionate tones of mourning.

The emphasis on loss and decline may seem inevitable in any discussion of Bashevis Singer's work: the gloom is in either the subject or the writer, or both. Idyllic stories of the East European Jewish *shtetl*, like "Short Friday" or "The Little Shoemakers," vivify a world whose beatific fictional existence is set into fiercely tragic perspective by its historical extinction. Most of Singer's stories inspire a fresh awareness of human malignancy and remorseless fate. The author's fatalism is prominent in large novels, like *The Family Moskat*, which trace the disintegration of modern Jewish society through a series of characters who gravitate unerringly toward their doom. As Singer has often remarked, the pessimist is the realist. His unblinking realistic eye has noted this century's unholy marvels, including those special revelations it has offered the Jew.

Yet the progress of Singer as a professional writer is an unusually happy study. His first published story, submitted under a pseudonym to the literary contest of a Warsaw weekly in 1925 when he was twenty-one, was a prizewinning entry.[1] A year later he was the youngest of forty-six contributors to the massive anthology, *Warshever shriftn*, establishing his literary presence among the major Yiddish writers of the period. His first novel, *Satan in Goray*, published serially in a local magazine, was issued in book form by the Library of the Yiddish PEN Club in 1935, the first volume of what was to have become a series of annual stellar publications. Singer had the prescience and good fortune to leave Warsaw in the mid 1930's for New York, where, after a period of dislocation, he became a regular contributor to the *Jewish Daily Forward*, the only moderately secure affiliation ever afforded to the Yiddish writer. He was able, on the *Forward*, to cultivate two literary voices—that of "Warshavsky," the feuilletonist and personal chronicler, and that of "Bashevis," the writer and novelist—finding for each an appreciative audience. Lastly, and by no means least, he was "discovered" in the early 1950's by Irving Howe, the editors of COMMENTARY and *Partisan Review*, and the late Cecil Hemley of the Noonday Press, and set aloft on the wave of fame that nowhere swells so high and fast as in America. The Nobel Prize for Literature confers international recognition and honor upon a writer who has gone "from strength to strength."

More compelling than the story of his reputation is that of Singer's literary progress. Though he presents himself to his American audiences as a rather puckish character, musing about demons, asking for explanations of a difficult term like "modernism," parrying with quips and aphorisms the questions addressed to him as if to an oracle, Singer is really a thoroughly professional literary man who has carefully considered the nature of his craft. Plunged into the thick of Jewish cultural life in his late adolescence, he served an excellent artistic apprenticeship, becoming one of the first and few Yiddish writers to make his living—meager though it sometimes was—solely by the pen.

Bashevis Singer became a writer in the heyday of Yiddish literature in the 1920's at what was undoubtedly its geographic center: Warsaw, capital of the new Republic of Poland, a city whose 300,000 Jews constituted about one-third of the total population. The classical period of Yiddish literature had come to a sudden end with World War I, when the three giants—I. L. Peretz, Sholem Aleichem, and Mendele Mocher Sforim—died in rapid succession between 1915 and 1917. Under Peretz's guiding and often autocratic rule—his disciples called him their *"rebbe"*—his home in Warsaw had become the heart of a spirited cultural renaissance. Although emigration and shifting political borders in the postwar years greatly affected Jewish demography, Warsaw remained the mecca of Yiddish letters until the 1939 German invasion.

When Singer first began to publish in 1925, there were in Warsaw a number of important Yiddish dailies, representing the spectrum of Jewish ideologies and a considerable journalistic range from photo-express sensationalism to high-quality coverage and editorial analysis. Singer found employment with *Literarishe Bleter*, the most prestigious literary weekly ever published in Yiddish. He was soon a full-fledged member of the Union of Jewish Writers and Journalists, which boasted a membership of about 300 professionals, sponsored hundreds of literary evenings, published its own anthologies, and provided an around-the-clock meeting place for discussion and drink. To be a Yiddish writer in Warsaw, said the poet, Melekh Ravitch, when he arrived there from Vienna after World War I, was "to feel the Redemption at hand, and to be at its center."

In addition to being well situated for a literary debut in Yiddish, Singer also witnessed in his own family a microcosmic drama of the conflict between Jewish tradition and worldliness, which was the main subject and stimulus of modern Jewish writing. Few writers, whether in Hebrew or Yiddish, have emerged from so thoroughly "old-fashioned" and learned a home. As Singer himself has explained, the Jewish *shtetl* of Poland experienced the Enlightenment, the *Haskalah*, much later and with greater suddenness than did similar communities of Russia and Lithuania, where so many Jewish writers had originated:

> Until 1914 most *shtetlakh* in Poland remained observant (*frum*). Jews lived as they had hundreds of years earlier. . . . The Enlightenment as a mass movement came to Poland with World War I, and because of its delay and momentum, assumed almost epidemic proportions. The revolution in Russia, the arrival of the Germans and the Austrians, the creation of the Polish Republic, the Balfour Declaration—all of this had a simultaneous impact. Processes that elsewhere lasted several decades here transpired virtually overnight.[2]

Singer's first-hand familiarity with the "pre-Enlightenment" Polish *shtetl* and his upbringing in a bookish as well as a pious home gave him immediate access to Jewish folkways and literary sources from which Jewish writers, even of the preceding generation, had felt themselves rather removed. Back in the 1890's, I. L. Peretz and his friends were already collecting from outlying areas folk materials that could be reworked in modern literary forms. Some of the impetus for S. An-ski's haunting drama, *The Dybbuk*, derived from the ethnographic expedition that the author had undertaken to gather materials thought to be in danger of disappearing. As Singer has described his home, much of this endangered lore was the daily stuff of his life, his for the taking.

If his parents, a small-town rabbi and rabbi's daughter, and the various visiting and visited relatives remained a wellspring of tradition, Singer's older sister, Esther, and his brother, Israel Joshua, soon introduced the challenge of secular modernity. Israel Joshua, a draft evader during the war for reasons of conscience, was caught up by the excitement of the Bolshevik revolution and began his literary career under its spell. Later in Warsaw, he was a prominent companion of "The Gang" (*Di Khaliastre*), a determinedly innovative group of Yiddish writers who took as their bible the *Ethics* of Spinoza, and as their literary model the expressionistic bravado of the Russian poet, Mayakovsky. Before Bashevis Singer attempted the passage from home, his older brother had already publicly rejected the Jewish God and braved the heady atmosphere of the artistic world. Of the clashes between generations in his home, Singer was to say: "Although later in my life I read a great deal of philosophy, I never found more compelling arguments than those that came up in my own kitchen."

While the example of Israel Joshua no doubt facilitated the transition of young Isaac from *Yeshiva bokher* to Yiddish writer, it also preempted some of the younger writer's independent initiative in this direction. In order to step out on his own, Bashevis had not only to reject the assumptions of his parents, but also those of his brother who was intimidatingly talented and famous. It was necessary to separate himself from both his home and from both his home and from the new "revolutionary" circles in which his brother played such a prominent role. And, in fact, though Singer fell in with some trends of his day—the naturalistic impulse to show the seamy side of life and to emphasize its sexuality; the attraction to Spinoza, vegetarianism, pacifism—he was among the very few to oppose political ideologies, whether nationalist or socialist. Even more solitary was his opposition to literary modernism as a means of expressing the unease and disjunction of the 1920's. His earliest published story, about a man's precipitous decline, ends in a shocking scene: the ailing father is asked by his daughter, a prostitute, to roll over in bed so that she might use its other half for her trade. This was certainly an attack on the values of modesty in which Singer was raised. At the same time, the spare, direct narrative style of this and all the rest of his work repudiated current vogues of impressionism and expressionism, while the emphasis on character rather than social conditioning called into question all faiths in a new world order.

His position between the contending values of a traditional past and an ideologically-impelled future seems to have endowed Singer with a curious detachment, curious certainly within the mainstream of Jewish literature which took any number of directions but was invariably *engagé*. More onlooker than participant, Singer has seen the forces of opposing ideas canceling one another out, much as in his works the charm of one beloved is soon deflected by the lure of another and then, invariably, by yet a third. Singer has referred to himself as "unsentimental." He did not nurse ideals that could be shattered, or trust the human condition enough to believe in ultimate remedies. The habit of skepticism, though it has sometimes chilled Singer's work to the bone, made him an exceptionally steady recording secretary for his times.

From the outset, Singer defined his craft not in terms of possibilities but in terms of limitations. In the manner of a proper *halakhic* Jew, he first set up the fence of restrictions before exploring the opportunities within its bounds. Though he has experimented in a number of genres over the years, and expanded his two original locales, the old world and the new, to include a third, the beyond, he remains surprisingly true to his earliest literary ideas.

For Bashevis Singer, literature is realism and realism demands a narrative that depicts and speaks for itself. "The description, the given fact, was always the attribute of the realistic narrative," wrote Singer in a 1927 essay, "just as sentiment and mood are dominant in the lyric."[3] The poet may *react* to events, but the prose realist sets up the events themselves, leaving reaction to the reader. The fiction writer is sentenced to details, and "the subtler the intended mood, the more details . . . he must artfully combine." The realist must deal with objective facts; only in dialogue, in the exchange of voices, do we have a "tiny window" into the unseen inner life of the characters.

Singer's endorsement of realism is in large measure an attack upon the moderns, particularly the expressionists, who wished "to tear down all barriers and penetrate directly to the very essence." He considers their exhibitionistic art intrinsically inferior to that of the consistent realist like himself, who accepts the binding limitations of narration as the first condition of success. "In graphic form it isn't possible to render everything, but everything in a realistic narrative must be given graphic form."

While submitting to its restraints, Singer raises some traditional objections to realism which also express his own impatience. Can objective descriptions really communicate the full complexity of the individual? What about the intellectual who thinks more than he acts: can realism do him justice, or must it favor the folk type? Is there no other direct source for the artist apart from the natural world, apprehended through the senses? These questions clearly anticipate the author's attempted solutions. Like the libertines of his stories who require a social context of propriety, Singer defines a thoroughly conservative norm which he may then bedevil and transgress.

He soon began to use historical chronicles, folk tales, and the supernatural to explore those subjects and ideas that could not be treated with sufficient freedom in contemporary realistic settings. His "chronicles" do obey the laws of objective narration, his imps are kept dutifully subject to the same laws of fiction that govern their human victims. Yet in these stories, the very normalcy of the form undercuts the assumptions of materialism and natural reason on which literary realism rests. Erotic impulses and subconscious desires are embodied in androgynous, lesbian, sadistic, and murderous creatures whose substantive existence is portrayed in such "authentic" and charming detail of language and setting that they seem not only real, but commonplace. The apparent simplicity of Singer's narrative form, like the innocence of his characters, is only the better to call them into question with.

Satan in Goray, the greatest of Singer's novels, moves into a semi-legendary past to draw a bead on contemporary reality. Hailed upon its appearance for its incomparable mastery of language and style, the book was called an "anachronism," a judgment for which the author himself was largely responsible. Singer subtitled his novel, "a story of long ago," and drew attention to its antique properties.

In an article, "On the Question of Poetry and Politics," which was published almost concurrently with the novel in *Globus*, the same magazine where it first appeared, Singer lashed out against the political pressures that were demanding allegiance from the writer. One side cries, how can *you*, of all people, look calmly down from your Olympian heights while the poor and dispossessed rise up against their oppressors? The other side cries, how can *you*, creator and bearer of culture, witness the destruction of European culture without coming wholeheartedly to its defense? Each side exhorts the writer to produce works that set men against one another, class against class, group against group. Well, says Singer, the true artist will never become a propagandist. "Not only will he refuse to incite the rich against the poor, he will even refuse to incite the poor against the rich." Singer is particularly cynical about the pressure applied to artists in the Soviet Union. With some foresight, he writes:

> The recent easing of demands for a Prolet-Cult in the Soviet Union is merely the result of a temporary pacifistic and constructive mood. . . . As soon as the battle is joined, there will certainly be categorical demands made upon the writer to serve as effectively and single-mindedly with his pen as the soldier must with his rifle. Similar demands will undoubtedly be made by the other side.

Taking for his motto the proposition of Spinoza that "Hatred can never be good," Singer insists that the writer is too pessimistic, or realistic, to trust the promises of politicians, who have amassed enough power without the writer's help.

Of course in the narrow sense, *Satan in Goray* is an entirely apolitical book. It tells of the messianic fervor that seizes and corrupts a small 17th-century Polish town, unleashing passions that the Law and the calm of reason had formerly kept in check. It shows the community of Goray, weakened physically and hence spiritually by the devastation of the Chmielnitski pogroms, unable to withstand the apocalyptic ideology of the followers of Sabbatai Zevi. The poison of false hope infects the town and then runs its course like an epidemic before its power is finally spent. So thickly embedded is the book in historical detail; so intricate are its recreations of the old Jewish epistolary, homiletic, and chronicle styles; so richly individualized are the characterizations of even the minor figures, that it resists any notion of "allegory": it is too much itself to be the symbolic representation of something other than itself.

Yet this may well be the most powerful political novel of the 1930's. Singer's hatred of ideologies, those sweeping solutions to the problems of mankind that lack all tolerance for the human reality, animates this "ancient chronicle" and transforms it into a frighteningly modern work. Singer had removed the artist from the political arena except as referee or judge, and praised the pacifist neutrality of Erich Maria Remarque, whose anti-war novel, *All Quiet on the Western Front*, he himself translated into Yiddish. His own modern parable rages not against war, but against the incendiary ideas that in the name of a higher spirituality flood the world with hatred enough to bring it to ruin.

The attraction to the frenzy of the Sabbatean movement finds its parallel in the works of many contemporaries, most important among them Gershom Scholem, whose historical interest was also spurred by his perception of contemporary obsessions. Whereas Scholem has dedicated himself to understanding the Sabbatean phenomenon in its precise detail and broadest social implications, Singer bends history to heighten the irrational—man's fearsome lack of control and susceptibility to mad persuasion. Once he has released the fiction, though, Singer reimposes upon it a strict moral and narrative rein. The novel concludes in the homiletic style of the chronicles, bringing villains to judgment, good men to easeful death, and the universe back to order: "Let none attempt to force the Lord."

Singer's most conservative literary pronouncements pertain to the uses of Yiddish. In 1943 the New York literary monthly, *Svive*, published his essay on "The Problems of Yiddish Prose in America" with a rare editorial footnote indicating that the opinions of the author were not those of the magazine and that contrary views would be expressed in the coming issues. The article touched off a barrage of dissenting replies and provoked more anger in Jewish literary circles than Singer's discomfiting eroticism.

According to Singer's analysis, Yiddish in America is a language in serious decline. A language is decaying when people consign it to particular functions. "Life itself is rich and varied, yet there is hardly a Jew in America who can name in Yiddish all that he sees or feels." What is more, Yiddish speakers in America represent only a small fraction of American Jewry, a limited class. How can the Yiddish writer depict Jewish doctors and farmers when no one uses the language in those spheres of work?

Singer compares the handicaps of the Yiddish writer in America with those of the Hebrew writer at the turn of the century who lacked the simplest idioms of everyday speech. It was clumsy when the Hebrew writer had his wagon driver curse his horse with the phrase, "Move thither, son of Belial!" It is equally inappropriate when rich Yiddish expressions flow from the mouths of contemporary American characters who would actually be speaking and thinking in English. This explains, says Singer, why the best Yiddish prose writers consciously or unconsciously avoid writing about American life. They don't want to fake the dialogue, and they are fed up with describing yet again the narrow circle of coarse, aging immigrants.

Not content with this severe circumscription of Yiddish fiction, Singer redefines the whole sphere of Yiddish, retroactively and for all time. Yiddish developed in the home, the House of Study, the shop, and the artisan's workroom. Those Jews who attained wealth or who aspired to be thoroughly worldly proceeded to other cultures and other languages:

A language that is not taught in elementary schools, high schools, and universities; a language into which the classic works of knowledge have not yet been translated; a language that is not used on the farm and in the factory, in the building of trains and bridges, automobiles and airplanes, does not serve any worldly interests.

Singer mocks the efforts of the philologists of the YIVO Institute for Jewish Research and others who are creating neologisms that no one will use.

This still leaves the Yiddish writer a marvelous 500-year heritage in which he will discover "Judaism in all its splendor." And Singer exempts from his prescription the lyrical poet, "who is not obliged to any hero other than himself." But the prose writer, who must develop a broad cast of characters, has to yield to linguistic pressures, recognizing that he is a slave to the past, where Yiddish was thoroughly at home.

Whatever its partial validity, the severity of the argument strikes the reader as forcefully as its truths. Taking his opposition to modernity one step further than before, Singer plucks Yiddish prose out of the 20th century to move it back to its roots, to a culture ruled by the impulses of evil and good rather than by the id and the superego, or fascism and democracy. In a way, Singer seems to be entering a linguistic monastery that will forever protect him from the ravages of earthly time. By voluntarily immuring himself in the Jewish past, he does not have to face the actual forces that had already, by April 1943, plucked Yiddish speakers out of the 20th century: the war is not mentioned. The displaced harshness of his analysis (he himself would later write a considerable body of American work) serves as a kind of justification for returning artistically to a world he had abandoned in fact.

As might be expected, the old-fashioned Yiddish stories Singer wrote during the war use an authentic Yiddish idiom for reasons other than the rediscovery of "Judaism in all its splendor." Such stories as "From the Diary of One Not Born," "Zeidlus the Pope," and "The Destruction of Kreshev," which were to have been collected in *Memoirs of the Spirit of Evil*, underscore the arbitrariness of evil, its imperviousness to the category of justice in which Jews so unyieldingly believe. For some readers the transposition of these categories of evil into a world that strove so vehemently to free itself from them, is insensitive or wrong. Reviewing Singer in 1965, Dan Jacobson wrote:

> I cannot help feeling that to some extent Singer is forced to import evil, as it were, into a world which cannot really contain or express it. The evil which obsesses him is far greater than anything his poor peddlers, ambitious rabbis, lecherous widows, grasping merchants, or their apostate sons are capable of committing . . . *they* did not gas children, burn them alive, machine gun them into pits.[4]

Others have justified Singer's method, noting that in these traditional Jewish settings, the demonic still retains the power to anger and shock. Whether or not the linguistic limitation of Yiddish actually forced Singer back to the Polish *shtetl*, that familiar setting provided him with the only convincing medium for the representation of sin on a still-human scale, with something like the "realism" the age required.

As his literary essays suggest, Bashevis Singer knows the sources of his strength. He is at his best within a conservative literary form, in an old-fashioned setting, and within tight linguistic constraints. Three of his finest works—the stories "Gimpel the Fool," "Taybele and Her Demon," and "The Spinoza of Market Street"—are tender tales of love. A solitary man or woman reaches out to an unlikely partner and finds, in the bitter sweetness of love, intimations of both mortality and transcendence. Some of Singer's plainest autobiographical sketches, published under the name of Warshavsky because they did not meet Bashevis's literary standards, have crashed American high culture with the charm of Cinderella at the ball.

In his long novels and contemporary stories, Singer suffers from some of his own biases. His distaste for modern secularism, abhorrence of ideologies, lack of interest in politics, and practical resistance to an updated Yiddish vocabulary make it difficult for him to treat with genuine complexity the characters he sets down in a complex world. A growing misanthropic tendency also limits his ability to breathe much compassion into his stories of passion. There is no lack of narrative suspense, though coincidence, impulse, and supernatural interference too often replace a reflective intelligence. The homey truths and sharp or soothing bits of wisdom that prove so satisfying in folk characters sound distressingly hollow in the mouths of modern Jews trying to make some sense of their fate.

Like his captivating magician of Lublin in the novel of the same name, Singer the artist does not feel wholly at ease in the big city. Yasha the magician leaves his faithful wife and the comfort of his *shtetl* to pursue the greater challenges of cosmopolitan Warsaw. Lusting after Gentile beauty and the homage of Gentile audiences, he falls ever deeper into sin in his efforts to attain them. Finally, to escape the world he both loves and fears, he returns home and walls himself up in penitential solitude. The choice between licentiousness and asceticism is made absolute, as if the only escape from the one were to the other.

The more Singer admits the modern world into his writing, the more forcefully he opposes its values and lures. In the most recent of his books to be translated into English, *Shosha*, a semi-autobiographical novel of pre-war Poland, the author actually rewrites his life. Singer's hero, Aaron Greidinger, who bears an obvious resemblance to the author, is beset in his debut as a writer and a lover by a number of literary and amorous opportunities among which he is invited to choose. The hero selects not the representation of the woman Singer actually married, but Shosha, a childhood playmate who has remained small in size and naive in spirit—an eternal child. Shosha had briefly appeared as a sweet companion of childhood in one of Singer's earlier autobiographical story collections, *A Day of Pleasure*. Here she becomes his symbolic wife, the repository of untouched, old-world innocence that never passes through the modern slime at all; and she dies, simply expires, as the Jews begin their forced march to extinction.

The introduction of so pastoral a character into a novel that otherwise throbs with the frantic tempo and maddening insecurity of interwar Poland—quite as though Gimpel the Fool had been turned into the hero of one of Singer's contemporary novels, like *Enemies*—disturbs the book's coherence and its sense of truth. But for Singer, the choice of Shosha is obviously the very point. The artist-magician renounces the tightrope of all his worldly quest and embraces the trustful ingenuousness of the past as his one true bride. A strange "autobiography," that follows the road not taken, as if atoning for an actual, successful artistic career in the modern world by yoking itself in its fiction to the poorest, most unlikely possibility of all.

Der Bal Tshuve ("The Penitent"), 1974, a novel intended for Yiddish readers that is not likely to succeed in English, turns its back on the present with even more shameless zeal. The book is so very didactic that its narrator, a certain Joseph Shapiro who has emigrated from America to Israel, apologizes throughout his narrative for his homiletic and moralistic digressions. Shapiro accosts the famous author, Bashevis Singer—where else but at the Western Wall?—and in two long monologues on successive days tells him the story of his life: his rapid climb to prosperity in postwar America, his inevitable descent into profligacy, and his total repudiation of the sinful "vanity of vanities" in a sudden flight to Israel. Shapiro finds in modern Israel no more than an extension of America. The fact that the language is Hebrew and the statesmen are Jewish is no protection against sin.

Only in Mea Shearim, the Orthodox section of Jerusalem that is the closest contemporary approximation of the pre-Enlightenment *shtetl*, does Shapiro begin to find his salvation. At first he finds it difficult, as a faithless Jew, to participate in ritual and prayer. His Evil Spirit protests, "You are play-acting." But before long he is captivated by the unsophisticated generosity of the people and the perfect purity of their daughters. He becomes convinced of the genuine superiority of the traditional Jewish way of life and of his own ability to live it wholeheartedly. At this point he marries, and settles permanently in the quarter; his only connection to his former life is the need to communicate its follies.

It is hard to enumerate all the facets of modern life and thought that catch the brunt of the narrator's disgust. Lacking in plot or invention, the monologues are sustained by the stunning energy of their antipathy—to culture, to sociology, to psychology, to the youth cult and the sex cult, and especially to humanism, "the greatest lie in the world." "Humanism does not serve merely one idol; it serves *all* the idols." Only the religion of the Talmud can civilize man, by keeping him subject to its moral code. Shapiro, who despite a technical separation from the author clearly speaks with his full blessing, concludes with the perception that even if death should prove him wrong, if he should face an end without Judgment or Judge, he will have lived the final part of his life according to his convictions and his taste.

Singer's work draws its power from the tension between containment and license, Thou Shalt Not and I Must. At one time the formal austerity permitted thematic intemperance. More recently, where the work has grown loose and self-indulgent, the characters reach out for order to the imposed restraints of the anti-modern or pre-modern Jew. As Singer himself is feted with more worldly honor than he ever granted his characters, even in their dreams, he strikes loud and ever louder the note of renunciation. For a modern writer with such a distrust of modernity, this may be the only balance possible.

Notes

1. For this interesting detail, I am indebted to Khone Shmeruk's introduction to *Der shpigl un andere dertseylungen*, a collection of Singer's first-person narratives, issued by the Hebrew University, 1975.

2. *"Arum der yidisher literatur in poyln"* ("Concerning Yiddish Literature in Poland"), *Zukunft*, August 1943.

3. *"Verter oder bilder"* ("Words or Images") in *Literarishe Bleter*, 1927, no. 34.

4. *Commentary*, February 1965.

Isaac Bashevis Singer; or, The American-ness of the American Jewish Writer

LESLIE FIEDLER

In his Nobel Prize acceptance speech, Isaac Bashevis Singer made it clear that he considered the award a tribute not to him but to the language in which he writes, a language without a homeland and—in the opinion even of most living Jews—without a future. There seems little doubt, moreover, that the Committee which bestowed that award must have agreed with him; since they could not otherwise have honored him so soon after Saul Bellow, another Jew who lives and writes in the United States. To that Committee, I must suppose, Bellow seemed an *American* novelist, and Singer a *Jewish* one; but the matter is by no means clear-cut. To the Jewish literary establishment, for instance, the majority of critics who read him in Yiddish, Singer's work seems too demonic and erotic to be properly "Jewish" at all; and they are, therefore, profoundly uneasy that he has been taken by the Gentile world as representing a culture they feel he traduces and betrays.

It was not the Yiddishists but precisely such Jewish-American writers as Bellow (who began the whole process by translating "Gimpel the Fool"), Isaac Rosenfeld and Irving Howe who introduced Singer first to a larger American public without Yiddish, then to the world. Singer has always insisted on his difference from such Jewish-American exponents of "modern" fiction, alienated from their folk roots and too highfalutin' to tell a simple story; so that there seems no reason to disbelieve him when he says he has never read any of them. But they have read and loved him, for the very reasons surely that his fellow fictionists in Yiddish have rejected him, finding in his obsession with sex and his evocation of demons an assurance that he is "one of them."

Much time has elapsed, however, between the publication of those earliest translations and the Nobel Prize; and our culture has changed so much that these days one is more likely to find a new Singer story englished in the *New Yorker* than in journals like the *Partisan Review, Commentary* or

Midstream, in which he made his American debut. He has passed, that is to say, from the pages of magazines devoted to building a bridge between secular Jewish culture or, more generally, secular European culture, and American culture, to those of one which aspires to be the epitome of *goyish* America; and seems more suitable, therefore, to the fiction of John Cheever, John Updike and Donald Barthelme than to fantasies dreamed in exile by a child of the Warsaw ghetto.

Despite the fact that he continues to write in Yiddish for *The Daily Forward* topical essays, reminiscences, uncollected tales, serial installments of novels, all under the name of "Isaac Warshafsky," Singer has created for himself—after forty-five years in the United States—another, an American persona called "Isaac Bashevis Singer." Under that name, he now publishes in English *for the first time* all his books, whether novels or collections of short fiction. Even when he still permitted full-length volumes of his work to make their initial appearance in Yiddish, he did so under a third name, "Isaac Bashevis," a matronymic he bestowed on himself in honor of his mother, Bathsheba. Son of his native city as a journalist, son of his mother as a Yiddish novelist, he is his father's son as an American author; or perhaps rather the acknowledged brother of Israel Joshua Singer, that beloved and resented sibling rival, who became an American author before him—creating for Isaac a writer's block he could not break from the moment of his arrival on this soil until the latter's premature death.

Though he still does the first version of almost everything he writes in Yiddish, what he chooses to preserve between hard covers the twiceborn Singer now turns before final publication (with the help of translators and editors, though, one gathers, more and more subject to his own final judgment) into English, American English, American. This seems fair enough, inevitable perhaps, in light of the fact that that language has become for the majority of surviving Jews the *mammeloshen*, a secular mother-tongue, filling the function once served by Aramaic, *Ladino* and Yiddish itself. But what this means in Singer's case is that his fiction is not merely read, received and reviewed in American English, but exported to Europe, East and West, and to the Third World along with other items of Jewish American culture, including the novels of Saul Bellow, Bernard Malamud and Philip Roth. It was, therefore, as an American as well as a Jew that most of the world perceived Singer at the moment of his receiving the Nobel Prize—whatever he or the Committee believed, or pretended to believe.

But he is, of course, though an American and a Jew and a writer, *not* a Jewish American writer like Bellow or Malamud or Roth. He is rather an American Jewish writer: the only truly distinguished fictionist, perhaps (his brother Israel Joshua and Sholem Asch once seemed contenders, but they fade fast from our memories), to have arisen from among ex-European Jews entering the United States after the closing down of mass immigration. In his own awareness and in ours, he has never seemed an "immigrant" as defined by earlier, first-generation Jews from the Pale, like Anna Yezierska or Abraham Kahan. Nor is he perceived as a "refugee." These came later, out of the heart of the Holocaust, which Singer is constantly aware of having missed, thus remaining unredeemably a survivor of but not a participant in the destruction of East European Jewry. In this sense, he is more like us second- and third-generation offspring of earlier immigrants,' than the escapees from Nazi Concentration Camps or Stalin's Siberia, who to be sure, populate his fiction.

Like them, however, and unlike us, his first tongue is Yiddish and his earliest memories belong to the *shtetl* and the Warsaw ghetto. He is, in short, an *emigré* (something for which there is no exact word in our language): one whose identity is involved with a dead past rather than an unborn future; one who seeks not to lose but forever to cling to his status as an unreconstructed greenhorn, unassimilated, incapable of assimilation to American culture. He remains eternally—in theory, at least—a member of no community except that essentially stateless one which remembers not only Yiddish and *Yiddishkeit*, but the alliances and rivalries, the parochial politics, the hates and loves of a Yiddish-speaking *intelligentsia*, made up of men and women, long dead, or reduced to silence, or scattered over the face of the earth. The aging survivors of that community, though rescued from terror and living in relative security, tend to think of themselves condemned to perpetual exile, whether they find themselves in Montreal or Buenos Aires or Tel Aviv or New York, or even a Kiev or Odessa or Warsaw transformed beyond recognition.

The protagonists of Singer's stories with a contemporary setting find themselves from time to time in one or another of those places of exile, chiefly, of course, New York, the city in which he has lived for some four decades and a half. He has, to be sure, moved back and forth across our land during that time, spending occasional semesters in residence at Oberlin and the University of Wisconsin, and making overnight lecture stops everywhere in the cornfields and wheatfields of the heart of the heart of this country. By and large, however, he portrays America—his second homeland—as a claustrophobic enclave, centered in the West Side of Manhattan, and bordered on one side by Coney Island, on the other by the resort towns of the Catskill Mountains. Nonetheless, more and more of his fiction takes place in that narrow American world, including three novels, *Enemies, A Love Story, Shadows by the Hudson* and *A Ship to America* (the latter two, ironically enough, never translated from their serialized Yiddish versions in *The Daily Forward*) and some twenty-five short stories. I have read most though not all of the shorter fiction, and, of course, only the novel in English; but that has been enough to pose for me—urgently, tantalizingly—the question of what exactly is American about Singer's American fiction?

Perhaps because I have spent many years speculating on the Jewishness of the Jewish American writer, and have vowed I will return to it no more,

I turn with a real sense of relief to the complementary one: What *is* the American-ness of the American Jewish writer? Minimal, I am tempted to say, thinking of Singer, almost non-existent: an American-ness Degree Zero, equal and opposite to the Jewishness Degree Zero of such vestigially Jewish American novelists as Nathanael West, J. D. Salinger, Bruce Jay Freedman, or, for that matter, myself. The characters in Singer's American stories and his American novel move through a putatively American landscape consisting of mean city streets, where the temperature is always too hot or too cold, and the grey rain ceases only to let the grey snow fall.

There are other American novels set in similar urban landscapes; but in Melville's *Pierre* or even Saul Bellow's *The Victim*, somehow we are aware that somewhere beyond the asphalt and concrete there is a Wilderness, unlimited space, the untamed ocean. But outside of Singer's half mythological city, we are permitted to imagine only squalid bungalows huddled on the slopes of alien hills; and if the sea laps the shores of his Coney Island, it remains always a sea seen from apartment house windows, into whose waves his protagonists are never moved to plunge. Those protagonists tend to fade into each other in the American tales, seeming at least variations of a single anti-hero who uncannily resemble his author.

Whatever alternative lives Singer creates for him, he sees always in his mirror the same face, white-skinned, blue-eyed, red-headed but balding fast. Moreover, he is inevitably a crusading vegetarian, a non-smoker, a moderate man without a passion for drink (in a land where whiskey is more myth than intoxicant, more Muse than myth); a Yiddish journalist and travelling lecturer; a reader of occultist magazines, forever questing for a God in whose goodness he finds it even harder to believe than in his existence. Endlessly, restlessly, though self-tormentingly polygamous, he is sometimes married and sometimes not, but always essentially a bachelor; and he yearns, even more than he does for God, for an equally polygamous female: a witch, a *revenant*, or a woman possessed, with whom he can achieve a kind of living *Liebestod*, a kind of *eros* undistinguishable from *thanatos*.

That protagonist—though his alter ego, the author, exists for his audiences only in English—lives in his dreams and waking fantasies only in Yiddish; and consequently, meets only speakers of Yiddish, *emigrés* like himself, in his wanderings through a psychedelic landscape, whose street signs and billboards are written in English, yet which remain in many ways disconcertingly non-American. Not only does he encounter no Red Men in the streets he walks (how could he, after all?); but though the city he haunts (or is haunted by) is recognizably New York, even Blacks remain always on the periphery, intangible, almost invisible: half-naked savages on the edge of vision—a trouble-maker in the subway, a bootblack tickling his toes as he slops polish on his shoes. Indeed, there are scarcely any white American *goyim* in his fictions, not as expected persecutors, not as improbable lovers.

Never a *shegetz*. And when a *shikse* enters the scene, she is likely to be a European, a peasant, a servant girl from the *shtetl*.

Small wonder, then, that the myth of inter-ethnic male bonding, present in all authentic American fiction from James Fenimore Cooper to Mark Twain and Ken Kesey (even turning up in Bellow's *Henderson the Rain King* and Malamud's *The Tenants*) is absent from his pages. There is, in fact, almost *no* male bonding in Singer's overwhelmingly heterosexual world. What we find instead is domestic strife and joy, demonic love; and, especially, a desperate metaphysical joining of male and female flesh, which goes beyond erotic mysticism of the *Zohar* into the realm of heresy: a triumphant celebration of what is perverse and forbidden in passion—incestuous, adulterous, necrophiliac, Satanic love in the mode of Shabbatai Zevi.

And yet—and *yet*, very occasionally, through the eyes of one or another of his tormented, vegetarian nympholepts Singer sees in America suggestions for new heresies, more appropriate to the end of the twentieth than the close of the seventeenth century, and discoverable perhaps only in a world in which he can never feel really at home. One notable instance occurs near the conclusion of an American story called "The Third One." The theme, an "unnatural triangle" involving the bonding of husband, wife and lover comes right out of Dostoyevsky; but its climactic moment of vision occurs in Times Square as his first-person narrator, sweltering in the subtropical heat of midsummer Manhattan, looks up at the electric billboard display:

"We walked out on Broadway," he tells us, "and the heat hit me like a furnace. It was still daylight but the neon signs were already lit, announcing in fiery language the bliss to be brought by Pepsi-Cola, Bond suits, Camel cigarettes, Wrigley's chewing gum. A tepid stench came up from the subway gratings." Though this begins like an infernal scene, it is presided over by no familiar European devil; only the image (portrayed on a movie house billboard) of "a half-naked woman four stories high, lit up by spotlights— her hair disheveled, her eyes wild, her legs spread out, a gun in each hand. Around her waist was a fringed scarf that covered her private parts." And when Selig Fingerbein, who has just told the tale of his wife and live-in lover, stops to stare, "one eye laughing and one tearing," the narrator beside him is moved to say, "If there is no God, she is our god." To which Zelig responds, shaking "as if he had been awakened from a trance. 'What *she* is promising she can deliver.' "

Though they can comment on, gloss the American scene, however, such choral voices cannot be understood by American passersby. The language they speak is dying or dead, though they do not know it, being themselves a kind of living dead; either living European Jews who do not believe they are quite living, or dead ones unwilling to believe they are quite dead. Their America is, consequently, neither earth nor heaven nor hell, but Limbo: a twilight landscape in which they can haunt only each other, being imperceptible to the wide awake inhabitants of daylight America. They influence nothing, in fact, change nothing, want to change nothing in the land to which they have come as semi-survivors, not-quite ghosts. They do not vote, sign petitions, put on uniforms; they do not protest anything, cheer anything, join anything. Occasionally they go into business, dealing chiefly with each other; more frequently they write or lecture; always they make love, incestuously, of course, and tell stories, true or false, to those who speak their language. But especially, they hide—or get lost.

Lostness. It is the *Leitmotif*, the compulsive theme of Singer's American tales. Especially his demi-autobiographical male protagonists, but by no means they alone, lose their wallets, their papers, their manuscripts (asserting the immortality of Yiddish), their keys, their way, themselves. They take the wrong trains, end up in the wrong hotels or the right ones on the wrong day. It seems to me apt, therefore, that Singer, for whose sake most of us, certainly I, were present in San Francisco, lost *us*—never making it to the meeting of the MLA group at which I delivered the first version of this paper.

But it is this theme which, paradoxically, makes him seem finally one of us, one more Stranger in a Strange Land; which is to say, one more American, as *Enemies, A Love Story*, his single novel set in the United States and published in English, makes abundantly clear—particularly in its last pages, where Singer actually loses Herman Broder, his main character. It seems at first glance the most astonishing, terrifying and satisfactory thing about that eminently astonishing, terrifying and satisfactory book. Yet it is clear from the first that no other fate can possibly await Broder except to vanish. He is by profession a ghost writer; but this means (as anyone who knows anything about Singer's narrative mode is aware) that he is a ghost who writes, as well as the author of works issued under someone else's name: not *symbolically* a ghost, let it be clear, but a ghost in all the super-actuality of popular fiction.

Singer writes still in the unfallen world before the invention of *symbolisme*: a world in which the archetypes have not yet been introjected, but are still Out There with the rest of us. In his stories, therefore, metaphor is not generalized into symbol or allegory, as in the works of literary Modernism; but specified in hallucinatory character and events, as in the fantasies of schizophrenics, or the best-selling fictions of Dickens, Conan Doyle and the writers of Daytime Serials on television. For this reason, my barely literate grandfather could read him out of his daily newspaper, and my quite illiterate grandmother listen to him read aloud with as much pleasure and understanding (more, in one sense at least) than I.

Entangled throughout the course of the novel with competing wives or quasi-wives with equal claims—Herman Broder seems for a long time utterly unlike the typical American protagonist in flight from the world of women. Toward the end, however, he is tempted, much as Dimmesdale was tempted by Hester in *The Scarlet Letter*, to flee the complexities and conflicts his own lies have created for a romantic Utopia *à deux* beyond the limits of law as he knows it. But if, again like Dimmesdale, he does not yield to that temptation, this is not because he has chosen to tell the truth and die; but because his Hester, who is called Masha, a hysterical survivor of the Holocaust, half Lilith and half Angel of Death, commits suicide at the last minute.

What ensues for Broder is not quite clear, since as I indicated earlier, he simply disappears from the final pages of the book; which is to say, Singer will not or cannot discern his ultimate fate. He leaves that task instead to one of the surviving wives, who speculates that her husband may have died, offstage, outside the fiction. It is too European an ending to bear; and I would prefer therefore to believe that he chose instead the truly American flight to total loneliness, an undefined territory ahead. If this makes him seem disconcertingly like Huckleberry Finn, that is fair enough in light of the fact that his strategy throughout the novel has been, not unlike Huck's, to "flee from evil, hide from danger, avoid showdowns."

And, after all, Singer himself suggests—or at least permits one of his characters to suggest—that maybe Herman is alive and hiding out in "an American version of his Polish hayloft": a reference which becomes clear when we remember that he had concealed himself under the hay in a peasant's barn throughout the whole of World War II; sleeping out the Holocaust, even as Rip Van Winkle had slept out the American Revolution. It occurs to me, moreover, that an "American version of a Polish hayloft" would be nothing more nor less than America itself: the Wilderness America of writers Singer has never read, like Melville and Twain, Hemingway and Faulkner, Mailer and Bellow—a mythic land as invisible to the other characters in Singer's novel as their world is to us, except in his pages where improbably our boundaries meet.

I. B. Singer—Alone in the Forest

Joseph C. Landis

The loneliness of the writer in exile from his homeland is hard to exaggerate. Greater by far, however, must be the loneliness of a writer who has decreed his own exile in the very midst of his world and his culture. Such is the loneliness that pervades the self-imposed spiritual exile of I. B. Singer, who has quarreled with his God and repudiated both the literature to which he belongs and the culture to which he must perforce address himself. In the very heartland of both Yiddish culture and orthodox piety, he declared the two-front war which he has fought all of his life and which mobilizes his creative vitality. Both quarrels are repeatedly recounted in the series of memoirs he has written in the course of several decades, narratives that fulfill the same psychic function as his fiction: to justify the ways of I. B. Singer to God. It is this quarrel with God, a quarrel unresolvable, irreconcilable, and endlessly repeated, that lies at the heart of all his creative work.

Quarrels with God, however, are rarely encountered in modern Yiddish literature. During the century of its great flowering, theodicy has rarely been an issue. As a result, a great many of Singer's Yiddish readers have failed to perceive the central concerns of his fiction and have been at a loss to account for his astonishing popularity in the "outside" world. That a writer who initially repelled so many Yiddish readers and left others indifferent or nonplussed should be so acclaimed by non-Jews baffled them. "What do *they* see in him?" Some have "said or implied that he concentrates his attention too much on repulsive Jewish types and practices, that the proportion of sensuality and superstition in his pages is offensive."[1] Others have shouted "Pornography!" an accusation that is not only unjust to Singer, the great anti-pornographer, as well as to his admirers; it is really rooted in the failure to perceive Singer's central concern; for what most concerns Singer is "utterly at variance with the warm-hearted humanitarianism characteristic of the fathers of Yiddish literature, I. L. Peretz, Sholom Aleichem and others."[2] What is central to Singer has from the very beginning been peripheral to the concerns of the modernist, rationalist, meliorist world of modern Yiddish culture in its bloom.

This deviation of Singer's from the broad tradition of Yiddish literature

From *Yiddish* 6 (Summer–Fall 1985): 5–23. Reprinted by permission of Joseph C. Landis.

has, indeed, been brought as a charge, even levelled as an indictment: He stands outside the mainstream of modern Yiddish literature; he rejects outright its central values.

> The fact is that, although the exaggerated sex repelled many Yiddish writers and his playing around with devils evoked impatience and repugnance, the essence of Bashevis Singer's strangeness and of his estrangement from Yiddish literature lay in that anti-humanism of his. This is where the basic dividing line was drawn between Bashevis Singer and the whole of modern Yiddish literature.[3]

Such outright rejection would be surprising enough in the case of a writer who has probably been more acclaimed by the world than any of his predecessors or contemporaries and who is certainly the most recognized and rewarded of all who have written in Yiddish. More astounding, however, is Singer's own fierce assertion of his estrangement from the great bulk of modern Yiddish writing and his low opinion, frequently expressed, of the overwhelming majority of its practitioners. Even as a young man newly arrived in Warsaw to seek a literary career, he felt himself alienated from the mainstream of Yiddish literature.

> I had already become acquainted with modern Hebrew and Yiddish literature. The writers of both languages were under the influence of the Enlightenment. These authors wanted the Jew to step out of his old-fashioned gabardine and become European. Their doctrines were nationalistic, liberal, humanistic. But to me such ideas were already obsolete.[4]

During the first quarter of the twentieth century there was hardly a Yiddish writer or intellectual who would have thought the Jewish Enlightenment "obsolete" or who would have repudiated "doctrines" on the ground that they "were nationalistic, liberal, humanistic." Indeed, those were the years when the Yiddish Enlightenment was just reaching its peak. As Singer himself observes, modern Yiddish literature had, in fact, grown out of the Jewish Enlightenment—the Haskala—which had reached its full force in East European Jewish life during the late nineteenth and early twentieth centuries. Two generations of young intellectuals had embraced it as a liberating, vitalizing force, which rejected Jewish pietism and medievalism and demanded, with a passion not always intellectual, the modernization of Jewish life. The Haskala had, in effect, promulgated a doctrine of the separation of religion and culture: Be a Jew at home and a man in the street. Out of the Haskala had emerged the possibility of a secular Jewish intellectual life and of secular intellectual careers. The very concept of a modern Jewish intellectual, of a concern with modern Yiddish culture, of a career as a Yiddish writer could take hold only in proportion to the breakdown of the self-contained, self-sufficient enclave of Jewish piety. In the world of piety, there was no room for modern literature. In a very real sense, therefore, modern Yiddish literature became possible only with the breakdown of that world, became viable only as a successor to that self-sufficient world. The progress of Yiddish literature and the aspiration of Yiddish culture during the century that followed the publication of Mendele's *Dos kleyne mentshele* (1864), the work that "inaugurated" modern Yiddish literature, was toward a modern, secular, rationalist, humanist, libertarian, meliorist cultural entity. Not one of these attributes was regarded by Singer as anything but spiritually destructive.

In a passage that still snorts with scorn a full half-century after the initial judgment, he renders an indictment not only of the entire literature but of the very language itself:

> The themes employed by Yiddish writers and the writing itself struck me as sentimental, primitive, petty. Too often it had to do with a girl whose parents wanted an arranged marriage while she really loved someone else. Quite often the girl comes from a wealthy family and the youth was the son of a tailor or a shoemaker. Would it be possible to describe in Yiddish the kind of [frankly sexual] relationship I had with Gina? Although Yiddish literature flirted with socialism and more recently [i.e., early 1920s] with communism, it had remained provincial and backward. Besides, Yiddish—the language itself—had become repugnant both to gentiles and to a great number of modern Jews. Even such Yiddish writers as Mendele Mokher Sforim, Sholem Aleichem, and Peretz called Yiddish a jargon.[5]

As though there were not enough here to startle and offend the Yiddish reader, he continues:

> Both the Yiddish literature and the Hebrew avoided the great adventures inherent in Jewish history—the false Messiahs, the expulsions, the forcible conversions, the Emancipation, and the assimilations that had created a condition in which Jews became ministers in England, Italy, and America, professors in large universities, millionaires, party leaders, editors of world-famous newspapers. Yiddish literature ignored the Jewish underworld, the thousands and tens of thousands of thieves, pimps, prostitutes, and white slaves in Buenos Aires, Rio de Janeiro, and even in Warsaw. Yiddish literature reminded me of my father's courtroom where almost everything was forbidden. True, Sholem Asch had in a sense created a minor revolution and had taken up themes that till then had been considered taboo, but he was and remained a rustic, at least that's how I saw him then and still do to this day. His stories personified the pathos of the provincial who has been shown the big world for the first time and who describes it when he goes back to the town where he came from.[6]

A closer inspection of the bill of particulars reveals both a telescoping and a reshuffling of history—for example, Jews did not become professors in large American universities in any perceptible numbers until after World War II—as well as outright inaccuracy about Yiddish literature, which had, in fact, already dealt with and was very soon to deal even more with "false Messiahs, the expulsions, the forcible conversions, the Emancipation. . . ." By 1922, when Singer was eighteen, Sholem Asch had already published *Sabbatai Zevi*, Pinski, *The Mute Messiah*, and Leivick had written two messianic works with the Golem as redeemer, to name only a few of the better known works. In fact, as far back as 1908, when Singer was four, Asch had already shocked Warsaw with his *God of Vengeance*, a play set in a brothel, peopled by pimps, whores, and brothel owners, with a second act centering around a scene of lesbian love. And Yitzkhok Leybush Peretz, while pointing to serious defects in the play, had also praised it highly and had urged his readers to "buy the book. . . . *God of Vengeance* is, to my taste, a wonderful work."[7] In 1916, Asch had again returned to the subject of the demimonde and the Jewish underworld of pimps and whores, thieves and murderers in his *Mottke the Thief*. Indeed, if anything, the Jewish underworld was a staple of the Yiddish penny dreadfuls and of the *shund* melodramas of the early Yiddish stage.

Such denigrations without regard to accuracy have never ceased. Writing recently on the Yiddish theater, Singer observed that the plays he had seen as a young man of twenty-one were "ridiculous":

> I was already a young writer and an ardent reader of world literature when I began to attend plays in Yiddish. . . . These plays were folkish, utterly naive and sometimes even ridiculous. . . .
>
> It was true that every Yiddish play needed a heart-rending recital of Kaddish and a wedding ceremony in order to keep the noisy audiences quiet for some time.
>
> If someone were to ask me what was essentially the topic of Yiddish theater, I would say it was basically a love story—the tale of human love oppressed by religious asceticism and supposedly freed in an epoch of enlightenment. The protagonists of both the Yiddish theater and Yiddish literature were young men and women of the shtetl who refused to marry by arranged marriages and wanted to follow their own romantic desires. They craved to free themselves from their poverty-stricken and backwards environment. They yearned for the big world, secular education and for the right to wear modern clothes, to do away with the caftan, the wig and the whole burden of orthodoxy which they considered Asiatic.[8]

By 1925, when Singer was twenty-one, and having published his first story could legitimately describe himself as "a young writer," the Yiddish stage had produced, besides the *shund* productions he describes, at least three serious art theaters beginning with the Hirshbein Troupe in 1908 and followed by the Vilna Troupe, and the VIKT (Warsaw Yiddish Art Theater), with Esther Rokhel Kaminska as well as the Hebrew Habima, which initially drew from the Yiddish repertoire. By 1922 he could have seen or heard about the plays of Ansky, Asch, Gordin, Hirshbein, Leivick, Pinski, Sholem Aleichem, to name only the best known of the important Yiddish playwrights. Indeed, the 1920s were a period of almost frenetic theatrical experimentation and artistic earnestness.

The opening denigrating paragraphs of the article seem, in fact, to have no relation to the rest of the piece, which is not unlike the chronicle to be found in most encyclopedias: a galloping survey of Yiddish theater history. The facts, however, are not permitted to interfere with the judgment. The real Singer commentary is to be found in the introduction. The rest is filler.

On occasion, however, derision alone seems not to suffice. At such times his fierce contempt can scarcely be restrained as he mounts an *ad hominem* assault on Yiddishists themselves, the intellectuals who were the ideological architects and the activists of modern Yiddish culture: "To have anything to do with Yiddishists one had to be, as the saying goes, stronger than iron. Every Yiddishist was a party unto himself. All of them talked a blue streak. To deal with them was quite impossible, because keeping one's word and paying one's debts were totally alien to their nature."[9] The level of the argument is a measure of the emotional depths from which it springs. Very few were spared in Singer's war against "the radical, atheistic atmosphere of a Jewish culture that was ignorant and provincial besides."[10]

There were times, however, when the occasion demanded a more restrained and judicious analysis. In a Jewish Book Month address, feeling constrained to phrase his criticism more circumspectly, he traced the low estate of Yiddish letters to the ignorance of Jewish traditional learning that characterized writers after Mendele. Yiddish literature, he conceded,

> was created by people with great Jewish education. Linestski, Mendele, Sholem Aleichem, Peretz were possessed of much Jewish learning. Later, however, a disorientation arose in our literature. They began associating Yiddish with matters that had no organic connection with Yiddish. Coincident with that, the worth and the prestige of our literature began to fall. . . . It was a fatal decline. . . . I do not exaggerate a bit when I say that the tragedy of Yiddish literature was the result exclusively of the fact that it took a road that was contrary to our history, our spiritual and physical existence. The Jew is habitually a man of Torah. He wants to and must be continually studying. . . . The Yiddish writer must study Jewishness.[11]

What is ultimately illuminating about these and other passages in a similar vein is not the faulty recollection—or deliberate distortion—of the facts about the concerns of Yiddish literature and the state of Yiddish culture but the icy contempt for that literature of which he has become a part and, initially, for the language in which he creates, the smoldering hostility that still erupts some fifty years later as he writes his recollections. Rarely does he leave any doubt about his own separation from that literature or the grounds, often repeated, of his divorce: "Neither Aaron Zeitlin nor I fitted into Yiddish literature with its sentimentality and cliches about social justice or Jewish nationalism."[12]

With Yiddish as a language, however, he ultimately had to come to terms. It was, of course, never the jargon that the German Jewish Maskilim had asserted it to be. In fact, when Mendele, Sholem Aleichem, and Peretz had used the word *zhargon* for Yiddish, they had used it simply as a respectable synonym. The acceptance in Yiddish of the term *zhargon* had long since divested it of any pejorative implications or overtones of Maskilic scorn. Sholem Aleichem, for example, could matter-of-factly remark without the slightest hint of self-denigration, "ikh bin a zhargnisher shrayber," and mean simply "I am a Yiddish writer." There were, however, more obvious and more pressing reasons for Singer's reconciliation with Yiddish.

> My choice had to be between Yiddish and Hebrew. . . . After many trials I decided I could not convey in Hebrew a conversation between a boy and a girl on Krochmalna Street or even the talk used by the litigants who came to my father's courtroom. I turned to Yiddish, but I soon realized that this language had limitations and peculiarities inherent perhaps in no other language. Yiddish was never spoken by military men, police, people of power and of influence. It was the language of the tailor, the shopkeeper, the Talmud teacher, the rabbi, the matchmaker, the servant girl, but never of the engineer, the scientist, the army officer, the judge, the *grande dame*. . . . *Yiddish, however, was the language of the Ashkenazi Jewish exile. It was remarkably appropriate not only to my experience but also to my spirit.* [Italics added.] Yiddish had a *Weltanschauung* of its own. . . . It is the language of those who are afraid, not of those who arouse fear . . . a language of Jewishness, the expression of those who still view human behavior from the point of view of kosher and non-kosher, permitted and forbidden.[13]

> I cling to Yiddish because this language conveys my disbelief in worldly achievements and expresses my hope for redemption. . . . Yiddish shared and is still sharing the lot of the Jew who resigned from the promises of this world, its vanities, and its wickedness.[14]

His Nobel Lecture accepting the prize, acknowledged the honor as "also a recognition of the Yiddish language—a language of exile . . . that was despised by both gentiles and emancipated Jews" (thereby according to Yiddish its vindication and its ironic revenge over its denigrators). As the first and possibly the last Yiddish writer to receive the prize, the recipient might normally have been expected to make a generous gesture to the literature of which he was a part. Not Singer. His quarrel with Yiddish literature is not some crank letter to its Op-Ed pages. Its greatest, its unforgivable sin was that it had yielded to Singer's own temptation: it had rejected God and faith and humility and patient endurance. It had regarded Him as irrelevant. Singer could quarrel with God, but he could not ignore Him.

During the astonishingly swift transformation of Jewish intellectual life in Eastern Europe toward the end of the last century, when young Jewish intellectuals exited from the yeshivas in which they had studied to become secular Yiddish readers, writers, critics, and thinkers, young modernists and modernizers of a culture, under the intellectual leadership of I. L. Peretz, when pietism was regarded as the foe of modernization, the bulwark of resistance to change and a backwater of intellectual life, only two young writers departed that world with any deep regret: I. B. Singer and his older patron and friend, Aaron Zeitlin. And for Singer alone did that break become the mainspring of his creative life and the central concern of all his writing. It may well have made him into the greatest modern Yiddish writer; it certainly made him into the only major Yiddish writer for whom the confrontation of God and man is the central drama—as it has been the central drama of I. B. Singer's own spiritual life.[15]

That rejected legacy of faith and piety that was Singer's and his deeply felt regard for it permeates all of his recollections—the legacy of faith and the passion of doubt. Or, as he phrases it himself, "the wisdom of doubt and the fire of faith."[16] The opening pages of *A Little Boy in Search of God* sound these twin motifs of both his memoirs and his fiction: faith and doubt, *gloybn un tsveyfl*. *Gloybn un tsveyfl* is, in fact, the name of the several series of reminiscences that ran twice weekly in the *Jewish Daily Forward* from 1975 to 1979, the second such lengthy memoir (preceded by *Mentshn oyf mayn veg* and followed by *Figurn fun literatn fareyn*), and the one from which the two English volumes *A Little Boy in Search of God* and *A Young Man in Search of Love* are excerpted. *Gloybn un tsveyfl* seems hardly intended as an accurate record of events. It is more nearly a kind of Wordsworthian *Prelude*, the story of the growth of a writer's mind and consciousness, the tale of a writer caught in the contradictions of past and present, faith and reason, piety and the Enlightenment. It is not really the story of Itchele, the little boy from Lioncin and Warsaw's Krochmalna Street No. 10 searching for God, but of I. B. Singer, the writer of seventy, recalling once again his quarrel with God in yet another autobiographical reprise, retracing the origins of his doubt and trying once again to affirm the justice of his stance— or trying to exorcise the dybbuk of his doubt, to justify the ways of Isaac to God. His early questions really should be more childish than they are; his youthful wisdom, less wise. But the essential truth, the tortured truth of Isaac's struggle with God, emerges as he seeks again the vindication of Isaac Singer. If his comments on emancipated modern Yiddish literature and culture are acrid with disdain, his descriptions of his home and the *yikhes* of his family tree are redolent with affection, admiration, and pride:

I was born and reared in a house where religion, Jewishness, was virtually the air that we breathed. I stem from generations of rabbis, Hassidim, and cabalists. [His father was a rabbi and rabbinic judge of Krochmalna Street; his maternal grandfather, a pillar of faith and righteousness, was the rabbi of Bilgoray; Reb Dov Ber Meisels, his great-great-grandfather, was the Warsaw rabbi.] I can frankly say that in our house Jewishness wasn't some diluted formal religion but one that contained all the flavors, all the vitamins, the entire mysticism of faith. Because the Jews had lived for two thousand years in exile, been driven from land to land and from ghetto to ghetto, their religion hadn't evaporated. The Jews underwent a selection the likes of which has no parallel in any of the other faiths. Those Jews lacking strong enough religious convictions or feelings fell to the wayside and assimilated with the gentiles. The only ones left were those who took their religion seriously and gave their children a full religious upbringing. The Diaspora Jew clung to only one hope—that the Messiah would come . . . a spiritual deliverance that would change the whole earth, root out all evil, and bring the Kingdom of Heaven to earth.

In our house the coming of the Messiah was taken most literally. . . . My father had published a book in which there was a family tree tracing our descent from Shabatai Cohen, from Rabbi Moshe Isserlis, from Rashi, until King David. My brother Moshe and I would enter the palace where King David sat with crown on head on a golden throne and call him "Grandpa."[17]

His imagination glowed with vivid recreations of biblical scenes.[18] He rejoiced in the carnival of Purim on Krochmalna Street. He delighted in the mysteries his father revealed in the Cabala. With what admiration and love he describes that unworldly father, who was so submerged in Jewish piety that he refused any concessions to the gentile world around him, even at the expense of his own livelihood! All he needed to do to be licensed as an official rabbi was to learn a smattering of Russian, take an examination in it, and have a chat with the Governor. He refused. "Even at that time such unworldliness was rare."[19] He was a man of total and unquestioning faith, who rejected the very thought of doubt. "Father warned Mother that if she didn't stop abusing the Rabbi [his Hassidic *rebbe*] before the children they would proceed from doubting the rabbi to doubting God."[20] In this intensely gratifying Jewish world, "I actually *felt* that there was a holy soul inside me, a particle of the Godhead."[21]

The truth is that what the great religions preached, the [orthodox] Yiddish-speaking people of the ghettos practiced day in and day out. They were the people of the Book in the truest sense of the word. They knew of no greater joy than the study of man and human relations, which they called Torah, Talmud, Mussar, Kabballah. The ghetto was not only a place of refuge for a persecuted minority but a great experiment in peace, in self-discipline and in humanism.[22]

The ghettos teemed with saints, mystics, men of genius.[23]

In this world of old Jewishness I found a spiritual treasure trove. . . . Time seemed to flow backwards. . . . I lived Jewish history.[24]

Indeed, in this timeless Jewish universe, it was the surrounding world that was exiled as unfit. "In our home the 'world' itself was *tref*." And then the aged, reminiscing writer adds, with words that understate the deep regret, the lasting, living ache, "Many years were to pass before I began to understand how much sense there was in this attitude."[25]

It may not be immediately clear why a world so idyllic and so spiritually gratifying should have been rejected by anyone, much less by Isaac Singer, who had found in it so much spiritual peace. Yet this is the world from which he departed before he was out of his teens.

Singer offers various explanations for the ultimate crumbling of this spiritual fortress, a process that began, by his own account, some years after the family moved to Warsaw from the little shtetl of Leoncin, in 1908. For brother Israel Joshua, eighteen at the time, the move opened a door to the modern world of Warsaw, and an escape from the world of piety which had become for him constricting and oppressive; for Isaac, only four at the time, it was hardly more than a move from one shtetl to another, from Leoncin to the confines of the intensely pious enclave on Krochmalna Street. It was during the nine formative years of his stay in Warsaw, however, where his father served as a rabbinical judge, especially during the war years, that Singer dates the growth of his doubts. "My brother and his worldly books had sown the seeds of heresy [i.e., doubt] in my mind," he notes at one point.[26] Elsewhere, he blames the intrusion of the real, intriguing outside world into his life for tarnishing the luster of his piety: "Between Ostrzego's studio [where he used to visit his brother who was hiding out as a deserter from the unbearably anti-Semitic Polish army] and the disinfecting station, the heder, Father's courtroom, and the study house lost their attraction for me."[27]

In a still later memoir, however, he reports that the great blows which battered his faith derived ultimately neither from his brother's books nor from the seductive breadth of the great world. They had begun earlier and had grown out of his observations of the cruelties that both nature and man inflicted without reproof or punishment from the Almighty, observations that had deeply affronted his moral sense since childhood. The utter indifference of God to the gratuitous pain and undeserved suffering of life was incomprehensible to him. His own observations supported his brother's argument that

Nature demonstrated no religion. . . . It apparently didn't concern nature that the slaughterers in Yonash's Market daily killed hundreds or thousands of fowl. Nor did it bother nature that the Russians made pogroms on Jews or that the Turks and Bulgarians massacred each other and carried little children on the tips of their bayonets.[28]

And "boys caught flies, tore off their wings, and tortured them in every manner only men could conceive while God the Almighty sat on his Throne of Glory in seventh heaven and the angels sang His praises."[29] The young Singer often felt "an unbearable pity for those who were suffering and who had suffered in all generations. . . . I lived in a world of cruelty. . . . I was a child, but I had the same view of the world that I have today—one huge slaughterhouse, one enormous hell."[30] Why did God permit this cruelty? He could "find no answer in the Scriptures."[31] These doubts and questions when, according to his own report, he was only eight or nine, awakened a terrifying thought: "I am becoming a heretic!"[32]

Israel Joshua had given up trying to "fathom the truth of the world" and urged Isaac "Eat, drink, sleep, and if it's possible, try to create a better order."[33] Neither eating nor drinking nor improving the world held any interest for Isaac Singer then, nor do they now. He continued to be tortured by the problem of God's dereliction of duty, of "why people and animals must suffer so. This to me was the question of questions."[34] Again and again the challenge, sometimes the very phrases re-echo in his memoirs: "The question of questions was the suffering of creatures, man's cruelty to man and to animals. . . . These were my feelings then, and those are my feelings still."[35] And again, the "problem of problems is still to me the suffering of people and animals."[36] The problem gave him no peace. "If God were indeed full of mercy and benevolence, He wouldn't have allowed starvation, plagues, and pogroms."[37] Isaac could not escape the shattering conclusion: " 'God is evil,' I said, astounded at my own words. A good God wouldn't arrange it that wolves should devour lambs and cats should catch innocent mice."[38] The outcome of such heretical thoughts might have been a denial of God. But denial was beyond his capacity. The only alternative for Singer was war.

War with God, on the one hand, and war with the Yiddish modernists on the other, left Isaac Singer the Yiddish writer in almost total isolation, an exile from both the world of piety and the world of modern Yiddish culture, caught forever between them like a dybbuk.

A Prometheus chained, he fought his private war with God. An exile, he fought his war with his world:

> I often spoke with rage against God, but I never ceased to believe in His existence. I wrote about spirits, demons, cabbalists, dybbuks. Many Yiddish writers and readers had cut loose from their Jewish roots and from the juices upon which they had been nourished. They yearned once and for all to tear away from the ghetto and its culture—some as Zionists, others as radicals. Both factions preached worldliness. But I remained spiritually rooted deep in the Middle Ages (or so I was told). I evoked in my work memories and emotions that the worldly reader sought to forget and factually had forgotten. To the pious Jews, on the other hand, I was a heretic and blasphemer. I saw to my astonishment that I belonged neither to my own people nor to any other peoples. Instead of fighting in my writings the political leaders of a

decadent Europe and helping to build a new world, I waged a private war against the Almighty.[39]

His war with God broadened into a war that included His creatures as well. Political reform and social progress were illusory. Oppression

was the essence of human history. Today the Poles tormented the Jews; yesterday the Russians and Germans had tormented the Poles. Every history book was a tale of murder, torture, and injustice; every newspaper was drenched in blood and shame.[40]

I had often fantasized about redeeming the human species, but it became obvious to me that the human species didn't deserve redemption. To do so would actually be a crime. Man was a beast that killed, ravaged, and tortured not only other species but its own as well. The other's pain was his joy, the other's humiliation was his glory.[41]

Unable to deny God yet equally unable wholly to accept Him, he sought a kind of equilibrium in a stance of continuous protest:

I said to myself: I believe in God, I fear Him, yet I cannot love Him—not with my whole heart and soul as the Torah commands nor with the *amor dei intellectualis* that Spinoza demands. Nor can I deny God as the materialists do. All I can do is to the best of my limits treat people and animals in a way I consider proper. I had, one might say, created my own basis for an ethic— not a social ethic nor a religious one, but an ethic of protest. . . . The moral person protests not only when he is personally wronged but also when he witnesses or thinks about the suffering of others. If God wants or feels compelled to torture His creatures, that is His affair. The true protester expresses his protest by avoiding doing evil to the best of his ability.[42]

[Indeed,] I had even related my philosophy of protest to Jewishness. The Jew personified the protest against the injustices of nature and even those of the Creator. Nature wanted death, but the Jew opted for life; nature wanted licentiousness, but the Jew asked for restraint; nature wanted war, but the Jew, particularly the Diaspora Jew (the highly developed Jew), sought peace. . . . Even if he had to wage war against God, the Jew would not desist.[43]

"With this view of life and in this mood I went to Warsaw [1923, age 19] to become the proof reader of the *Literary Pages*"[44]—and to take up his quarrel with modern Yiddish literature and culture.

It is clear that the resolution in this "ethic of protest" really resolved nothing. To deny God can be final, to defy him is forever. The "ethic of protest" was only a name and a frame for a continuing inner conflict, for a state of constant warfare with God and man. It neither cured him of his desperate need to believe nor did it provide a rationale for an uncompromising faith. A stranger in the world, he belonged neither to the secular world of modern Yiddish culture nor to the world of Jewish religion. He had rejected the one and found himself unable to belong to the other, to that world for which his heart yearned. He was in total exile.

For all his bravado about defying God and man on behalf of righteousness, Singer admitted the terrifying proviso:

> Well, but this kind of strength lay only within the Jew who observed the Torah, nor in the modern Jew who served nature like the gentile, was subservient to it, and placed all his hopes upon it.[45]

Neither a "Jew who observed the Torah" nor a "modern Jew who served nature," what identity could Singer claim? An artist, he is fond of observing, must have roots, must have an address: "An artist is a person who is rooted in his milieu; he does not deny his parents and grandparents."[46] And Singer himself? "Identity I got at home. I knew exactly who my father was—the rabbi in Warsaw. My grandfather was the rabbi in Bilgoray, and so on and so on."[47]

But is this really Singer's identity, embraced without conflict or qualification? Is he a Jew who observes the Torah as did his pious forefathers "Since at an early age I forsook the code of laws according to which I was raised"?[48] What does it mean not to "deny his parents and grandparents"? Singer's pious ancestors did not write novels, and modern Yiddish novelists are at best only intellectually enamored of their pious ancestors. Did his father even read the Yiddish newspapers that printed both his sons' work? "Father said that the newspapers were full of blasphemy and heresy."[49] And to the end of his days Father pretended that his sons were in the newspaper business, not writers for the Yiddish press.

Wordsworth's pantheism, Milton's Ptolemaic cosmos were constructs that created for each a stability, an aesthetic calm, a tranquility in which to recollect emotion, and a frame to contain their work. Singer's construct, however, his "ethic of protest," served his creativity by establishing an unresolvable, continuing tension that propels almost all of his works along all or part of a trajectory: a need to believe contending either with an inability to believe or with a dereliction from faith; a resulting, sometimes rampant evil; and a final containment of evil and moral chaos, a containment that is real in the works of fancy and conceptual in the realistic fiction. Those who do not complete the cycle are destroyed. Those who do find not an easy peace but the means of eternal vigilance against Satan, a cell to contain the waywardness of the inclination to evil, a humility that to Singer is the central virtue of the traditional Jew, a recognition, as Shlomo Bickel phrased it, that this is the least evil of all possible worlds, an acceptance of the ultimately unfathomable nature of God and his ways,[50] and a total rejection of that Promethean boldness, that modernist daring to question the ways of

God to man for which the punishment is of necessity Promethean. Only a rigid conservatism of faith—and of social and political vision—only a steadfastness as firm as that of his grandfather, the Rabbi of Bilgoray, who singlehandedly had held the world at bay during his lifetime,[51] could serve to withstand the total moral anarchy that attends on the slightest deviation from the path of Torah. And only a rigid social and political conservatism makes sense in a world that is *tref*, whose unclean ways are forbidden, where change is impotent to change and therefore really changes nothing, a world in which man's nature and temptations are constant. Such is the resolution in Singer's fiction, a resolution he cannot effect in his life. "I am not an observant Jew," he remarks, abashed and sad. For Singer, the conflict is beyond resolution. But, the effort to resolve it, to explain the dereliction of Isaac, is endless. The fiction goes on.

Whatever the cost to the man, the gain to the artist was incalculable. Almost from the very first, Singer had his theme and his universe, his characters and his plots. Like Michelangelo's, his struggle was to liberate them from the marble. Each work springs from the inner tension which is never resolved and never relaxed. That unresolved psychic struggle of this writer in spiritual exile leaves a state of unremitting tension, a heightened sense of man's audacity and guilt, of the enormity of the evil when bodily hungers and spiritual pride are unleashed by diminution of faith, an acute sense of the awesome danger of doubt and a terrifying awareness of the capacity—human and personal—for evil. The two sins of sex and slaughter so common in his fiction become opposite sides of the same coin, evils in themselves as well as symbols of temptation and evil. Add the inevitable third and there emerges the vicious trinity of sin: doubt, sex, and slaughter. These are at the core of his fiction. These are the forces that must be chained lest they run amok in a crescendo of evil.

The basic Singer plot that begins along the continuum of an unstable stability, followed by a volcanic eruption and ending in an exhaustion of the demonic ferocity—"Even the fire of the Evil Inclination does not burn forever"[52]—and the final vindication of a moral order and stability that are rooted in Jewish tradition repeats itself incessantly. There is almost always a Goray, either individual or collective, that has been rocked by a cataclysm: almost always a Satan that enters, a Satan that is neither Rechele nor Gedalye but Promethean self-assertion, the audacity of doubting the Lord and his wisdom, of forcing the Lord to either secular or religious redemption, of Promethean urges; and always the possibility of the exhaustion of the Promethean defiance and either a return to tradition and humble acceptance or destruction and death.

If *Satan in Goray* and a multitude of other demonic tales illustrate in phantasmagoria the consequences of the slightest deviation from traditional morality, the realistic and social novels do the same in their own mode.

Satan and *The Magician*—the "autobiographical" core Singer novel—

reveal most clearly the essential pattern: doubt—a daring, modern Prometh-eanism—whose cosmic aspirations are chastened and which then finds a humble reconciliation in faith. *The Slave* is relatively rare in its portrayal of the huge exercise of will needed to retain faith against the onslaught and temptations of the world. But both Jacobs—Jacob the slave and Jacob Yasha the magician—spiritual wrestlers both, find freedom in servitude to the Torah: Jacob in the successful struggle to retain faith, Yosha after the unsuc-cessful effort to reject it.

As Yasha the magician demands of his wife, Esther, in an early exchange that foreshadows the climax of the novel:

> "What would happen if I became an ascetic and, to repent, had myself bricked into a cell without a door like that saint in Lithuania?" . . .
> Esther said, "It's not necessary to seal one's self in a cell to repent."
> "It all depends on what sort of passion one is trying to control," he an-swered.[53]

Yasha's final self-immuration in his cell becomes the central metaphor of Singer's fiction. For those—for modern men—who are caught in the aftertow of the great Promethean self-delusion and self-assertion of the Enlighten-ment, the Messiah is either a penitential return to faith, the faith of Shosha and Krochmalna Street, or death, as in *The Family Moskat*.

If, as has been suggested, many a story seems really unresolved, if endings sometimes seem inconclusive, it is because no resolution is possible for all those who, like Singer, are tainted, who, though they hunger, can neither believe nor disbelieve, who are driven to doubt by the cruelty of God and man yet who cannot bear the guilt and uncontrollable sin of that doubt. The story is repeated in numerous disguises, but "it's the same story you told us last time." "The little rogue!" says Gimpel. "He was right."

Is it any wonder that much of Isaac Bashevis Singer's Yiddish audience, a product of the Jewish Enlightenment, has read him with, at best, grudging admiration, at worst, downright hostility? He so often leaves those readers puzzled. His world seems so familiar. His universe is so strange.

Within a century of its "birth," modern Yiddish culture had completed a cycle not of its own making. Having seen Western barbarism, it recoiled briefly from its faith in the Western Enlightenment and the golden promises of Western culture. But it never returned to the faith of its pious ancestors nor did it even long for that faith. When Yankev Glatshteyn in the 1930s thundered, "Good night you great big stinking world! I return to the ghetto because I wish to," his words proclaimed the moral superiority of "backward" traditional Jewish life and morality over the bestiality which the Western world revealed; they did not, however, affirm the need for a return to traditional piety. Like his literary colleagues and his readers, he was too much a product of the Enlightenment, too much committed to modern life and its premises for a return to ghetto piety. The tears and regrets, the kaddish for the destroyed shtetl world that resonates in postwar Yiddish writing, mourn the loss of a Jewish world—not the loss of Jewish faith. Indeed, the world of modern Yiddish culture remains untroubled by its departure from faith; it remains committed still to the Enlightenment and to secularism. The hunger for faith, the plague of doubt—these are passions that do not trouble it. But these are precisely what trouble Singer and what has troubled much of Western culture in our time. The irony: the victims retain their faith in the Enlightenment; the world at large is not so sure. And so Yiddish readers read Singer and are untouched by what is central to him. His conflict is not theirs. The sex that in Singer is the apex of man's sin, the encompassing symbol of evil and the instrument of his fall once he strays from obedient faith, the archetypal plot of Eden is, for the Yiddish reader, obscured from its cause and becomes for him, falsely, the central focus of the work. "Pornography?" the secular Yiddish reader wonders. "*Shund!*" he sometimes cries, "a desecration of the world destroyed and the millions martyred!" For the non-Yiddish reader, Singer tells it like it is. For the Yiddish reader he maligns a martyred world.

The issue was, in fact, raised at the very outset of Singer's career, though the two critics, Shmuel Niger and Singer's friend Aaron Zeitlin, could hardly have guessed at the dimensions either Singer or their differences would later assume. Shmuel Niger, in his reviews of Singer's first work,[54] hailed the power of the young artist but wondered about his increasing distance from the mainstream of Yiddish writing: the forces of evil are too often unpunished and unrebuked. Satan increasingly rules unchallenged. The Enlightenment faith in the progress of men, in the ultimate victory over evil however long the struggle, the spirit of the doomed but unconquered Jewish World War II partisans—"Never say this is our final fight"—all these premises of the modern Yiddish world are absent from Goray and the towns and tales around it. And Shmuel Niger feels he must call this lack to the attention of the brilliant young neophyte.

It is Aaron Zeitlin, however, who perceives that such admonition is irrelevant to what is central in Singer. Singer's stories, he writes, "breathe with the uniqueness of an artist whose basic theme is the strange, the weird, the tortured, the God-needy,"[55] and their author, he asserts, is "a prose poet who digs deep, sees Satan and is terrified of him, senses what is concealed from sight and calls to God after his own fashion, calls to him, fearful, out of the dark."[56]

Even as he did then, so does Isaac Bashevis Singer still.

Notes

1. Milton Hindus, "A Monument With a Difference," review of *The Family Moskat*, The New York *Times Book Review*, March 14, 1965, p. 4.
2. *Ibid.*
3. I. Goldberg, *Esayen* (New York, 1981), p. 422.
4. "Yes . . . ," *Esquire*, Vol. LXXXII (December, 1974), pp. 196 and 250.
5. *A Young Man in Search of Love* (Garden City, 1978), p. 7.
6. *Ibid.*, p. 10.
7. I. L. Peretz, *Literatur un Lebn*, Vol. X, *di verk fun yitskhok Leibush Peretz* (New York, 1920), pp. 193 and 195.
8. "Yiddish Theater Lives Despite the Past," The New York *Times*, Sec. 2, January 20, 1985, p. 1.
9. "Gloybn un tsveyfl," *Jewish Daily Forward*, October 4, 1979, p. 3.
10. *A Little Boy in Search of God* (Garden City, 1976), p. 157.
11. "Tsum khoydesh fun yidishn bukh" (On Jewish Book Month), *Jewish Daily Forward*, December 16, 1968, p. 2.
12. *A Little Boy in Search of God*, p. 164.
13. "Yiddish, the Language of Exile," *Judaica Book News*, Vol. VI (Spring/Summer 1976/5736), pp. 25–26, reprinted from *Next Year in Jerusalem* (N.Y.: Viking Press, 1976).
14. *Ibid.*, p. 27.
15. For a detailed discussion of the surprising contrast between I. B. Singer and his brother Israel Joshua in their responses to the world of Jewish piety, see my "The Brothers Singer: Faith and Doubt," in *Blood Brothers, Siblings as Writers*, ed. Norman Kiell (New York, 1983), pp. 365–82.
16. "Yiddish, the Language of Exile," p. 27.
17. *A Little Boy in Search of God*, pp. 1–3. With good reason, his older brother, Joshua, was not included in the reunion.
18. *In My Father's Court* (New York, 1962), p. 60.
19. *Ibid.*, p. 51.
20. *Ibid.*, p. 56. As Gimpel discovered, first you doubt Elke, then you doubt God.
21. *Ibid.*, p. 79.
22. "Yiddish and the Spirit of Jewish Life" (Nobel Lecture), *Jewish Daily Forward*, December 24, 1978, p. 28.
23. "Yiddish, the Language of Exile," p. 23.
24. *In My Father's Court*, p. 290.
25. *Ibid.*, p. 68.
26. *Ibid.*, p. 243 (1914–1916).
27. *Ibid.*, p. 259 (1916).
28. *A Little Boy in Search of God*, p. 12.
29. *Ibid.*, p. 20.
30. *Ibid.*, p. 49.
31. *Ibid.*, p. 55.
32. *Ibid.*, p. 57.
33. *Ibid.*, p. 71.
34. *Ibid.*, p. 77.
35. *Ibid.*, p. 88.
36. *Ibid.*, p. 89.
37. *Ibid.*, p. 91.
38. *Ibid.*, p. 102.
39. *Ibid.*, pp. 113–17.
40. *Ibid.*, pp. 133–36.

41. *Ibid.*, p. 136.
42. *Ibid.*, pp. 127–31.
43. *Ibid.*, pp. 179–80.
44. *Ibid.*, p. 131.
45. *Ibid.*, p. 180.
46. *Isaac Bashevis Singer on Literature and Life*, an interview with Paul Rosenblatt and Gene Koppel (Tucson, Arizona, 1971 and 1979), p. 24.
47. *Ibid.*
48. "Yiddish, the Language of Exile," p. 24.
49. *A Little Boy in Search of God*, p. 59.
50. *Shrayber fun mayn dor (Writers of my Generation*; New York, 1958), p. 360.
51. *In My Father's Court*, p. 302.
52. *Ibid.*, p. 10.
53. *The Magician of Lublin* (New York, 1960), p. 25.
54. S. Niger, *Yidishe shrayber fun tsvantsikstn yorhundert (Yiddish Writers of the Twentieth Century)*, Vol. II (New York, 1973), pp. 299–308.
55. *Der sotn in goray un andere dertseylungen (Satan in Goray and Other Stories;* New York, 1943), p. 11.
56. *Ibid.*, p. 12.

Death by the Word: Victims of Language in *Enemies, A Love Story*

Marilyn R. Chandler

Isaac Singer's *Enemies, A Love Story* (1972) is a poignant tale of life amid the ruins of language. In it Singer reflects the concern George Steiner, George Orwell, and many other critics of postwar culture have expressed about the inflations and distortions of language in recent history that threaten to leave us all inarticulate.[1] Language, they claim, has become divorced from the sources of spiritual vitality that give it power. The living word has become a corrupted and corrupting agent, and those who deal in words are endangered by the infectious plague of meaninglessness: those who live by the word shall die by the word.

The story of Herman Broder, talmudic scholar and writer, illustrates how tragically "the letter kills" when cut off from the living spirit of the tradition it encodes. Herman is a man who lives by words: he interprets Talmud, writes sermons and books, edits manuscripts, reads incessantly, and writes compulsively. In fact, he treats his own life as a fictional narrative, weaving a web of lies that literally creates the environment in which he lives, suspended between his two mistresses, alternating between them as an author might between plot and subplot. Gradually Herman loses "authorial control" over that life: the stories he tells his women conflict; his fictions become unconvincing, his promises hollow. He no longer knows how to make language connect with experience either in scholarly discourse or through storytelling. Herman's loss of authorial control reflects loss on a much grander scale: the loss of a language capable of accurately reflecting and adequately ordering experience.

The postwar New York ghetto in which Herman's story is set is a scene of considerable social disorder among displaced Jewish survivors. Every survivor has a story, and all their stories lack context. Communication breaks down in the mélange of different languages and conflicting accounts of the shattering experiences all have undergone. It seems impossible to ascertain historical truth. Words serve not so much to connect, affirm, sustain, or

From *Studies in American Jewish Literature* 7, no. 1 (Spring 1988): 105–17. Reprinted by permission of The Kent State University Press.

enlighten as to confuse, obscure, and deceive. Herman's quest for the authoritative Word has led him through a variety of belief systems, but behind the many words of religious and philosophical texts the voice of God has remained silent. Herman's earlier vocabulary of experience was drawn from Judaic theology and secular philosophy, but in this new setting both seem to fail him. There seems to be no ultimate way of determining or validating the truth of those texts—in fact the Holocaust seems ultimately to invalidate them. As Herman's wife, Tamara, declares, "If God was able to watch all this horror and remain silent, then He's no God" (82). So Herman finds himself caught between meaning-making traditions and an overwhelming sense of meaninglessness, isolation and cosmic silence:

> The silence rang in his ears. . . . Through a hole that had once been a window, he could see the dark sky—a heavenly papyrus filled with hieroglyphics. Herman's gaze fixed upon three stars whose formation resembled the Hebrew vowel 'segul.' . . . They were all silent: God, the stars, the dead. The creatures who *did* speak revealed nothing. (122)

Herman desperately wants God to speak. He wants a revelation or a directive. He wants the security of tradition; he wants to bury himself in sacred texts like the ancient scholars he sees bent over their books in a little basement room—

> a group of white-bearded men studying the Talmud. Their eyes under heavy brows expressed scholarly sharpness. The wrinkles on their high foreheads reminded Herman of the ruled lines of parchment scrolls used by scribes to guide their letters. The faces of the old men reflected a stubborn grief as ancient as the books they studied. For an instant Herman toyed with the idea of joining them. (66–67)

He wants, like the old men, to be absorbed in tradition—in a sense, to become a living text himself. But he cannot shut out the silence or the doubt; he cannot participate in his tradition with good faith because he has lost his faith. So he does not enter the room, but continues to wander the streets pondering his loss:

> The thought occurred to Herman that Jewry was a hot-house growth—it was kept thriving in an alien environment nourished by the belief in a Messiah, the hope of justice to come, the promises of the Bible—the Book that had hypnotized them forever. (52)

Before the war, we are told, Herman had been a scholar, a "disciple of Schopenhauer" who had "shown a leaning toward philosophy even as a youngster," and had "read all the philosophic books he could find in the Tzivkev library" (29). Even then his search for truth had been thwarted by the confusion of contradictory and inconsistent systems of thought. Now his very need for consistency and truth pushes him further and further into a morass of fictions. He chooses to follow Otto Weininger because he considers him to be "the most consistent philosopher," though the narrator immediately exposes the absurdity of Weininger's philosophy by reciting one of its basic tenets: that Weininger considered woman to be "a creature with 'no sense of logic, no memory, amoral, nothing but a vessel of sex' " (30). Though the philosophy's internal consistency appeals to Herman's desire for the reassurance of an ordered system, it is not in fact consistent with Herman's actual experience. In the pursuit of consistency he becomes not only progressively divorced from his own perceptions, but also, ironically enough, progressively inconsistent. Successive disillusionments with philosophical systems which fail to explain the world and provide an adequate description of experience leave Herman a "fatalistic hedonist who lived in presuicidal gloom." He realizes, "Religions lied. Philosophy was bankrupt from the beginning. The idle promises of progress were no more than a spit in the face of the martyrs of all generations" (30).

As a scholar, Herman approaches life through the mediation of the written word; he is so tied to texts and conventional language that his imagination is completely bound by them, and he cannot function without their mediation. Words have placed feeling, affection, and empathy at one remove. When words fail him he is left vitiated and impotent.

But Herman's facility with words is only effective in a context of fantasy or philosophical abstraction. When his wife, Tamara, missing since the war and presumed dead, suddenly shows up, he cannot answer her simple questions because they penetrate directly to the vacancy at the center of his life that he is trying to conceal. Tamara pierces through the balloon-like insulation of his multiple fictions, and the deflation of that balloon threatens to leave Herman in a state of complete despair, deprived of even the illusion of meaning.

It is not only in sacred and scholarly texts that those who have been uprooted like Herman have lost their faith, but even in the ordinary organs of communication like newspapers. Newspapers, which appear repeatedly throughout the novel, are presented as a kind of secular scripture which to the naive are vehicles of truth and meaning—as to Shifrah Puah, the mother of Herman's mistress, Masha, who tells him, "If they put it in the paper, it must be important" (59); but to the enlightened or disillusioned, newspapers are agents of falsehood whose many words, like the words of the sacred books, are masks to cover a sinister emptiness. Herman reads them faithfully, but recognizes them as propagandistic and false. When Yadwiga, his present wife, an innocent, illiterate woman, asks him, "What's in the newspaper?" he typically replies, "Oh, they've made a truce, but it won't last. They'll start fighting again . . ." (14): the newspaper is a purveyor of lies about lies. Picking up an abandoned Yiddish newspaper in the subway, Herman reads accounts of Stalin's false promises, war in China, and exposés of atrocities in Germany and Russia. He reflects on the shallow optimism with which the article concludes that one day the sickness of the world will be cured: "So? They are still intent on curing?" Dropping the paper, he muses on the inanity of such words of hope:

> Phrases like a 'better world' and a 'brighter tomorrow' seemed to him a blasphemy on the ashes of the tormented. Whenever he heard the cliché that those who sacrificed had not died in vain, his anger rose. "But what can I do? I contribute my share of evil." (19)

Herman's "share of evil" is, of course, his writing. "His livelihood," the narrator observes, "was as bizarre as everything else that had happened to him. He had become a ghost writer for a rabbi. He, too, promised a 'better world' in the Garden of Eden" (19).

Herman's skill with words becomes a definitive factor in each of his relationships. He serves his employer, Rabbi Lampert, by providing a false front or mask of words behind which the rabbi conducts his "real" work as a social activist. Lampert, a modern man of the world, and the one character in the novel who seems to have emerged from the war unscathed and to have adapted admirably to secularized postwar American life, has departed radically from his traditional role. He is not a man of words, but a man of action, alienated from the very tasks which traditionally define his role: reading, writing, and interpreting texts. These are, for him, obsolete activities to be delegated to a subordinate while he engages more directly with the world around him. "The rabbi had neither the time nor the patience to study or write" (20). His sermons and lectures, which Herman writes, are a concession to traditional expectations of him as teacher and spiritual leader. But his real effectiveness lies in social action rather than in preaching or interpretation of scripture: ". . . he loved doing favors—finding jobs for the needy . . ." (22).

Though he dignifies Herman's work with the term "research" in public, privately the rabbi refers to it as "scribbling." Herman ghostwrites the rabbi's books, articles, and speeches in Hebrew or Yiddish, a second person translates them, and a third person edits them. None of the three works closely with the rabbi himself. The end product is connected with Lampert's rabbinical authority only in the most tenuous way. Herman is scandalized by this abuse of authority and ashamed of his own role in it, though it is the only available vocation for which he is fit:

> The rabbi was selling God as Tebra sold idols. Herman could find only one justification for himself: most of the people who listened to the rabbi's sermons or read his essays were not completely honest either. Modern Judaism had one aim: to ape the Gentile. (19)

Herman sees the words he authors as mimicry, pretense, and deception. They no longer propagate a living faith, but only cosmetically create a semblance of life on the face of a moribund tradition. Herman's writing therefore is both a betrayal of Jewish tradition and a betrayal of himself— and by this time he is so inured to those acts of self-betrayal that they have become a morbid habit to which he is enslaved as to a drug.

There are, in fact, numerous indications that Herman uses writing precisely as a drug—to deaden the pain of contact with reality. He quiets his nerves at the dinner table by writing: "Between the fish and soup courses he took a notebook and pen from his breast pocket and jotted something down" (105). After one acutely upsetting confrontation with the rabbi, Herman grabs a pen compulsively and starts "writing quickly in small letters," just as a smoker would reach for a cigarette to ease tension (22). At one point this analogy is made explicit:

> Just as Masha always had to hold a cigarette between her fingers, so Herman had to hold a pen or a pencil. He wrote and made notes even in the hayloft in Lipsk, whenever there was enough light coming through the cracks in the roof. He practiced an ornate calligraphy, elaborating the letters with flourishes. . . . He even wrote in his dreams—on yellowish paper in Rashi script, a combination of a story book, cabalistic revelations, and scientific discoveries. He sometimes woke up with a cramp in his wrist from too much writing. (41)

Herman's writing is an expression and an extension of a life of abstraction and fantasy, but it produces real consequences. Masha tries to impress upon him what destructive power his fantasies have: "I shouldn't say this, but compared to you Leon Tortshiner [Masha's estranged husband] was an honest man. He lied too, but he bragged harmlessly and thought up silly fantasies" (95). Herman's lies, on the other hand, shape the lives of four people: his own and those of his three women.

Herman's power over his wife, Yadwiga, a simple Polish peasant, resides in his knowledge of languages she does not know. His exercise of that power is essentially benevolent, if misguided, but his lies create a prison for her. She is entirely dependent on him to explain, translate, and interpret the alien world around her. It is Herman who teaches Yadwiga to sign her name "with three little circles" and offers to teach her the alphabet (though he never does, that being another of his empty promises), but it is also Herman's lies which keep Yadwiga penned up in isolation awaiting a fate over which she has no control because she is illiterate and foreign. Not only can she not speak English, she cannot even speak Yiddish. She is a Gentile among Jews, with no access to the language of Jewish life which would enable her to establish a bond with the women around her.

Ironically, however, Yadwiga's very illiteracy and primitiveness are also sources of strength. Somewhat romantically, she is represented as close to the earth, to the source of things. She communicates in non-linguistic ways. Elemental things have more significance for her than words. Though she must rely on Herman's mediation to write letters to her mother and sister, for instance, and to read the replies, "written by the village teacher," real communication with her family seems to consist of symbolic gestures as when her sister, Marianna, "enclosed a kernel of grain in the envelope, a little stalk with a leaf from an apple tree, or a small flower—reminders of Lipsk in faraway America" (8).

Yadwiga seems, moreover, to have access to some prelapsarian language that Herman cannot speak, conditioned and corrupted as he is by a "civilizing" process of which she has remained "free." At one point the narrator indulges in a romantic paean to her primitive peasant nature and its mystical inarticulateness:

> . . . sometimes at night, when she was overcome with passion, she would chatter a village gibberish that he couldn't follow—words and expressions he had never heard before. Could it be the speech of ancient peasant tribes, perhaps from pagan times? Herman had long been aware that the mind contains more than is gathered in one lifetime. The genes seem to remember other epochs. (14–15)

The passage continues, comparing Yadwiga to the parakeets, and ending with Herman's own reflection that "the sermons he wrote for Rabbi Lampert were a disgrace and mockery" (15). The implicit contrast between the corruption of Herman's intellectual activity and Yadwiga's prelinguistic purity and innocence is highly suggestive, and in fact is the first statement of a major theme to which the novel returns in the end: the necessity of a radical new beginning, a return to the Adamic act of naming and a whole reorientation of language, this time through women and womanly experience.

Yadwiga's pregnancy, which occurs despite Herman's conscientious efforts to prevent it, underscores the regenerative power of life principle independent of language which will, it is suggested, produce a new language out of its own vitality when conventional and traditional systems of language fail. Yadwiga's naming of her child, Masha, is the beginning of a new story of redemption—a new "word made flesh"—this time as woman, whose naming is a renaming—an appropriation and transformation of a name which in the world of the novel has signified negation, life-denying intellectualism, and death. Yadwiga, the illiterate peasant, thus becomes a standard of goodness in the novel and, like Billy Budd, a stumbling block for those around her. Herman calls her "truth itself" (88). In the act of naming her child, Yadwiga has the proverbial "last word" in the novel which is at the same time a profoundly significant "first word" which, being uttered, initiates a new order.

That utterance is preceded by the suicide of Herman's mistress Masha, a symbolic enactment of the death of an old order. Masha is Yadwiga's opposite, characterized as much by her literacy and intellectual sophistication as Yadwiga is by her illiteracy and simplicity. Masha signifies a principle of negation, Yadwiga of affirmation. Like Herman, Masha lives by words; for her, words are also instruments of self-deception, of power over others, and of perversion. Through them she betrays herself, as Herman does himself. She identifies so completely with her father, Meyer Bloch, a scholar, poet, and linguist, that she loses touch with her own womanhood and is profoundly alienated from her mother, who in her simplistic piety literally speaks a different language. Masha has been caught in a complicated version of the family romance which has left her in a state of self-alienation reflected in the conflicting modes of discourse between which she is forced to choose. The importance of language is highlighted in the history of the mother-daughter conflict:

> Their grievances dated back to the time when Meyer Bloch was still alive. He had carried on an allegedly platonic love affair with a Hebrew poetess, a teacher of Masha's. Masha would say jestingly that the love affair had started with a discussion about some rule in Hebrew grammar and had never gone any further. (44)

Masha, like Herman, insulates herself with stories—fictional versions of her past that seal her off from immediate experience. Words are her insulation against cold despair, as they are his.

Herman's room at Masha's apartment is littered with texts: "Books, manuscripts, and scraps of paper covered with Herman's doodles lay scattered about" (40). In this room Herman and Masha come together to make love—a ritual always preceded by storytelling. Herman learns to expect these stories. They are the offspring of a sterile woman weaving a world in which to give herself significance as an escape from one in which she is totally alienated:

> Herman knew that she was preparing some unusual story for their love play. Masha compared herself to Scheherazade. The kissing, the fondling, the passionate love-making was always accompanied by stories from the ghettos, the camps, her own wandering through the ruins of Poland. Through them all, men pursued her: in bunkers, in the forest, in the hospital where she had worked as a nurse. (44–45)

Masha's stories have two purposes: to illustrate her seductive powers and to confirm her nihilistic outlook. "The moral of all her tales was that if it had been God's purpose to improve His chosen people by Hitler's persecution, He had failed" (45). Herman, who writes sermons in which he does not believe, has met a strangely fitting partner in Masha, his "enemy" and lover, who sermonizes endlessly on her unbelief. Their conversations are demonstrations of the spiritual sterility in which they both live—like their love-making, their arguments generate heat and passion, but are neither conclusive, nor regenerative:

> They quarreled, made up, quarreled again. As always, their conversation abounded with promises they both knew would never be kept, with fantasies of pleasures not to be achieved, with questions asked as a spur to their mutual excitement. (56–57)

Arguments lead nowhere. Masha's many words, like Herman's, engender discord or deception, and subvert language so that finally Herman finds it impossible to establish truth between them, even when he wants to: "Masha was so complicated, stubborn, and neurotic that he couldn't tell her the truth either" (23). His lies and her suspicion make the truth impossible to hear. This problem is amusingly illustrated when Herman, tired of deceiving Masha about his wife's sudden arrival in New York, sardonically declares the truth: "My dead wife, Tamara, has risen from the grave. She's polished her nails and come to New York" (95). Masha's response is a dismissive, "Of course." Habitual deception and rankling mistrust have made all communication oblique and suspect. Herman and Masha ask one another time and again, "Is that the truth?" "Are you telling me the truth?" They inflate their devalued discourse with solemn oaths, which are also broken and rendered meaningless.

The pathos of both characters lies in their yearning for truth. The traditions that promised them truth have failed them and they are, in their respective ways, so bound to those traditions as the only accessible vehicles of truth that they are dying with them. Lacking either the self-knowledge of Tamara or the innocence of Yadwiga, they seek truth in external forms and try to express it in a language which is a product of those forms, but which is no longer vitally linked to experience.

There is real tragedy in their blindness and inability to change. Both are clinging to a past that once gave them meaning. For Masha that past is vividly present in her dreams, where she is visited by her father, the poet, who recites stanzas of his verse to her (46). She substitutes the voice of her father for her own voice with formulas like "Papa always said . . ." (37). And she dismisses her mother's words without a hearing. When Shifrah Puah asks her sadly, "Are my words worth nothing to you?" Masha retorts, "You have a story for everything!" (92), forgetting that she herself lives by stories as well.

Shifrah Puah is not at war with herself and the past in the way Masha is. Though her piety manifests a certain limitedness and ignorance, she has a worldly common sense that protects her from the labyrinthine traps of language and argument in which Masha is ensnared. She complains to Herman,

> Listen to her carrying on. Ask her what she's talking about. . . . She has to say something contrary, that's all. She inherited it from her father's family— he should rest in the Garden of Eden. They all loved to argue. My father . . . once said, "Their Talmudic arguments are brilliant, but somehow they end up proving that one is allowed to eat bread on Passover." (35)

While Shifrah Puah's simplistic piety spares her the anguish of existential despair, her many prayers and "mumblings" are no more effectual than Masha's arguments. If Masha's empty language leads to nothingness, Shifrah Puah's seems a mere vestigial enactment of a one-sided dialogue with a silent God, a remnant of obsolete ritual—annoying, obsessive, and just as self-deceptive as Herman's and Masha's elaborate fictions. Masha recalls that when her father was alive Shifrah Puah had "insisted that Meyer Bloch perform the sanctification ceremony and sing the Sabbath hymns, although after the meal he would lock himself in his study and write poetry in Hebrew" (42). Shifrah Puah's own audible prayers are consistently described as "mutterings" and "mumblings." Her pious practices are accompanied by an obsession with the past nearly as morbid as Masha's cynicism is bitter. "She saved money from her food budget," we are told, "to buy books about Majdanek, Treblinka, Auschwitz" (43).

The connection between food and books is a frequent one, and doubly ironic. Books, supposed to be nourishment for mind and soul, are, in this novel, mere reminders of defeat and despair. They fill, but do not nourish, like food grown in depleted soil. Shifrah Puah, a survivor of war-torn Europe, has known enough of starvation to value food highly. To deprive herself of food money for books, therefore, suggests a real urgency in her hunger for some key to understanding, which she presumably hopes to find in them. But they are texts which can only provide her with visions of horror and defeat.

Shifrah Puah's obsession with the past is an effective foil for Tamara's willingness to face the future. Tamara enters the novel after the constellation of relationships among the other characters has been clearly established. Herman is caught between two women who represent extremes. He is paralyzed, impotent, and helpless—caught in a maze of contradictions. Tamara steps into a similar position—between similar extremes—with humor, honesty, and the adaptability that comes from having nothing more to lose, and rather than becoming trapped by contradiction, she seems to be energized by paradox. She enters the narrative as a "dead woman come to life," and indeed represents a spirit of resurrection.

Like Masha, Tamara is intelligent, literate, articulate, and polyglot. Like Shifrah Puah she is willing to use the forms of Jewish piety, though she is no longer "hypnotized by slogans." It was Tamara who supported Herman in his odyssey through secular philosophy, though with serious misgivings: "she even typed his dissertation, although in her opinion it was anti-humanistic, anti-feminist, and depressing in outlook" (64). Her own vocation, during the same period in their lives, was as an activist, not a writer. Tamara also shares something of Yadwiga's life-giving and life-affirming vitality. She, too, bore children by the same unwilling husband, and though they are dead, her children remain the vitalizing force in her existence. As a mother Tamara represents continuation and survival; her identity as mother survives the death of her children. Thus Tamara is Herman's counterpart and opposite—as incorporative, energetic, and adaptive as he is limited, vitiated, and brittle.

As a "ghost" returned from the dead, Tamara seems immune to many of the ills of the "living," including the deceptions and corruptions of words. Her "descent into hell" has given her a penetrating vision which enables her to see through the fictions men use to protect themselves from horror and despair. An unbeliever, she does not make a fetish of her unbelief like Masha, or hide behind equivocations, like Herman. She knows that truth will never be told whole, and is neither a naive optimist nor a philosophical pessimist, but simply a courageous woman who has made a decision to go on living. She would doubtless agree with Masha's cynical formula, "If the Jew is God and the Nazi is God, then there's nothing to talk about" (38). But unlike Masha her response to that statement has its own practical logic: not to talk about it—to do something else. When Herman inquires about her past, she shakes her head "as if to indicate the futility of relating what was beyond belief." And Herman realizes, "This was not the garrulous Tamara he had known. . . ." (73).

Instead of conversing Tamara acts, and tries to get Herman to act, too. She introduces him to Reb Nissen who, unlike Herman, has successfully adapted to practical necessity without forfeiting the semblance of intellectual life:

> In Lublin he had owned a small establishment that published rare religious books. He had traveled to Oxford to copy an old manuscript that had been discovered there. In 1939 he had come to New York to enlist prenumerants for printing this manuscript and was prevented from returning by the Nazi invasion.

When the war thwarts his plans, he adapts, like Tamara, and goes on with life:

> He lost his wife, but in New York had married the widow of a rabbi. He had given up his plan to publish the Oxford manuscript and instead had begun to work on an anthology of the writings of the rabbis who had perished at the hands of the Nazis. His present wife, Sheva Haddas, helped him. (67)

Reb Nissen has transformed words into action and thereby survived. For him the printed word is a part of life, not a place to retreat into from life. He provides another foil for Herman, whose descent into oblivion we are called upon to witness from so many angles. Tamara tries to revitalize Herman on the model of Reb Nissen, by channeling his proclivity for books and writing into a practical endeavor. She helps him take over Reb Nissen's bookstore. But Herman, who all along has been loath to engage in "selling God," resists—this time more from indifference than idealism. So Tamara stocks the store and runs it. The fact that in doing so she caters to beliefs she no longer shares bespeaks not only a willingness to compromise for the sake of a living, but, perhaps more significantly, a certain tolerance. She is able to accept religion and philosophy as part of the wide spectrum of means people use to cope with the mysteries, pains, and inanities of existence. She enters into the commerce of the community in a spirit of disinterested laissez-faire, but with full engagement; her disinterest is wholly unlike Herman's indifference. If Herman is a tragic victim, Tamara is a heroic victor—but heroic precisely in her refusal to adopt heroic stances or attitudes. She does not dramatically "accept the universe," nor does she hide her head in the sand, but simply, in a spirit not unlike that of Beckett's heroes, "goes on." She is a woman with vision, but not a visionary. She simply sees clear-sightedly what is and makes the most of it.

The three main women in this novel represent three modes of existence: action, speech, and simple being. Each functions as a catalyst in Herman's tragic odyssey. Through Yadwiga, Herman survives, first by her rescuing him during the war and later in the person of the little daughter he never sees. She gives him life and the continuation of life. Through Tamara, Herman is summoned into a vital dialectic of contemplation and action which, were it a fully realized pairing, would have great productive potential. But through Masha, his Lilith, he is drawn into a world of unreality, succumbing to the seductions of ungrounded intellect and imagination and passion detached from life-giving love, which in the end destroys them both.

There is a terrible blackness in the vision presented in *Enemies, A Love Story*, but also a current of hope. In this novel Singer ingeniously combines an indictment of language, tradition, and philosophical discourse with a limited but hopeful vision of regeneration. This vision is feminist in that it is embodied in the characters of two women and a baby girl who survive the disintegration of a dying patriarchal tradition. It is radical in that it suggests, by imaging that hope in a primitive, illiterate peasant woman and her newborn child, and a woman "returned from the dead," that renewal must begin at the very roots of civilization.

The final note of the book is provocatively ambiguous. Informed that she is free to marry again, Tamara replies, enigmatically, "Perhaps, in the next world—to Herman." It is either an ironic refusal and denial, or an inexplicably touching affirmation of loyalty both to a man she has ceased to love and to a tradition she has ceased to honor. Perhaps it is both.

Notes

1. See Steiner 3 and Orwell 127–140.

Works Cited

Orwell, George. "Politics and the English Language." *In Front of Your Nose: The Collected Essays, Journalism and Letters of George Orwell, 1945–1950*. Eds. Sonia Orwell and Ian Angus. New York: Harcourt, 1968.
Singer, Isaac Bashevis. *Enemies, A Love Story*. New York: Farrar, 1972.
Steiner, George. *The Death of Tragedy*. New York: Oxford UP, 1961, 1980.

Passivity and Narration: The Spell of Bashevis Singer

DAN MIRON

Isaac Bashevis Singer, last of the great Yiddish story-tellers, passed away at a ripe old age, crowned with international success and renown. His death seems to carry a note of half-reconciled farewell to a rich and vital literary tradition that won neither the appreciation nor the longevity that it deserved.

The beginnings of this tradition appeared about a hundred and thirty years ago in the form of the juvenile works in Yiddish of Mendele Moykher-Sforim and Yitschak Yoel Linetsky: *The Pupil {eye}, The Magic Ring, Fishke the Lame,*and *The Polish Lad.* From these roots Yiddish fiction flowered into its "classical" age with the mature Mendele Moykher-Sforim, Sholem Aleichem and Peretz. The decades between the two World Wars saw the great branching out of this tradition in the works of maestros like Dovid Bergelson, Der Nister and Moshe Kulbak, and in many other talented writers, such as Sholem Asch, Itshe Meir Weissberg, Yonah Rosenfeld, Yisrael Yehoshua Singer,Yosef Opatoshu, E. M. Fuchs and their colleagues. During the war and after it, in the dark, final days of Stalin's rule, the Yiddish literary tradition succumbed to the axe-blows of murderers and tyrants, and now it seems to have reached its final hour. In the long chain of brilliant and colorful reflections, highly diverse and yet complementary, of the life of the Jewish Ashkenazi tribe of eastern Europe as it was mirrored in the minds of the tribe's most talented members, soaked through with the essential juices of its unique historical presence and yet cut loose from their cultural moorings, open to the culture of their times—in this chain the final link has been closed.

These days, it is said, prophecy is the privilege of fools alone, and this rule may apply even to the prophecy regarding the future of the Yiddish tongue and its literature. Nevertheless, it seems safe to say that the spiritual-literary reality that found its last concentrated expression in the works of Bashevis Singer is no longer. This was clear to all, long before Bashevis himself reached the pinnacle of his literary successes with the receiving of

From *Judaism* 41, no. 1 (Winter 1992): 6–17. Reprinted by permission, copyright © 1992 American Jewish Congress. Translated by Uriel Miron.

the Nobel prize for literature in 1978. This witty, skeptical Jew, devoid of all pathos and full of humor, who combined sarcasm with tragedy and fatalism, traveled across the American and international literary scene like a "last of his kind." The international cultural community that lavished its appreciation upon him (as opposed to the servings of envy and hatred that he received from the rapidly shrinking Yiddishist cultural establishment), did so, of course, because of his ability to tell stories that conquered hearts almost in any language, and in any place where they were told; but it did so, among other reasons, as a gesture of farewell to a literary culture that was rich and vital in its day, and as a gesture of grief and regret for the horrifying circumstances that brought that culture to the point of extinction. Isaac Bashevis was the last great emissary of the kingdom of Yiddish to the world of western culture in the second half of the twentieth century.

Because of this historical representivity, which, by the way, was thrust upon Bashevis neither to his benefit nor by his consent, and without taking his qualities and character into account (he possessed none of the attributes of a "cultural leader"), it is perhaps fitting that we turn our attention to the fact that he was *not* actually a typical representative of modern Yiddish literary culture. Even though he grew up in the heart of this culture during the peak of its development in Poland, in the period between the two World Wars, he remained a stranger and an oddity within it. This, and not just the almost insane personal envy, might be the reason for the suspicion and even aversion with which he was held by the Yiddishist establishment.

In its essence, the difference between Bashevis' work and the whole of the modern Yiddish literary corpus (apart from a few very narrow and marginal segments of it) reveals itself in one crucial aspect. Bashevis approached the act of literary creation with a base-experience of underlying awareness that falls under the sign of fatalism and nihilism. Human existence and, certainly, Jewish existence appeared to him suffused with evil and suffering, torn apart from within by internal conflicts that cannot be resolved, pervaded by an absurdity both comical and tragic. Moreover, he was convinced that any organized effort to correct and improve man's lot, any will to guide it towards some "salvation" according to an ideological-eschatological program, was doomed to failure. Not only would such efforts fail to right life's wrongs, they would even increase the suffering and evil to the point of holocaust. Bashevis "understood" the twentieth century as an age in which a suffering humanity was forced to follow lethal ideological-eschatological agendas which gave birth to a murderousness unequaled in viciousness and horror by any evil known to man throughout all of history. He was opposed with all his heart (and that even without pathos and with the awareness that opposition itself was hopeless) to any eschatological human organization and especially Soviet and international Communism, and almost to the same degree any Jewish eschatological movement such as Zionism, national socialism (the *Bund*), etc. The only spiritual position that he accepted was passive-fatalistic.

By adopting this stance a person might achieve a certain "saintliness," to the degree that he or she gives up from the very start any attempt to control his or her own destiny, let alone that of others, and this out of the awareness of the moral superiority of surrender over initiative or over the desire to steer the course of events in the "desired" direction. Bashevis' "saint" is the "fool" who is not a fool at all. Gimpel the Fool, the hero of his early story of the same name, that, in its superb English translation by Saul Bellow, opened for Bashevis the door through which he could address the American and international audiences and capture their hearts, is in the framework of the Bashevian story-telling art, the most complete human being. He is not the fool that those who exploit him throughout his entire life believe him to be. He sees through their lies. He knows of their malice towards him. He knows that his wife is deceiving him and that his children are not of his seed. He knows full well that he has always been cheated and exploited in everything, yet he accepts this state of affairs in his awareness that any response on his part would only serve to increase the wickedness and suffering.

In the eyes of Bashevis, Gimpel is the archetypical Jew, just as he is the embodiment of the Yiddish language—a language with no territory, no protection, no cultural-political alliances, no prestige and no army or any military terminology—the language of the weak, the victims. It is as a representative of *this* Yiddish and its speakers that Bashevis trod the paths of the modern world of power-struggles and protest, the world of the demanders of rights and the "discrimination-gruntled." As such an emissary he reached Stockholm to receive the Nobel prize for literature and, likewise, he arrived in Israel for his famous conversation with Menachem Begin, in which he demonstrated to the prime-minister how ridiculous military pomp would be if it were carried out in Yiddish. Neither Begin nor the Israeli public caught on that, in his ironic-humorous way, Bashevis was expressing his reservations towards Israel as an authentic Jewish entity, as though he were saying: A real, authentic Jew who thinks and behaves as you do, my dear Israeli friends, is nothing but a joke, an incongruity, a Yeshiva-Boher brandishing a sword and clutching a general's staff as if it were a broomstick.

This moral and philosophical position (not, however, the opposition to Zionism itself) was utterly alien to the mainstream of the new Yiddish literature. Like much of modern Jewish culture, the central tradition of Yiddish literature had sprung out of the opposition to what appeared to be the inertia and passivity of the old, traditional Jewish way of life. This is not the forum for a deliberation of the degree of truth in the claims made over the last two-hundred years against Jewish inertia and passivity. Modern Jewish culture and the new Yiddish literature as a whole operated under the assumption that the Jewish people, who had for centuries refused to take an active part in the formation of history, and had thus relegated themselves to the passive position in its most extreme sense (the position of the victim), must break out of their national passivity. To achieve this they must also abandon their static adherence to the religious-halakhic tradition, to which they clung in their effort to preserve their distinctiveness and exclusiveness and to worship their God (their only *desiderati*). This new culture and literature asserted that the Jewish nation must open its world to humanistic ideas that place man, his values, qualities and needs, at the center of life and culture: ideas that point towards ways of attending to these needs while improving man's qualities and realizing the positive potential hidden in the "human condition."

Modern Jewish culture demanded that the people of Israel apprehend life through the lens of humanism, and by this willful act of comprehension break through to the heart of historical becoming. It hoped for the awakening of a national will ("Awake my people, how long will you slumber?"), recommended activity, vigor, readiness to struggle and effort to change. Yiddish literature endorsed these recommendations with the best of its talents, all of its earthy vivacity and all of the immediacy of its contact with the Jewish masses. When Yiddish literature sprang from the ideological soil of the Enlightenment (*Haskalah*) in the nineteenth century, or when it reflected, at the turn of the century, the birth of modern Jewish nationalism, or when it played a central role, later in the twentieth century, in the burgeoning Jewish socialist movements, its call to the Jewish people was a call for change and awakening. The voice of this call was not mitigated even when this literature appeared to be clinging with nostalgia to the popular-traditional Jewish milieu with its religio-cultural underpinnings and its colorful folklore which had already acquired an "exotic" flavor, as it were. It can be shown that Y. L. Peretz's hassidic tales and folk-like-legends, for example, not only infuse the pseudo-folk narrative material with modern humanist referents, but also cast doubts upon the validity of the traditional culture that they presumed to represent or duplicate, and even undermine it. The call of Yiddish literature was not just against halakhic-religious rule and the control which it exerted over every aspect of Jewish life, or against hassidic supernaturalism (although these did inform a major part of its message throughout the nineteenth century); it was primarily directed against the passivity, weakness, inertia, and stagnation that encumbered any process of awakening or overcoming.

Into this cultural continuity, that cast its lot with change, will-power and "the courage to transform," entered Isaac Bashevis Singer, bringing with him both as innate qualities and as a fully developed world view, a deep distrust in human will-power and an absolute aversion for both the Nietzschean "will to power" and the liberal faith in "progress." He brought an aversion to any overly vigorous human activity—individual and even more so collective, national or class activity. He was suspicious of the motives of such activity and predicted catastrophic results for it. He didn't believe that penetration into the "heart of history," which was nothing more than the heart of a dark and murderous power struggle, would bring the people of Israel any profit, let alone relief. He was willing to accept—and this is very rare in both modern Yiddish literature and its Hebrew counterpart—complete passivity. Y. L. Peretz wrote the story "Bontshe Shweig" as a bitter satire on Jewish passivity, although it has also been given a sentimental, non-satiric interpretation in the service of which editors of readers and anthologies have seen fit to excise parts of the original text. (When Bontshe reaches the after-life and the heavenly court of justice offers him all the luxuries of the earth and the heavens, he is content to have a buttered roll.) Bashevis, however, took Bontshe to his heart, relieved him of his intellectual numbness, and transformed him into Gimpel the Fool. He accepted Bontshe's attitude as a moral and Jewish stance; he refused to accept Peretz's derision.

Sholem Aleichem, in his marvelous monologues (including the series of Tevye's monologues), presented archetypes of Jewish passivity: men and women in the gravest distress who experience terrible trials and are unable to envision a way of extricating themselves from their hellish situation, other than the act embodied in the telling of their tribulations in rich and digressive speech, a narration that advances in a nervous and absurd zigzag motion that, in itself, reveals the pattern of the scuttling from wall to wall of the prisoner who knows not how to break through his prison-walls. The great author's criticism lay in this very rhythm, arising from the words of geese-herdesses and Yeshiva-students still sitting at their in-laws' table, Jews who had supposedly won the lottery, or, on the contrary, Jews who had been "burned" and are suspected of having themselves acted out the blessing *"Barukh borei me'orei ha'esh"* (Blessed be the Creator of the fiery lights). Out of these frenzied monologues rises a cry that even the juiciest humor cannot conceal; a cry that calls, without the speaker's awareness, for change, for salvation. Bashevis, who in many respects carried on Sholem Aleichem's great art of the monologue to achievements that do not fall short of those of the creator of the model, also presented, in tens of monologues, situations of great distress, but deprived them utterly of the nervous, tortured rhythm, of the hopeless internal scrambling. In Bashevis' monologues the flow of speech is the tempestuous or relaxed flow of the human soul that is carried upon the waves of a current over which it has no control. The demons, great and small, that often make their voices heard in these monologues, are none other than expressions of the speaker's awareness that his or her attempt to fight the current will not end successfully. Bashevis' monologues are, in this respect, not just a continuation of Sholem-Aleichem's monologues but, also, their inversion.

There is a certain proximity between Bashevis and Agnon (reflected in the elegant insights that Bashevis made in his article on Agnon that was published in *The New York Times* on the occasion of Agnon's receiving the Nobel prize for literature, together with Nelly Sachs). Agnon's love is given wholly to the lost man, the cornered individual who is passive and inarticulate, the victim of cruel manipulation at the hands of his environment, who is carried, willy-nilly, upon the waves of historical developments. He, too, in fact, introduced into Jewish literature the figure of the "fool" who is no fool, but is no resounding intellectual either. There is an intimate proximity between some of Bashevis' folk-heroes and Agnon's Ovadiah the Cripple, or between his most educated and aware heroes and Hershel Horovitz from Agnon's *A Simple Story* or Yitzhak Kummer from *Yesteryear*. The similarity is, however, limited and, actually, superficial. Agnon's work is shaped entirely by the powerful tension between a Zionist-religious belief in salvation and a dark, bitter, chilling disappointment in the heavenly order of the world and the slim chances that the people of Israel have of survival in the framework of this order. Agnon's passive heroes are tragic in the sense that, in the possible framework of a "correct" world order, their passivity would be appropriate and would produce no ill effects. The "wheel of time" that rolled off its axle is the force that crushes Agnon's heroes. Accordingly, if the Zionist effort were to bridge the pernicious rift between salvation and the savior (according to Agnon the world of the second *aliyah* was split into two groups: those who struggle for salvation but are estranged from God the savior, and those who attach themselves to the savior yet refuse to lift a finger for the sake of salvation), Yitzhak Kummer could have found his place between Jaffa and Jerusalem and would not have died insane. If the Jewish community that is described in *A Simple Story* were not dissociated both from the spirituality of authentic faith and from modern humanistic endeavor (and not devoted solely to provincial materialism), Hershel could have found a cure for his suffering either in the strength of religious faith or in the realization of his romantic love for Bluma—and would not have become, at the end of the story, a shell of a human fly that a spider has sucked dry of all vitality.

In Bashevis' work, on the contrary, passivity is not the result of a malfunction in the social or the cosmic mechanism; rather, it is the only correct stance in the face of the essential order (or disorder) of things, be they what they may, always and everywhere. Chaos is in a superior position everywhere. It engulfs man in tidal waves from without (historical events) and from within (lusts, perversities of character, internal conflicts, and unexplained distortions in the existential flow of the psyche). The conscious man (like the hero of *The Moskat Family*) faces reality and himself while gripped by boundless terror and curiosity. He knows full well that he can control neither himself nor his environment. He is bound to commit every possible blunder to which external circumstances and his own incomprehensible lusts and desires drive him. No rational life-plan of his will ever reach fruition; in all his actions he will always be swept, led, and discharged further and further towards some unclear goal determined by an unknown force; and, like that hero, Yehoshua Heshel Banet, so the rich and influential Moskat family and the whole of Polish Jewry, in their journey towards extinction.

In many of Bashevis' novels and stories, this basic feature repeats itself: a person watches, as if from afar, his own existence driven by forces which he does not recognize or by wild currents that he cannot fathom. While, objectively, this person participates fully in the destructive activity which brings about his downfall, his subjective sense of existence is passive and semi-detached. Often, the author introduces some tragic occurrence which supposedly explains this separation between the objective and subjective "I," such as the death of Arturo, Max Barabander's only son in *Scum*, or the loss of Herman Broder's entire past (as a result of his experiences during World War II) in *Enemies—A Love Story*. However, this does not mean that Bashevis regards passivity and the paralysis of the will as characteristic of a certain type of person or as a result of a specific set of circumstances. Rather, the people who react this way to loss and bereavement, as Barabander and Broder do, represent for him the human norm.

Here, by the way, is the place to comment on the sexuality in Bashevis' stories which won him so many denunciations (the Yiddish critics could not swallow it, and some saw it as an intentional sullying of Jewish life by an author who was libeling his own people), and was thought of as the spice by which Bashevis contrived to "sell" his wares to his millions of readers. This last claim is, of course, utter hogwash. Explicit and implicit sexuality can be found in the works of hundreds of writers of whom only a handful achieved true popularity; sex itself has yet to sell a single scrap of paper outside of the prescribed and highly specific domain of the pornography industry and its audience. At any rate, even the presentation of sexuality in Bashevis' stories is entirely different from its presentation in the whole tradition of modern Jewish literature. In this tradition, sexuality appears— usually in a positive role—as the representative of an oppressed vitality, of an internal libidinal energy, individual and national, that was repressed by an ascetic culture and now, with the relaxing of that culture's norms, is capable of bursting out and realizing itself not just via pure sexuality, but also through a whole system of earthly and human pathways of vitality— even national, sovereign vitality. For Bashevis, sexuality is none other than that absurd force that pulsates within the human body and mind, and exerts its maddening influence which is intended to break apart any order in life, any logic and any rational intentionality. Humankind is subjugated by sexuality as it is subjugated by historical events.

Singer's attitude towards sex is actually compatible, up to a point, with that of traditional religious puritanism, which identifies the sexual drive with the disruptive presence of Satan. However, whereas the religious tradition demands, if not complete repression, at least a channeling and controlling of sexual drives, Bashevis, in his fatalistic way, does not believe that such measures are possible. Accordingly, even in his stories that are set in traditional Jewish society, many of the characters are completely overwhelmed

by their sexual instincts. His work is completely devoid of any moral impera-
tive of continence, as it is devoid of didacticism.

Indeed, the halakhic code did make an heroic effort to assist Jews in
conquering their sexuality and in ruling their lives by a transcendental and
spiritual logic. This struggle, in Bashevis' view, was lost from the beginning,
and became hopeless as historical events utterly undermined the power of
the religious code. The demons had always haunted the abandoned cellars
and attics of the Jewish psyche. With boundless cunning, patience, wisdom,
humor, with threats and temptations, they diverted this psyche from its
proper path. Now that the psyche has been all but murdered and hardly
exists in the world, the demons remain, lonely and wretched, in the crumbling attics of the ruined homes of Israel. Together with the Yiddish language, they are fading away, becoming transparent, spiritual, ephemeral
beings, melting into nothingness.

The sober, self-aware man in Bashevis' works, both those that unfold
against an East-European background and those that take place in America
(particularly in the American book of memoirs and, also, to a certain degree,
the novel, *Enemies*)—this man is thrown about, surprised, from wave to
wave like driftwood from a shipwreck on stormy seas. Each time he is taken
by surprise anew, even though he knows that anything is possible in this
existence of his. His only recourse is to wonder at the world and about the
meaning of the will of "God," if such a one exists. He is distinguished by
his power of memory, but his memories can neither guide nor teach him;
they can only torture his soul. Often, the intellectual point of departure of
the Bashevian protagonist is the teaching of Spinoza that interprets human
existence and nature alike as expressions of the will and presence of God.
This was the most logical philosophy for someone who had just emerged
from the world of religious tradition. The typical Yeshiva student, having
lost his faith in a personal God, clutches at the compromise of pantheism. The
life experience of the Bashevian protagonist, however, completely negates
Spinozian optimism. It points, rather, at an existence devoid of all will or
directed divine presence. Thus, a kind of philosophical debate is built into
the stories; but, the Spinozan way of thinking does not really represent in
this dispute a positive or even possible alternative. It merely constitutes a
connecting link between the guileless religious faith that the traditional Jew
carries over from the past and the absurd existential amazement that envelops
him in the present. Furthermore, it acts as a foil to emphasize this absurdity.
The amazement is existential, but not existentialist. A vast distance separates
the belief in the Camusian "rebel," the existential absurdity, or the Sartrian
necessity of choice and commitment in the face of existential meaninglessness,
from the Bashevian view of a human existence that runs from birth without
will to a death without choice.

* * *

Bashevis began creating in the late Twenties and early Thirties, in a Poland squeezed between the U.S.S.R. and Nazi Germany. The political and social horizon appeared grim and the future of Polish Jewry, particularly after the closing of the American doors to mass immigration in 1924, appeared very grim, indeed. It was clear that this great Jewry, although much of it had undergone processes of modernization that had unleashed tremendous creative forces, was walking a dead-end street, that its fate was catastrophical (although no one dared imagine the utter destruction that it underwent during World War II). Caught in an ever-tightening economic stranglehold, exposed to hatred that periodically exploded in the form of pogroms and murders, discriminated against in every possible way, in fact, locked into a country that bore it only malice—this Jewry, with its deep historical roots and richly diverse traditional and modern culture, existed in a state of constant pressure and depression. There were those who announced the way out of the siege: the Communists (the best of the Jewish youth flocked to them) pointed towards the revolution that would negate the class structure of society and, together with it, presumably, the "Jewish Question"; the Bundists called for a struggle "here" on the historical raising-ground of Polish Jewry in the name of socialism and national Jewish and Yiddish distinctness; the Zionists spoke Hebrew and pointed out the way to Eretz-Yisrael, even though the crisis of the third and fourth *aliyot*, together with the immigration limitations declared by the British in the Thirties, precluded the possibility of a Jewish evacuation of Poland to Israel.

Bashevis absorbed the grim despair of stress-burdened Polish Jewry, but he didn't "buy" any of the popularly disseminated "solutions." He lived in an atmosphere similar to that described in Agnon's "A Guest for the Night," but he lacked the eschatological-Zionist perspective that informs the Agnonic novel, and that situates its deep gloom in the context of a "positive" perspective. Bashevis picked up mostly the feeling of no-way-out, of being swept away by a grim and uncontrollable current towards a catastrophic future.

He gave this feeling powerful expression even in his first novel, *Satan in Goray*, a masterpiece of stylization and dramatic symbolization that, even today, it seems, is still his most concentrated, coherent and complete work in the genre of the novel. Going back through history, as it were, to the days of Shabtai Zvi, Bashevis described the wretchedness of Polish Jewry after the Chmelnitsky massacres, its spiritual and physical collapse, the terrible fears that haunted its conscious and subconscious. On the background of these sorrows, the old rabbi tries in vain to reinstate the rule of rabbinical law over the congregation of Goray, this law being the only shield of historical Jewish life.

The crisis breaks out in his own home. Belief in Shabtai Zvi, the false messiah, gains a foothold in his family, and the expectation of the imminent arrival of the messiah soon engulfs the entire town. For a while, the reality of the town becomes a wondrously harmonic, messianic reality. The town is unified and happy. It is led by an authoritative man who radiates charismatic sexual vigor, prepares the town, as it were, for the arrival of the messiah, and has intercourse with the "prophetess," Rachel, a physically deformed and terrified young woman who had been married to an impotent Kabbalist and became a hearer of voices and seer of visions. In truth, however, it is Satan who takes over the Jews of Goray, the Satan of false salvation, and only now, not in the days of Chmelnitsky, does the town approach its complete disintegration. The disappointment of the false messiah who converted to Islam breaks the strength of the town and it can no longer face its pain. The destiny of the town is mirrored in that of Rachel: she is recognized as being possessed by a Satanic "dybbuk," and she dies at the moment that her "dybbuk" is supposedly exorcized by means of consecrations. The criticism of the novel points primarily to the Communist promise of salvation and Stalin's seductive charisma, but it protests, in fact, against all human and Jewish eschatological hopes. The novel can be compared to the play, *The End of Days*, by Haim Hazaz on the one hand (written during the same period), and the famous prologue of *The Jews of Zierndorf*, the work by Jakob Wasserman, on the other.

Hazaz's play and Wasserman's prose-poem describe, as does *Satan in Goray*, the tremendous excitement that, like fire, seizes the ancient and long suffering Jewish-Ashkenazi community when news of the coming messianic salvation breaks. These pieces also end with the destruction of the Jewish town—in "The End of Days" with the actual burning of the town by the messiah's emissary, Yuspa. This comes out of the assumption that, as long as the exilic condition remains, Jews will cling to it, and that only a complete dissolution of this condition can bring about salvation. In *The Jews of Zierndorf* the entire community of the town of Fürth sets out on a so-called journey to Eretz Yisrael, but this journey turns quickly into a disaster that finishes off most of the community. In both pieces, at any rate, destruction is accompanied by a vision of renewed integration. In Hazaz's play it is the vision of Zionist salvation, in Wasserman's work the vision is of Jewish integration within a "prophetic," liberal European culture as embodied in the figure of the half-Jew, Agathon (the hero) and in the village of Zierndorf, which was founded by the survivors of the Fürth Jews who had set out on their false messianic journey. Bashevis, however, is unique in that, in his novel, destruction is not followed by any vision of, or direction towards, a possible salvation. *Satan in Goray* ends in the author's "escape" to the stylized texts of traditional "dybbuk" stories, but this, nevertheless, holds no hint of a return to a naive, folkloristic religious faith.

Satan in Goray is still the best key to understanding the Bashevian grasp of reality, according to which the sufferings of humanity are solemn truth but its "salvations" are complete lies. *Satan in Goray* is also a key to the stylistic qualities of Bashevis' work, for his world view bears unique poetic and stylistic results that achieve their full development even in his debut novel. His fatalism finds its expression in an opposition to any structural or syntactic complication of the continuity of the story. Since no event or gesture has the power to change the course of events, there is no point in describing them with tangled structures and complex sentences that, by their very hypotactic quality, confer primary significance onto others. Everything can be expressed in simple sentences that follow each other in the either loosely or tightly knit flow of the story "as it is." Likewise, there is no point in splitting hairs or piling on relations of cause and effect or precedence and antecedence. It is better to put the events down on paper as they are in their finality and arbitrariness in a free-flowing and evenly rhythmed narrative sequence. Thus, Bashevis brought the modern Yiddish narrative back from the superlative structural and syntactical complexity of writers like Dovid Bergelson and from the self-aware stylistic and structural virtuosity of maestros like Der Nister and Moshe Kulbak, to some sort of basic, epic simplicity. It would seem that one can hear in this narrative yet again and with great force the voice of the "naive" narrator, who treats every event with respect and unfolds before the reader event after event, apparently of equal significance, in a single, moderate tone, accepting everything, knowing everything, wondering at everything, resigning itself to everything. This so-called naiveté is actually the understanding that no sophistication can explain a baffling reality, and that the gesture of sophistication is superbly naive.

There can be no doubt that this simple, basic story-telling tone, when it is applied to a universe full of conflicts and complexities, is one of the secrets of the spell that Bashevis' stories cast over millions of readers, and it goes a certain way towards explaining the ability of these stories to live a full life in translation. In spite of its untranslatable, idiomatic juiciness, Bashevis' Yiddish demands of the translator primarily a responsiveness to the feeling of basic narrativity that is actually embodied in the rolling of simple sentences one after the other. The sensitive translator need only revive in his heart the epic, rhythmic sequence of the folk-like tale in his own idiom and he immediately comes upon the recipe that enables a living duplication of the Bashevian narrative charm.

* * *

This is the place to bring up another point regarding the tremendous popularity of Bashevis' stories as the creations of a Jewish identity that is exotic, fascinating, alien, and seductive. We are forced to ask ourselves whether it is merely by chance that the great author who presents the historical Jewish identity as passive and victimized is the one who captured the hearts of so many non-Jewish readers. In posing this question I have no intention of belittling the virtues of Bashevis' work at its best, and yet it seems that these virtues are accompanied by a certain "weakness" that the non-Jewish reader seems particularly comfortable with. It is no accident that the view of the human condition that the non-Jewish world absorbs from Jewish culture comes mostly from a passive vantage point; the common denominator of passivity encompasses a broad spectrum of Jewish culture, from Kafka's "Metamorphosis" to "Fiddler on the Roof," supposedly after Sholem Aleichem's "Tevye" cycle. In the eyes of the non-Jewish world, it seems, Bashevis is not just a marvelous story-teller, but, also, some kind of wandering Jew, a modern Ahasuerus whose terrible destiny (the curse of Jesus) drives him on his endless journey and drags him through strange and wild experiences and events—all of them out of the realm of his control.

In this respect we can expect a certain degree of understanding of Bashevis, though uncomfortable and not as accepting as that of the "Goyim," by the Israeli and Zionist readership. It is doubtful, however, whether we can accept Bashevis' gospel which preaches surrender, being swept away, paralysis in the face of extinction, as basic truths—although, in the heat of our naive faith in our power to control our destiny, perhaps we should keep this truth in mind and accept something of its coolness and melancholy.

Nevertheless, it is impossible not to be enraptured by Bashevis' narrative art, not to be drawn into the melancholy and mystery of his fatalism, not to identify, if only for a moment, with the nihilistic undercurrents hidden by the deceptive simplicity of his narrative frameworks. All the same, we cannot wholeheartedly accept all of these. A substantial critique from a Jewish-Zionist vantage point will have to struggle with Bashevis' work.

At any rate, it is clear that the best of his stories will live long literary lives—even though the author himself never thought of his work in terms of any literary-aesthetic immortality. Bashevis' attitude towards literary creation was devoid of any pretense or mystification. He knew that he was a great artist, who tells stories better than most of the raconteurs of his generation. But this knowledge represented nothing more than excellence in a craft and not a spiritual virtue that can overcome time and the spiritual chaos of human existence; it is like the knowledge of a master carpenter who is sure that the object emerging from under his hand is more finely crafted and beautiful than any produced by another carpenter. Nevertheless, his pessimism was honest and real, and his fatalistic world view did not allow him to develop illusions about the timelessness of aesthetic achievement. He saw literature as a perishable thing, a human product given to destruction, wear, confusion, and insignificance, like any other product. Sometimes he made the appearance of viewing his craft in terms of mere *parnuseh* (livelihood). This was an ironic pretense, of course, under which, nonetheless, lay more than a grain of seriousness. There was no mistaking the look with which he would fix speakers and experts who extolled his works in public, composed orations about them, split hairs, and generally waxed verbose. Reflected in his blue-green eyes was a combination of derision and pity. Theirs was, once again, the particularly touching *naiveté* of the sophisticated in which Bashevis himself never took part. One can safely assume that this commemorative statement did not fully avoid the pitfalls of such *naiveté*. However, one hopes that it does retain some of the simplicity and straightforwardness of the master himself.

NEW ESSAYS
◆

Secularism and Yiddishkeit in Abraham Cahan's "The Imported Bridegroom" and Isaac Bashevis Singer's "The Little Shoemakers"

David H. Hirsch

Reviewing Henry Adams's autobiography in 1919, T. S. Eliot asserted that Henry's "very American curiosity was directed and misdirected by two New England characteristics: conscientiousness and scepticism. . . . Conscience told him that one must be a learner all one's life. . . . This is conspicuously a Puritan inheritance."[1]

We should bear in mind that this belated heir of the Puritans was powerfully attracted to the French Catholic shrine at Chartres and the image of the Virgin, and if he did not worship shrine and Virgin as symbols of religious transcendence, he at least worshipped them for the results they brought about in art and architecture. Having lost the faith of his fathers he spent most of his adult life seeking to recover it.

Adams was not a person to ignore the Enlightenment onslaught on "things invisible," but it was not until the process of his education was very far along that he discovered he was really seeking to regain his lost faith:

> Of all the conditions of his youth which afterwards puzzled the grown-up man, this disappearance of religion puzzled him most. The boy went to church twice every Sunday; he was taught to read his bible, and he learned religious poetry by heart; he believed in a mild deism; he prayed; he went through all the forms; but neither to him nor to his brothers or sisters was religion real. Even the mild discipline of the Unitarian Church was so irksome that they all threw it off at the first possible moment, and never afterwards entered a church. The religious instinct had vanished, and could not be revived, although one made in later life many efforts to recover it.[2]

Much as Adams worshipped the energy generated by religious faith, he was too skeptical to feel at ease in any particular faith himself. He observed

This essay was written specifically for this volume and is published here for the first time by permission of the author.

that "the twelfth and thirteenth centuries believed in the supernatural, and might almost be said to have contracted a miracle-habit, as morbid as any other form of artificial stimulant; they stood, like children, in an attitude of gaping wonder before the miracle of miracles which they felt in their own consciousness."[3] Henry Adams's reflections in *The Education* exemplify the gradual loss of faith and the shift in New England (and American) culture from a Puritan to Enlightenment mentality, from piety to secularity.

In *The Education*, Adams conceived his own life in a pattern that is the very opposite of Benjamin Franklin's, whose *Autobiography* has become the paradigm of the secular success story, in which virtue, hard work, and prudence assure the attainment of fame, material riches, and success in the public and private life.

For Jewish immigrants from Eastern Europe, the cradle of Jewish piety, both patterns came into play, as is apparent in the writings of Abraham Cahan, best known to American readers as author of *The Rise of David Levinsky*. Cahan was born and raised in Lithuania. His grandfather was a rabbi and his father a Hebrew teacher. Cahan himself received a thorough "Jewish" education. He came to the United States in 1882, at the age of twenty-two, worked as a laborer in a sweatshop, as a labor organizer, and as a journalist for Socialist Yiddish weeklies. He published his first story in English in 1895 and the story discussed here, "The Imported Bridegroom," in 1898.

The protagonist of the tale, Asriel Stroon, is a Lithuanian immigrant with an unmarried daughter, who, having made his fortune as a flour merchant, converts his wealth into real estate and then retires. With time on his hands, he becomes more pious than he has been in the past, spends more time in prayer, and one day decides to return to Lithuania to visit the *shtetl*, Pravly, in which he was born and raised. The reason the narrator gives for Asriel's desired return to his birthplace is revealing. "Numerous as were the examples of piety within the range of his American acquaintance, his notion of genuine Judaism was somehow inseparably associated with Pravly. During all the years of his life in New York he had retained a vague but deep-rooted feeling that "American piety was as tasteless an article as American cucumbers and American fish. . . ."[4]

Asriel the boor is recognizing a fact of American life that also disturbed the highly educated and highly refined gentile consciousness of the patrician Henry Adams, the fact that in America "the religious instinct had vanished, and could not be revived, although one made in later life many efforts to recover it." Adams does not perceive the problem in the same earthy, sensuous terms as Asriel—he does not compare piety to fish and cucumbers—but he too knows that religion in America has no taste. It exists in an environment that takes away its flavor. For all the difference in expression, the Jewish fictional boor and the historical Boston Brahmin are describing the same phenomenon.

While in Pravly, the town of his birth, Asriel finds a young man for his daughter to marry, a nineteen-year old prodigy of Talmudic lore. Asriel knows that his daughter, who has been assimilated to American life, would not want to marry what she thinks of as one of those "queer fellows, whose broken English had kept their own sweethearts chuckling. . . . She craved a more refined atmosphere than her own, and the vague ideal she had was an educated American gentleman, like those who lived uptown." Flora yearns for authenticity as a middle-class American and does not want to associate herself with the European past. But lacking a son, her father needs a pious son-in-law to say Kaddish (the prayer for the dead) for him (120).

As Asriel is leaving Pravly with the prospective bridegroom, an old acquaintance remarks, "May the Uppermost bring you home in peace and bless the union. . . . And Shaya [the groom]—may the Holy One—blessed be He—grant him the will and the power to spread His Law in America. The Jews there want a young man like him" (118–19).

The first thing Asriel does back in America is remodel Shaya, taking him directly from the ship to a "clothing and gents' furnishings store," where he decks Shaya out "in the costliest 'Prince Albert,' the finest summer derby, and the most elegant button shoes the store contained. This and a starched shirtfront, a turned-down collar, and a gaudy puff-tie set into higher relief the Byronic effect of his intellectual, winsome face." Shaya emerges from the store, in the narrator's words, "completely transformed" (120).

Flora, the daughter, eventually falls in love with Shaya and determines to make him an American doctor. She exposes him to the strong winds of Western learning, which, thanks to his phenomenal memory, Shaya absorbs quickly. Getting wind of what Shaya and his daughter are up to, Asriel shadows Shaya, and confronts him in a restaurant, where he finds him violating the rabbinical dietary laws.

Asriel realizes that his kaddish is lost and later expresses his plight to his housekeeper, a widow he employs for the sake of "her piety and for the rabbinical learning of her late husband." His words to her are both pathetic and revealing: " 'Yes, he is dead and buried and gone from the market place. . . . It's all gone Tamara!' he repeated gravely. 'I have just seen him eating treife in a Gentile restaurant. America has robbed me of my glory' " (154). Ironically, but perhaps characteristically, it is America that conquers Shaya, not Shaya America. If the "Jews want a young man like him" it is not for his rabbinical learning. Flora and America have destroyed his piety.

Though he edited the *Jewish Daily Forward* for half a century, till his death in 1951, Cahan wrote his short stories in English, not Yiddish, and he happened to be the editor of the *Forward* who first published the Yiddish writings of Isaac Bashevis Singer. Cahan and Singer came from a more or less common background (both Singer's grandfathers were rabbis), and both had to make the transition from Eastern European/Yiddish culture to American society.[5]

Singer's short story "The Little Shoemakers" (Yiddish, 1945; English, 1954) takes up Cahan's preoccupation with the transformation from East European Jewish piety to American Jewish secularism. In this bittersweet parable, the eponymously named Abba Shuster (i.e., Father Shoemaker), latest in the line of a family of *shtetl* shoemakers, has trained his seven sons in the family craft. But when the eldest son, Gimpel, is grown he decides to emigrate to America in defiance of his parents' wishes. As he prospers in the New Land, Gimpel brings his brothers to America one by one, till Abba and his wife, Pesha, are left in Frampol by themselves. Even after Pesha dies, Abba refuses to join his sons in America. Not until after the Nazis bomb Frampol does he flee to Rumania, and from there to Italy, where, thanks to the intercession of his wealthy sons, he is "put on board the last ship for the United States."[6]

In the luxurious lifestyle of suburban New Jersey, Abba deteriorates physically and mentally, till he discovers his abandoned shoemaker's tools in a closet and returns to working at his old trade, whereupon his health and vigor return. Inspired by their father's example, the sons, who had stopped practicing their craft to become owners and managers of a shoe factory, also return to the direct practice of their old skill.

At one level, Singer seems to be writing another variant of the Ben Franklin American success story in praise of the enterprising self-sufficient Jewish immigrant who finds a way to reconcile the fruits of freedom and prosperity in a modern secular culture with the world of Jewish piety he has left behind. This is how the story has been interpreted by the critics. Edward Alexander, for example, finds that

> "The Little Shoemakers" is one of the few Singer stories to allow for the possibility of a collective Jewish identity in the United States. For Abba and his sons survive not merely as individuals, but as a Jewish community. "No, praise God, they had not become idolaters in Egypt. They had not forgotten their heritage, nor had they lost themselves among the unworthy" (118–19). The lyrical rise of the story's end is a hymn to the Jewish power of survival which gains its special force from the fact that it is built into an elegy over a destroyed civilization.[7]

Lawrence S. Friedman endorses Alexander's view: "Gathered around the cobbler's bench with his seven sons and singing an old Frampol song once again in America, Abba thankfully concludes: 'They had not forgotten their heritage, nor had they lost themselves among the unworthy.' The story's ending is a paean to the survival of the individual through the reestablished Jewish family."[8] Friedman, however, sees "The Little Shoemakers" as something of an anomaly:

> Little of Singer's fiction invokes the earthly paradise awaiting Abba with his sons in New Jersey. Far more often the hope of heaven alone makes life on

earth bearable. Because this is so, the problem of belief is central to Singer's work. Belief in God was a natural by-product of shtetl life. . . . Jews who moved to Warsaw faced challenges to their beliefs undreamed of in Bilgoray. And when many of these same Jews emigrated, most often to America, their consequent loss of Jewish identity shook their belief still further. With the dissolution of social bonds comes the chaos that Singer eventually equates with the loss of belief.[9]

Both Alexander and Friedman feel that in this story at least, Singer is making the point that it is possible for Jewish immigrants from Eastern Poland to reap the benefits of the American experience without paying the price of giving up at least some aspect of their East European Jewish identity. Of course, "Shoemakers" is a parable, and consequently it is easy to oversimplify its moral. But even in his parables Singer is a complex thinker. He was too incisive an observer not to perceive that the change of venue from Poland to the United States was in many ways highly advantageous to Jewish immigrants.[10] America was truly a land of opportunity for them, and also a country in which persecution was minimal compared to what they had experienced in Eastern Europe.

Singer, however, was not blind to the downside of the Jewish immigrant experience. To avail themselves fully of the opportunities America offered, Jews often had to sacrifice at least some part of their old-world identity. "Piety" was an early casualty. Sometimes, for example, it was necessary to work on the Sabbath in order to prosper, and no "pious" Jew would have considered doing such a thing merely for material gain. Furthermore, the American suburb was not the Polish *shtetl*, and in a motorized society with suburban sprawl it was often necessary to desecrate the Sabbath to keep it (one might have to drive to Temple). As Cahan's Asriel observed, "American piety was as tasteless an article as American cucumbers and American fish."

Of course, many Jewish immigrants from Eastern Europe were happy at the prospect of leading a more liberated and less constrained lifestyle, but it was also true that diminished piety frequently resulted in the deterioration of family and community ties and a disintegration of tribal solidarity. To take a small example, Abba is shocked by many aspects of the "order" of the suburban synagogue to which his sons bring him; among other things he is disappointed to find "there was no courtyard, no faucet for washing one's hands, no stove to stand around" (117). That is, the suburban synagogue does not offer opportunities for socializing as well as praying. The spacious American continent and the ideology of American individualism are great isolaters of persons.

We should not be surprised, then, to find that the "moral" of "The Little Shoemakers" is more ambiguous than the critics have allowed. The ending is less euphoric than either Alexander or Friedman find, and the story itself is much less optimistic about the possibility of maintaining the ways of traditional East European Jewishness in America. While there may be a "lyrical rise" in the flow of the last paragraph, the closing words of the story introduce a note of ambivalence. The story closes with the "chorus" of a song that Abba used to sing in Frampol:

> "The tenth one was called Judele . . ."
> And Abba's sons came in on the chorus:
> "Oh, Lord, Judele!" (119)

The song that Abba sings to his sons, which the narrator attributes to Frampol, appears to be a variation of the Yiddish folk song, "Ten Brothers." The actual song is a dirge, and the Yiddish version in "Shoemakers" ends, not as it does in the English, invoking of the name of the Lord, but with a cry of anguish: "Vay, Gevaldt, Judele!" ("Woe, Horror, Judele!").[11] In Yiddish, it should be added, the name Judele is also a pun on "little Jew," which makes the dirge-like quality of the song even more pronounced. This "old Frampol song" (97) serves as a kind of Greek chorus. It is sung three times in the story, and its lyrics (largely untranslatable because they are an acrostic) are both melancholy and pointless. The acrostic runs as follows. In Hebrew, each letter of the alphabet has a numerical equivalent; hence aleph $= 1$, beth $= 2$, gimmel $= 3$, etc. The names of the ten sons, then, proceed alphabetically from aleph to yod (1–10). The first time Abba sings the song he names the first five boys; the second time he sings an intermediate verse about a goat and a slaughterer (reminiscent of a well-known song in the Passover Haggadah); the third time Abba sings, at the very end of the story, he names the last five sons, ending with Judele (whose name begins with yod, which equals 10).

Abba's song seems to be pointless in the sense that it merely names the brothers, tells us nothing about them, and then ends with the lament, "Woe, Horror, Judele!" In the actual folk song, the brothers are not named, but in each verse one of them dies ("We were ten brothers, / Who dealt in wine; / One died, / Then there were nine," etc.) until the tenth and last remaining brother sings "I was one brother, / And I dealt in wheat, / I die / each day, / Because I have nothing to eat."[12]

If we look at the events in the final section of the story that lead up to the last paragraph, the evidence suggests that Abba's perception that his sons "had not forgotten their heritage . . . nor lost themselves among the unworthy" is either wishful thinking on Abba's part or an unwarranted and contradictory shortcut by the author, for if this last section makes anything clear it is that Abba's sons, and even more so his grandchildren and great-grandchildren, have indeed forgotten their heritage.

The narrator has made a point of specifying that "the feast . . . prepared in Abba's honor was to be held in Gimpel's house, in full compliance with the dietary laws." The implication, of course, is that the dietary laws will be observed at this particular meal for Abba's sake, but that ordinarily they are not. Such a reading is made even more explicit in the Yiddish, which would read in a more literal translation: "They especially bought strictly kosher meat and used new dishes" [39] (*"m'hut eigns gekoift glat-koosher fleish un genutzt nei gefays"*). Clearly Abba's children have not been living up to the traditional standards of "purity" transmitted to them by their father, since they not only have to make a special effort to buy "strictly kosher" meat, but they also have to use "new dishes," indicating that the children have been less than fastidious in maintaining the ritual cleanness of the dishes they normally use. We must not forget that Singer is a great ironist, and here the entire feast begins to take on a grotesque air; for this simple, pious man these people grown foolish in their prosperity are going to stage the kind of ostentatious display of excess described so devastatingly in Philip Roth's novella, *Goodbye, Columbus.*[13] Unaccustomed to all this glitz (multicolored candles, glittering silverware, crystal glasses), Abba becomes completely disoriented, falls asleep over his food, and spends the next several weeks in bed.

Describing the preparations for the "feast," the narrator informs the reader that "Gimpel's wife, Bessie, whose father had been a Hebrew teacher in the old country, remembered all the rituals and observed them carefully, going so far as to cover her head with a kerchief." One element of Singer's comic genius is to say things by leaving them unsaid. The fact that Bessie must dig the rituals out of her deep European past is a clear indication that she does not practice them in America. "Abba's sons," the narrator continues, "put on the skullcaps they had once worn during Holy Days." The implication is that unlike pious Jews such as Abba, who wear their skullcaps at all times, Abba's sons wear them only in synagogue during the high holy days. There is also the further implication that the high holy days are the only time of year Abba's sons attend synagogue, unlike Abba, who prayed morning and evening every day of the year.[14]

It is surprising that the critics have not noticed Singer's irony, since even Abba, the central character in the story, does not escape it. He is seemingly presented as the embodiment of virtues associated with the highest ideal of the *shtetl* Jew. He is pious, honest, unprententious, industrious, a master craftsman, content with his lot in life. In his little hut in Frampol, "looking up at the summer sky, losing himself in contemplation of the clouds, . . . he felt the presence of God, His providence and His mercy"(99). Abba's Frampol lifestyle is portrayed as materially modest but spiritually rich. Though his occupation is humble and earthy, his thoughts fly up to heaven. But the narrator undermines this description with sly contradictions.

The reader is told, for example, that Abba "was a man of learning. Every day he read a chapter of the Torah in Yiddish translation and occupied his free time with chap-books"(92). But among Polish Jews, who maintained very high standards where Jewish learning was concerned, "a man of learning" read and understood the Torah in its original Hebrew. Singer's ironic intention may be clearer in the Yiddish text, which refers to Abba as a *yoideah sefer*, a Yiddishized Hebrew phrase meaning literally "one who knows the book," and specifying someone who is a student of Torah and Talmud in the originals. Abba's knowledge of "the Book," however, is somewhat less than authentic, since he "knows" it primarily in Yiddish translation.

The narrator, then, is conveying the information ironically that Abba is not actually a learned man but a simple pious Jew with a minimal East European Jewish education. The English translation blurs the irony somewhat by indicating that Abba read "chap-books," which are "collections . . . consisting chiefly of small pamphlets of popular tales, ballads, tracts, etc.," whereas the Yiddish conveys a sense of Abba's actual reading with two titles: *mnoras hamaor* and *nachalas tzvi*. The former is a fourteenth-century treatise on ethics written in Hebrew and translated into Yiddish; the latter is a generic title signifying, among other things, a Yiddish translation of the mystical book, *Zohar*. Both books were apparently aimed at nonlearned Yiddish readers, and had a widespread circulation among East European Jews.

Any question that the narrator is being ironic is removed a little later on, when the reader is told that, "The town soon learned of [Abba's] virtues, and though he was nothing but a plain shoemaker, and, if the truth be told, something of an ignoramus, they treated him as they would a distinguished man"(96). "Plain shoemaker" and "ignoramus" translate the Yiddish, *pooshit sishterl, a halber am-ha'aretz*. The adjective modifying "shoemaker" is the Yiddishized Hebrew word *pashoot*, better translated here, perhaps, as "simple." The term translated as "ignoramus" is another Yiddishized Hebrew phrase, *am-ha'aretz* (literally, earthy person), which is used to designate someone who is ignorant or illiterate, and which is a kind of perfect reverse mirror image of *yoideah sefer*. Later, when Abba starts to free-associate between his own experience aboard the ship to America and the biblical images that populate his mind, the narrator prefaces his mental state by saying, "Abba had little learning, but Biblical references ran through his mind" (112).[15]

Contemplating the juicy irony of Singer's Yiddish style, one is struck by the seamless integration of Hebrew into Yiddish, reflecting the equally seamless integration of the religion of biblical-rabbinical Judaism into the everyday life of the *shtetl*. Though Abba is not one of those renowned formidable Talmudic sages of Eastern Europe, he nevertheless thinks the Hebrew Bible automatically, having heard it chanted again and again every Sabbath, having prayed parts of it every day, and having read it on his own in translation daily. If Singer were writing "an elegy over a destroyed civilization," then surely he was acutely aware that nothing is more damaging to the survival of a culture than the loss of its language. The passing of the language/culture of Eastern Europe is reflected nowhere more ironically (and unwittingly) than in the English translation of Abba's last words to Gimpel as the latter is departing for America: "Abba called after him, into the darkness, 'Good luck! Don't forsake your religion!' " (102). But a more literal rendering of the Yiddish reads, "Succeed and prosper! Don't forget [your] Jewishness (Yiddishkeit)." ["*Zei matzliach! Fargess nish' 's yiddishkeit!*" (28)].

The civilization whose passing Singer elegizes was not simply a "religion," but a unified totality compounded of religious beliefs, family and social relations, behavioral patterns, shared rituals, accepted traditions, all of which were embodied in and unified by a common language.[16] All translation has its limitations, but no limitation is more difficult to overcome than the presence of different language elements in the original; nineteenth-century *shtetl* Yiddish is particularly "polyglot," drawing its vocabulary from a wide variety of languages: a Germanic base bountifully enriched with biblical and talmudic words, as well as words from a variety of Slavic languages.

So although Abba is described as a rather feckless scholar and an ignorant man who cannot understand the Bible in the original Hebrew, simply by speaking Yiddish and by virtue of having learned to pray (which East European Jewish males did only in Hebrew), he has acquired a familiarity, even an intimacy, with the "Holy language." For example, in the distress of his voyage across the Atlantic, Abba associates his experience with his reading of the Creation story in Genesis: "The ship would leap up as if mounting the sky, and the torn sky would fall as though the world were returning to original chaos" (112). In Abba's Yiddish thoughts, however, the world is returning not to a highly conceptual "original chaos" but to the "*tohu bohu*" (i.e., to the richly descriptive biblical phrase "waste and void").[17]

Abba's subsequent thoughts, liberally sprinkled with biblical phrases, culminate in Abba's "making his confession, beating his knotty fist on his chest and exclaiming, 'Forgive me, Father!' " (113). Here again, the Yiddish is more graphic and more revealing of Abba's mentality. Beating his chest, Abba is quoted as saying, literally (Yiddish words in brackets), "[Oh, woe, Father! It is] They are come the waters to [my] soul." (["*Oy, Vay, tatte! S'iz*] *bo'u mayim ad nephesh*" [37]), a corruption, or at least a modification, of a verse in Psalm 69 ("Save me, O God; for the waters are come in unto my soul" [Ps. 69:1, King James version]). Abba's mixture of colloquial Yiddish and the sublime biblical Hebrew of the psalm contains a delicious humorous touch, as well as a psychological truth.[18]

I would like to make clear, however, that it is not my intention to criticize either the translation or the translator of this story. What I wish to point out, rather, is that the translator had to leave some things out because they would not have made sense to an audience of American readers, Jewish or gentile, and that certain kinds of transferences just could not have been made from the pious Torah-saturated Yiddish culture of Eastern Europe to the primarily secular liberal culture of America. One more instance of this saturation, if I may. Upon arriving in America, Abba "blindly embraced one of his sons and sobbed out, 'Is this you? Alive?' He had meant to say: 'Now let me die, since I have seen thy face, because thou art yet alive' " (114). Most difficult to convey in translation is the fact that what Abba actually utters is Yiddish, while what he had hoped to say, had he been able to remember it, would have been a quotation of the Hebrew of Genesis 46:30, Jacob's (Israel's) words to his restored son, Joseph.

Whatever his initial intention, there is no question that at some point Singer became conscious not only that he was writing a story of a culture forever lost, but also that as long as he wrote in the language of that culture he would be writing for a diminished and perhaps soon to be extinct audience. In the story, this realization is reflected in the fact that Abba finds his grandchildren and great-grandchildren totally ignorant of even the rudiments of Jewishness—the Hebrew letters and the Yiddish language (as it is put in the English translation, they do not know "the elements of Hebrew and piety").

In fact, the ignorance of Abba's progeny is so extensive that it is difficult to see the children's joining their father in shoemaking as sufficiently compensatory to make the story "a hymn to the Jewish power of survival." And to attribute "special force" to this so-called hymn because "it is built into an elegy over a destroyed civilization" is to overlook Singer's abbreviated handling of the Holocaust. When the first Nazi bomb falls, Abba thinks it is "the Messiah's trumpet." The narrator disposes of both the ordeal of the Holocaust and the Jewish religious past in three curt symbolic sentences: "The walls collapsed. Abba turned about and saw the shelf of sacred books go up in flames. The blackened pages turned in the air, glowing with fiery letters like the Torah given to the Jews on Mount Sinai" (109). It is as though all of creation itself, which came through the word, has been destroyed; but Singer in 1945 is perhaps still too numbed by the magnitude of the tragedy to speak about it at length.

After the bombing, Abba "re-entered the house and packed a sack with his prayer shawl and phylacteries, a shirt, his shoemaker's tools, and the paper money he had put away in the straw mattress. Then he took up a stick, kissed the mezzuzah, and walked out the door" (109). He eventually escapes to Rumania, where an old woman takes him into her house and sends a "telegram to Abba's sons in America, informing them that their father was safe." They then pull some strings and grease some palms in Washington to get him to the States.

Notwithstanding Singer's temporary bracketing of the tragic events of the Holocaust, Irving Howe feels that Singer's parable "sums up the whole of contemporary Jewish experience from tradition to modernity, from the old country to the new, from the ghetto to the camps," and subsequent commentators on the story seem to agree with him.[19] Actually, Singer circumvents the painful thought of the ghettoes and camps to get on with his main purpose, which is to describe the loss of Jewish piety in America, without attempting, at this point, to come to terms with the Holocaust.[20] But Singer's ambivalence, and also, I believe, his pain, in having to deal with the Jewish Holocaust experience, even summarily, is reflected in the closing paragraphs of the story. Emulating Abba's example after he has rediscovered his shoemaker's tools and returned to his craft, the brothers all "spread sackcloth aprons on their knees and went to work, cutting soles and shaping heels, boring holes and hammering pegs, as in the good old days. The women stood outside, laughing, but they took pride in their men" (118–19). I am not certain why the translator felt the need for the conjunction "but"; he apparently understood the text to say that the wives were laughing not joyfully but derisively at the foolish behavior of their husbands. The Yiddish, which contains no "but," is more appropriately rendered, "Their wives stood outside laughing, brimming over with satisfaction."

As Henry Adams and Abraham Cahan realized (and as I am sure Singer must have known), medieval piety does not thrive in modern technological societies. It is highly unlikely that these suburban New Jersey housewives would have taken joyful satisfaction in watching their husbands regressing to the craft and primitive economics of a *shtetl* Judaism in which, as it appears in the story, piety and good works are valued above material accumulation. As Thorstein Veblen pointed out in *The Theory of the Leisure Class*, it is much easier to move upward on the scale of consumption than it is to reduce one's standard of living, and it is doubtful that these suburban wives would rejoice at the thought of stepping down to a more demanding and more primitive way of living for the sake of nostalgia.

Abba's happy thought that his sons "had not become idolaters in Egypt, [and] had not forgotten their heritage, nor . . . lost themselves among the unworthy" (118–19) is a sad self-deception, for the return to the workbench indicates only that his sons have not lost their skills, not that they have rediscovered their *shtetl* heritage. A heritage, after all, is a language and a culture, and Abba Shuster's progeny have assumed a new language and a new culture.

To reach the conclusion that his sons have not become heathen in a secular land, Abba has had to overlook some powerful evidence to the contrary (their clean-shaven appearance, their not wearing skull caps nor saying daily prayers or blessings over food, their worshipping in a nondescript impersonal temple, etc.). If Abba is deceiving himself, however, is Singer equally bemused? I think not. But how, then, are we to account for the sudden turn in the story—how explain Abba's taking up his old tools and returning to his old craft in a heathen land, thus seeming to redeem himself, his descendants, and Yiddishkeit in America?

The answer may lie in Singer's personal situation in 1944 or 1945, the time he would have been writing the story. Irving Buchen has pointed out that the death of Singer's brother, Israel Joshua, in 1944, "was a great loss.

In light of Singer's later career, however, it evidently was also a great release."[21] I believe that in an unexpected way the demise of East European Jewry and Yiddishkeit in the Holocaust became a kind of release for Singer, as well. In a 1963 interview in *Commentary*, Singer says that early in his writing career, he "came to the conclusion that I must write in Yiddish [rather than Hebrew] because it was my mother language and the language of the people I wanted to write about."[22] Much has been made of the fact that Singer was writing in what was quickly becoming a dead language. In the same interview, Singer answers a question about the dwindling Yiddish-reading audience by saying, "You don't feel very happy about writing in a language when you know it dies from day to day."[23] But while the extermination of Polish Jewry may have taken away one potential audience, it may have given Singer his "subject," as Henry James would have called it.

Singer's early years in this country were not fruitful, especially if one compares them to the highly productive period of 1945 and later. Singer had explained this hiatus in his productivity by alluding to the dearth of Yiddish culture, and especially Yiddish literature, in America. "I came from Poland in 1935," he said in a 1966 television inverview, "and my first impression was here that Yiddish literature was of no avail; it's dead. This is what people told me and I felt so myself. And suddenly, I felt that I was in a cemetery."[24] In the 1963 *Commentary* interview, Singer said something similar: "When I came to this country I lived through a terrible disappointment. I felt then—more than I believe now—that Yiddish had no future in this country. In Poland, Yiddish was very much alive when I left. When I came here it seemed to me that Yiddish was finished: it was very depressing. The result was that for five or six or maybe seven years I couldn't write a word. Not only didn't I publish anything in those years, but writing became so difficult a chore that my grammar was affected. I couldn't write a single worthwhile sentence."[25]

Taken together, Singer's comments in these interviews are a little puzzling. In 1935, he found that the United States was a cemetery of Yiddish literature. He then says that for his first five or perhaps seven years in the States he was unable to write. But although in the mid- to late thirties he felt that there was no future for Yiddish (or Yiddish writers) in America, in 1963, he felt more optimistic about the future of Yiddish. That is certainly strange. In the mid- to late thirties, New York still had a thriving Yiddish community. The lower East Side of Manhattan was still thickly populated with Yiddish speakers, Yiddish theater, Yiddish movies, Yiddish vaudeville, and restaurants and cafeterias that catered to a Yiddish-speaking clientele. Several Yiddish newspapers were widely circulated. But by 1963, Yiddish had practically disappeared from the East Side and from the States. Why, then, did Singer believe in 1963 that Yiddish might still have a future in America? The answer would seem to be that the Yiddish writer, in the person of Singer, now had a future in America. By this time he was a recognized author whose works were being read in English translation by American readers. So the future of "Yiddishkeit," in the person of Singer, was assured.

The prospects for Yiddish had not improved by 1945, a highly productive year for Singer. In fact, they had grown much worse. So perhaps it was not the expectation of the revival of Yiddish but the certain knowledge that the Yiddish language and culture of Eastern Europe would not revive that gave Singer his theme. As long as there remained a vibrant Yiddish culture in Poland, Singer had no donnée. He would have to write for Yiddish readers in America about an ever-changing Jewish life in Poland that he knew less and less about. He would have been trying to write about a dynamic society from which he was growing increasingly remote.

Cahan's story of the transition from old-world piety to American secularism described the evolutionary process of modernization. In the wake of the extermination of Polish Jewry, however, the evolutionary process had been short-circuited, and the promise of modernity had turned into a nightmare. Singer recognized that, like the sylvan historian of Keats's "Ode on a Grecian Urn," he was now destined to become the chronicler of a culture that would no longer change. In 1945, the same year "The Little Shoemakers" was published, he began serializing *The Family Moskat* in the *Jewish Daily Forward*. Is it possible that in writing about Abba Shuster, Singer was in a sense writing about himself? As he tells it in the interviews, he had permitted his tools to lie fallow for seven years. According to his own account, it had become difficult for him to write grammatical Yiddish sentences. In taking up his tools again, through his storyteller's art, Singer would be able to bestow eternal life on the culture in which he was raised and which no longer existed in this physical world.[26]

Notes

1. "A Sceptical Patrician," *Athenaeum* (23 May 1919): 361.
2. Henry Adams, *The Education of Henry Adams* (1906; Boston: Houghton Mifflin Co., 1961), 34.
3. Henry Adams, *Mont St. Michel and Chartres* (1904; Garden City, N.Y.: Doubleday Anchor Books, 1959), 278.
4. Abraham Cahan, "The Imported Bridegroom," *Yekl and Other Stories* (New York: Dover Publications, 1970), 99; hereafter cited in the text.
5. There were, of course, differences in their backgrounds, Cahan coming from Vilna and Singer from Warsaw and Galicia. Also, Cahan was a socialist, and in general a rationalist, while Singer was more of a mystic and fantasist. To my knowledge, this relationship has not yet been the subject of scholarly investigation. See, however, David Neal Miller, *Fear of Fiction* (Albany: SUNY Press, 1985), 27–28.
6. Isaac Bashevis Singer, "The Little Shoemakers," trans. Isaac Rosenfeld, in *Gimpel the Fool and Other Stories* (New York: Noonday Press, 1957), 111; hereafter cited in the text.
7. *Isaac Bashevis Singer* (Boston: Twayne Publishers, 1980), 134. Alexander quotes

himself in *Isaac Bashevis Singer: A Study of the Short Fiction*, Twayne's Studies in Short Fiction (Boston: Twayne Publishers, 1990), 34, and provides a more extensive analysis of the story.

8. Lawrence S. Friedman, *Understanding Isaac Bashevis Singer* (Columbia: University of South Carolina Press, 1988), 20.

9. Ibid., 21.

10. Unlike Cahan, Singer was not a socialist and hence did not write stories about exploited workers in capitalist economies, even though he was obviously aware that many immigrants lived in poverty and were forced to toil in sweat shops He complained at one point that his editor (presumably Cahan at the *Forward*) told him, " 'Why do you write about things the readers have already forgotten? These things might have been valid two hundred years ago, but not today.' I kept on writing in the same way and didn't listen to my editor. In many cases, he fought me, tried to convince me what he wanted me to be, a social writer, to write about the situation of tailors in New York, how badly they live and how they fight for their existence." "A Conversation with Isaac Bashevis Singer," *The Eternal Light*, 6. A television interview on 6 November 1966 (printed by NBC and the Jewish Theological Society of America, T-138, 1–14). Cited by Irving Buchen, *Isaac Bashevis Singer and the Eternal Past* (New York: New York University Press, 1968), 19 n. 16.

11. Yitzchok Bashevis, *Gimpl Tam un andere dertzeilingen* (New York: Central Yiddish Culture Organization, 1963), 43; hereafter, cited in the text.

12. "Tzehn Brider, folkslied." "Ten Brothers, Jewish Folk Song," arr. Max Persin. Published by Joseph P. Katz, New York. I am indebted to Leo Greenbaum of YIVO for finding, and sending me, a copy of the music and lyrics of the song. It is no accident that a version of this song was sung in the concentration camp at Sachsenhausen. "When in October 1942 the Jews in Sachsenhausen found out that they were soon to be 'transferred' to Auschwitz-Birkenau, [Rosebery] d'Arguto composed his terrible 'Jewish Deathsong,' based on the tune of an old Yiddish folksong, 'Ten Brothers' " (text accompanying Folkways Records Album No. FSS 37700, *Songs from the Depths of Hell, Sung in German, Polish, Ukrainian, Yiddish, by Aleksander Kulisiewicz*).

13. Philip Roth's novella *Goodbye, Columbus*, appeared in the 1958–59 *Paris Review* and as the title story in the book in 1959. Some of the characters in *Goodbye, Columbus*, sound a lot like the New Jersey Shusters.

14. We are told explicitly, at least, that "Every day he read a chapter of the Torah in Yiddish translation . . . , [and] he never missed a single sermon of the traveling preachers who came to town, and he was especially fond of the Biblical passages which were read in the synagogue during the winter months [Genesis and Exodus]" (90). We are also told that every day "Abba would rise from his work, wash his hands, put on his long coat, and go off to the tailor's synagogue for evening prayers" (94).

15. Again, the Yiddish seems more precise: "chotsh Abba iz keinmol nisht geven kein lamdn, iz im itzt der kop ful geven mit fargleichenishn fun chumish un pusik" ("Though Abba had never been much of a talmudic scholar, now his head was filled with parallels [between his present situation and images] from the Pentateuch and the weekly Torah readings").

16. It may be worth noting that the highly successful musical *Fiddler on the Roof*, based on the writings of Sholom Aleichem, is also a lament for an exterminated culture. Of interest are the lyrics of the song "Tradition." Written by an American Jew, the lyrics reflect the very Emersonian view that [East European Jewish] "tradition" is rooted wholly in unthinking repetition rather than in continual study and modification to meet new circumstances.

17. Interestingly, Abba recalls the terms in the original Hebrew rather than the Yiddish translation (which translates the biblical "tohu bohu" as "vist un leidek"). But since Abba has been listening to the Torah chanted in Hebrew every Sabbath for some seventy

years, it is not surprising that he should think of the Hebrew phrase, even though he does his own private reading of the Torah in the Yiddish translation.

18. Paraphrasing, misquoting, and yiddishizing biblical and talmudic sources provides a particularly rich strain of humor in Sholom Aleichem's Tevye stories.

19. Irving Howe and Eliezer Greenberg, eds., *A Treasury of Yiddish Stories* (New York: Viking Press, 1954), 86.

20. Since the story was written before the founding of the State of Israel, Singer's view that the new center of Judaism would shift to the United States was plausible.

21. Buchen, *Eternal Past*, 22.

22. Joel Blocker and Richard Elman, "An Interview with Isaac Bashevis Singer," *Commentary* 36 (November 1963): 368.

23. Ibid., 364.

24. "Conversation," cited by Buchen, *Eternal Past*, 19 n. 16.

25. Blocker and Elman, "Interview," 369. Also cited by Buchen, *Eternal Past*, 19 n. 17.

26. So as not to be misunderstood, I wish to make it clear that I am not suggesting that Singer was dancing on the graves or that he would not have written great works of fiction had there been no Holocaust. Singer was a great and fertile creative spirit who could not have remained silent indefinitely. My point is simply that if history had been different he would have had to find, and surely would have found, another subject matter. As it turned out, he assumed the burden and the mission of giving eternal life to a destroyed culture. I should also like to make clear that what I have been discussing in this essay is Singer's perception of the passing of Yiddishkeit as both a religion and a way of life. I have not addressed the question of how Singer discovered possibilities of "redemption" in a secular world. For a discussion of this question, see Grace Farrell Lee, *From Exile to Redemption: The Fiction of Isaac Bashevis Singer* (Carbondale: Southern Illinois University Press, 1987), especially chapters 1 and 2. From the redemptive point of view, "the sacred books [that] go up in flames" have been destroyed by human beings inspired by the principle of evil, but the essence of the "sacred letters" can be restored by the creative spirit who chronicles their destruction.

Manuscript and Metaphor: Translating Isaac Bashevis Singer's Children's Stories

ALIDA ALLISON

In an essay reprinted by the American P.E.N. Center in its 1987 book *On the World of Translation*, Isaac Bashevis Singer makes a joke. Someone, he writes, once asked him at a lecture, "What would you do if you met God face to face?" Says Singer, "My answer was, 'I would ask him to collaborate with me on some translations.' " Tellingly, he adds, "I would not trust him to do it himself."[1] Beyond linguistic and creative considerations, the topics of metaphysical translation, the inevitability of error, and the struggle to get it right—all were of interest to the philosophical Singer.

In regard to Singer's children's stories, there was a highly noteworthy collaboration: not with *the* God, but with *the* translator, Elizabeth Shub. Without her, "Zlateh the Goat," Singer's first venture for children, would never have come into existence. Singer had many translators in his long career, from Saul Bellow to his own nephew Joseph Singer. But only Shub thought of him in regard to children's books. As Singer recalls:

> I had been writing for forty years and it never occurred to me that I would ever write for children. . . . But my friend, Elizabeth Shub, who was then an editor of juvenile books at Harper, had different ideas. For a long time she tried to persuade me . . . that I was, at least potentially, a writer for children.[2]
>
> The net result was that she translated many stories into English from Yiddish and now, whenever I get a check, she gets a check. Which proves that sometimes altruism pays off.[3]

Translation had always been crucial for Singer. Yiddish was a minority language if ever there was one, and his worldwide fame rested on his works in translation. Once he acquired an English-reading audience, he became, as he says, "one of those rare writers who works with his translators . . . I check my translators constantly—I mean those who translate me into English

This essay was written specifically for this volume and is published here for the first time by permission of the author. The text was read at the Modern Language Association, Toronto 1993.

or Hebrew. What happens to me in Italian, Portuguese or Finnish I will never know."[4]

Elizabeth Shub had known Singer since she was a teenager and he a young new immigrant to New York. Singer spoke no English when he arrived in 1935. By the time he began writing for children 30 years later, his English was fluent. But his was not native English; Shub's was. "It just seemed natural," Shub said, "when he asked me to translate for him."[5] In addition, Shub worked in and knew children's literature; Singer did not; as he observed, "It did not exist among the Jewish people in my time."[6] Shub's skills, her already having translated many of his adult stories, her tact with Singer, and, significantly, her familiarity (though second generation) with the world Isaac Singer had come from—all contributed to a solid working friendship.

Oddly enough, however, there was one thing Elizabeth Shub could not do; she could not read Isaac Singer's handwriting. "Other translators of Singer, such as Mirra Ginsburg, worked alone," Shub said. "Her Yiddish was better and she could read everything."[7] Shub spoke Yiddish and read it in typeset, but Singer's longhand was beyond her. As a consequence, Shub says:

> The way we mostly worked, at least on the first draft, is that he would come to my house and read it to me in Yiddish. He would sit in a nice easy chair and I would sit at the typewriter and do a rough immediate translation. If there was a word I didn't understand, he was there to help me. Then I would read it to him and he would correct whatever he didn't think was right. Then I would type the whole thing out clean and I would edit it to correct anything that I thought was wrong. And then he would go over it and correct anything he didn't like. Then I would read it to him and he would make corrections again or if I felt something wasn't working, he would immediately, if he agreed, fix it.
>
> Bringing the manuscript over didn't mean that as he read to me he didn't change things. He never felt that the manuscripts he brought over were just as they had to be. Once it was done, however, it was done. He wasn't a writer, like some of my others, who went back and said, "Oh, I hate this."
>
> Until I got used to working with him I would sometimes not understand what he was doing. I would have a questioning look or frown a little bit. He'd get very angry and he would say "Why do you look like that? How can I work when you look like that? . . ." I would smile and say, "I'm sorry." And then, by the end of the story, usually he had pulled it together and what didn't have any meaning to me in the middle certainly meant exactly what he wanted it to at the end. And that was a lesson I learned . . . not to take anything for granted till the story was finished. His instinct for the right word in another language was very, very keen.[8]

The spontaneous oral exchange between author and translator drew out the best of Singer's storytelling ability. Alternately he and Shub served as on-site audience. "My translators," says Singer, "are my best critics. I can tell by their expressions when they don't like a story of mine or any part of it."[9] Telling the stories aloud also drew out from him what Roderick McGillis calls "the speaking voice" of literature,[10] the narrative cadences of his young days in Eastern Europe as the son of a rabbi to whose drawing room all kinds of people came to tell their stories. Singer has often depicted himself in his memoirs as a child who listened carefully and consciously to the ways in which people told their stories.

Elizabeth Shub remembers when Singer finally agreed to try his hand at writing for children. He brought his first attempts, Hanukkah poems, to her apartment. It took her until the next day to find the courage to reject the poems, a response Singer wasn't at all pleased about.

Shub continues, "It was maybe a day and a half later when I got this phone call. He said, 'I wrote another story.' 'Oh great, that's wonderful, do you want to come to my house?' 'No, meet me at Famous' (his favorite deli on 72nd Street). So I met him in the cafeteria and he handed me 'Zlateh the Goat' and that's how we got started."[11]

Since Singer's debut as a children's writer won the first of his three Newbery Honor Medals—all three won for books Shub translated with him—theirs was a very good start indeed.

Briefly, "Zlateh the Goat" is about the Russian Jewish family of Reuven, the furrier. An unusually warm winter spells disaster for them, and reluctantly they are forced to sell their beloved old goat Zlateh to raise a few gulden for necessities. The task of taking her to the town butcher is laid upon young Aaron, but no sooner do he and Zlateh set off than they are caught in a blizzard. Their salvation appears in the form of a mound of snow, covering, Aaron realizes, a large haystack. He tunnels a way in for him and Zlateh and, during the three days they share there, they converse in their own way as Zlateh eats the hay and Aaron drinks her milk. The family is overjoyed when they return. The snow has alleviated the economic situation and Zlateh remains at home. The elements of Singer's own roots, family love and sacrifice, human/animal dependence, the warmth of the holiday, and harsh reality—economic and environmental—are all part of his first children's story.

New York University's Fales Library holds all the original English drafts of the seven stories of *Zlateh the Goat*, plus the stories Singer wrote specifically for *A Day of Pleasure*, his National Book Award—winning autobiography of childhood in Poland. The drafts are concrete documentation of a creative process that word processing has rendered quaint. Figures 1 through 3 reproduce draft pages from *Zlateh the Goat*. Shub, Fales Library, and the Singer estate have given their permission to reprint them.

There is very little editing on figure 1. The large signature on top is Singer's, appended when he donated the manuscripts; interestingly, it looks as if he spelled his last name wrong. The rest of the handwriting is Elizabeth

Zlateh, the Goat
by Isaac Bashevis Singer

At
~~Hanukah~~ Hanukah time the road from the village to the town is
usually covered with snow, but this year the winter ~~was a~~ had been mild
one. Hanukah had almost come, yet little snow had fallen.
The sun shone most of the time. The peasants complained
                    of the dry weather
that because ~~xxxxxxxx~~ ~~xxxxxxxxxx~~ there would be
a poor harvest of winter grain. New grass sprouted and the
peasants sent their cattle out to pasture.

For Reuven, the furrier, it was a bad year and after
long hesitation he decided to sell Zlateh, the goat. She
was old and gave little milk. Feyvel, the town butcher,
had offered eight gulden for her. ~~For that money one could~~
                                    Such a sum would
buy Hanukah candles, potatoes and oil for pancakes, ~~give~~ gifts for
and other   holiday   the
children ~~gifts and buy~~ necessaries for the house. Rueven
told his oldest boy Aaron to take the goat to town.
                                        to Feyvel
Aaron understood what taking the goat ~~to town~~ meant,
but he ~~couldxxxx~~ had to obey his father. Leah, his mother,
wired the tears from her eyes when she heard ~~xxxxxxx~~ the news.
                                cried loudly.
Aaron's ~~xxxx~~ younger sisters, Anna and Miriam ~~began to cry out~~
                                              ~~extravagant loud.~~
Aaron put on his quilted jacket, a cap with ear muffs, bound
a rope around Zlateh's neck, and took along two slices of bread
with cheese to eat on the road. Aaron was supposed to deliver
the goat by evening, spend the night at the butchers, and return
the next day with the money.

While the family said goodbye to the goat and Aaron placed
the rope around her neck, Zlateh stood as patiently and goodnaturedly
as ever. She licked Reuven's hand. She shook her small white
beard. Zlateh trusted human beings. She knew that they fed her

Figure 1.   First page of the edited manuscript of "Zlateh the Goat"
(Fales Library, New York University)

Shub's. The editorial improvement is clear: midpage, "For that money one could buy Hanukkah candles" becomes the more resonant "Such a sum would buy Hanukkah candles," and below, "began to cry out" becomes "cried out loud," and finally "cried loudly."

In figure 2, the collaborative translating is more evident; there is much more revision in Shub's hand. Midpage, one sees the dramatic "She could walk no longer" replacing the bulky and flat "She no longer wanted to or was able to walk"; the strongly cadenced "did not want to admit the danger" replaces the polysyllabic "was reluctant to admit the danger." And at the bottom of the page, "a large hay stack which the snow had blanketed" is the revised version of the bland "a large stack of hay covered with snow." The final page of the manuscript, figure 3, shows how spontaneous the working out of the story had become. In Shub's hand is written the final flawless paragraph of Zlateh: one can see "utter bleat" crossed out, replaced with "come out with a single sound which expressed," and the perfect last sentence is refined through crossings out from "all her feelings, all her thoughts, and all her love" to "all her thoughts, and all her love." Love *is* a feeling, after all, so why be repetitious?

There is a particularly lively page from one of the several draft versions in Shub's possession of Singer's 1983 *The Fools of Chelm and Their History*. The novella is an Orwellian Yiddish political comedy about the famous folklore fools, the so-called sages of Chelm, and the consequences of their harebrained imperialism. Humor is notoriously difficult to translate, and as Singer says, "Yiddish is a language with a built-in humor . . . [it] can take a lot of overstatement . . . English or French must be much more precise, logical, lean."[12] The deadpan and parody that begin with the inflated opening of the "history" of Chelm, that "God said, 'Let there be Chelm.' And there was Chelm" does translate, in no small part because of the tightening, the precision, of the editing. Artist Uri Shulevitz told me he was so tickled by Singer's opening that he chose to expand upon it in his illustration, which is the frontispiece of the published book: the illustration "Let there be Chelm."[13] About two-thirds down the page in question, for example, is humor that takes on evolution itself—all of history, from sea creature to Chelmite, is seen to have happened only to provide an explanation of why Chelmites like gefilte fish. At the bottom of the page, sentence structure and delivery are refined: "It is said that the first Chelmites were primitive people, or maybe just fools" becomes "It is said that the earliest Chelmites were primitive people. Some said they were just plain fools." Wording is definitely punchier the second time around. Singer's stories are good enough to be good in any language, but Elizabeth Shub made them good in *English*.

A theory of language contained in *The Fools of Chelm and Their History* effects a transition from a study of primary sources to a few preliminary Singeresque speculations about Language and Translation as metaphors for human—and divine—struggle. Indeed, language and translation were more

a peasant would ~~wait by~~ *come along* ~~itxxxxxntx~~ with his cart, but
~~he saw noone.~~ *noone passed by,*

The snow ~~became denser,~~ *grew thicker,* falling, in whole batches. Aaron
realized that he ~~kxixxxxnexxxfxxxxxxxdxxx~~ was no longer on the
road. Beneath ~~him~~ *his feet* his boots touched the softness of a
plowed field. He had gone astray. He could no longer figure
out which was East or West, which way the village *was* the
town. The wind whistled, howled, whirled the snow *about* in eddies.
It looked as if white imps were playing tag on the fields.
A white dust rose above the ground. ~~Zlateh~~ *Zlateh* stopped. She ~~no longer~~ *could*
~~wanted it on was able to walk.~~ *walk no longer. Suddenly* She anchored her cleft hooves
in the ~~ground~~ *earth* and bleated as if pleading to be ~~led~~ *taken* home. Icicles
hung from her white beard, her horns ~~to~~ *and* were glazed with frost,

Aaron ~~was reluctant~~ *did not want* to admit the danger, but he knew
just the same, that if they did not find shelter, they would
freeze to death. This was no ordinary ~~snow.~~ *storm.* It was a mighty
blizzard. The snow ~~had~~ *fell* reached his knees. His hands were numb.
He could no longer feel his toes. He choked when he breathed.
His nose felt like wood and he rubbed it with snow. Zlateh's
bleating ~~sounded like~~ *began to sound like* crying. Humans in whom she had had so
much confidence had dragged her into a trap. Aaron began to
pray to God for himself and for the innocent animal.

Suddenly he made out the outlines of a hill, ~~of snow.~~
What could it be he wondered? Who had piled ~~the~~ snow into such
a huge heap? He moved towards it dragging Zlateh after him.
When he came near it, he realized that it was a large stack *hay*
~~hay covered with~~ *which the* snow *had blanketed.*

Figure 2. Third page of the "Zlateh" manuscript showing the results of
the collaborative translation effort (Fales Library, New York University)

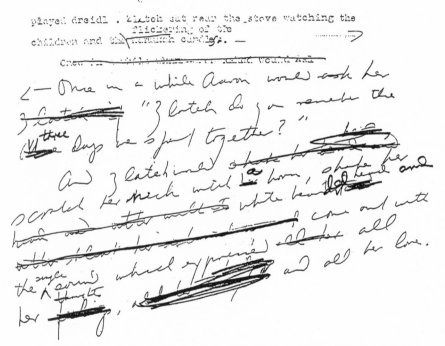

Figure 3. Eighth and final page of the "Zlateh" manuscript with working refinements (Fales Library, New York University)

than practical and artistic issues for Isaac Singer; they were central metaphors imbued with cosmological meaning.

Describing living and cultural conditions in Chelm, Singer writes:

> They walked around naked and barefoot . . . and hunted animals with axes of stone. . . . They often starved or were sick. [And this is Shub's writing] But since the word problem did not exist as yet, there were no problems and no one tried to solve them.
>
> After many years the Chelmites became civilized. They learned to read and write and such words as problem and crisis were created. The moment the word "crisis" appeared in the language, the people realized there was a crisis in their town.

These are the same Chelmite sages who, in another Singer story set during a year of deprivation when there is no sour cream for Hanukkah but plenty of water, solve the problem by decreeing that everyone call sour cream "water" and water "sour cream."[14] Thus, there is plenty of sour cream, and who cares if there's no water?

We—who are of course not fools—we know water is not sour cream no matter what it is called, and that the crisis exists whether we name it or not. But such is the manipulability of words and the possibility of confusion within one language—much less among languages—that words are associated literally and metaphorically not only with great power but with mistakes as well. Singer's example of a translator's error is the rendering of "She cried like a woman in labor" as "She cried like a woman in the Histadruth (union movement)," which has a certain logic to it, ultimately, but is nonetheless wrong.[15] With word, with existence, with the creation of the actual, comes the probability of error.

Singer had a lifelong passion for mystic ideas that embodied what George Steiner calls (in the "Language and Gnosis" chapter of *After Babel*) the affinity between Judaism and mystical linguistics: "Starting with Genesis 11.11 (the story of the tower of Babel) . . . Jewish thought has played a pronounced role in linguistic mystique, scholarship, and philosophy."[16]

In his Flora Levy Lecture, "My Personal Conception of Religion," Singer uses the mystical metaphor of God as primal writer of the universe, an idea derived from the *Sefer Yezirah*. Grace Farrell discusses this in her essay "Belief and Disbelief: The Kabbalic Basis of I. B. Singer's Secular Vision."[17] Singer writes in his Levy lecture that, as an artist, God is prone to all the strengths and weaknesses of authorship; Singer's God "experiments eternally . . . He creates and he fails—perhaps. He makes artistic errors, then rectifies them . . . God keeps on improving Himself . . . Godliness *is* struggle."[18]

In a typically Jewish fashion, I would like to base my conclusion on a quotation. This one is from an 18th-century Hasidic master whom young Singer would certainly have read, one Menaham Mendl of Vibetsk. Rebbe

Mendl said: "Man is the language of God."[19] A beautiful and thought-provoking statement, it is based on a belief in the primacy of language and humanity in the divine scheme. A Taoist teacher in Hong Kong compressed the same idea into three characters: Yun Yan Ji—"Profound ('s) Seal Man"—With "seal" in the Chinese sense of a carved signature. In other words, humanity is the imprint of God.[20] Existence is the Creator talking.

Typically Jewish, however, as opposed to Taoist, is the idea of a screw-up somewhere along the line. This experience-based attitude complements the exaltation of "Man is the language of God" with a resigned "So?—if man is the language of God, maybe it would have been better all around if God had kept his mouth shut."

But God did say, "Let there be," and from that a chain of linguistic imagery follows. For, if, as Mendl says, man is the language of God, then we can say that the writer, the author, is the language of man, the one who actualizes the human experience of existence, puts it into words and thus into memory and thus into as close to immortality as we humans can get. Steiner points out that language is a strange combination of the ineffable with the corporeal.[21] God chose to express his creative power through the medium of flesh and bone, the stuff of speaking, vocal cords and tongues, while the author requires the things of the flesh to give concrete form to his or her creativity. The writer imagines what he or she will, but to put that vision onto paper requires exactly that, paper, pen, hands typing, synapses coordinating: these are necessary . . . but they are prone to error.

To stretch this metaphorical string, if man is the language of God and the author is the language of humanity, can we then say the translator is the language of the author? The author requires the physical agency of another being in order to speak, to actualize, in another tongue. Singer understands translation in the broadest sense, as does Steiner, as the communicating not only of language but of ideas and arts: "In every field of human endeavor we are in need of translations."[22] Man is dependent on God, the author is dependent on humanity, and the translator is dependent upon the author, for the material circumstance. But God is dependent upon humanity to be expressed in a new world, and authors are dependent upon translators to make them exist in another universe of readership. But at the same time he or she opens a world, the translator creates the possibility for more error.

The world as a Translated Text is, as Singer's famous fool Gimpel says, at least once removed from the true world;[23] this secondary world is one of flaws and deceptions. In his essay "On Translating My Books," Singer brings the metaphorical and the mundane acts of translation together: "I sometimes suspect that the Universe is nothing but a bad translation from God's original. My cabalistic theory is that God trusted Satan to translate His creation and it was published before He had a chance to correct the proofs."[24]

Steiner says that translation is doubly removed from God—once because humanity has been exiled from the garden in which Adam spoke the language of God and himself named the animals, and again after Babel when humanity's linguistic oneness was forfeit to its arrogance.[25] The fact that we don't speak the same language reveals a spiritual state distanced from not only direct communication, but communion and community. How do we humans—and here the typically Jewish moral aspect entwines with the metaphorical and metaphysical—how do we get that already-once-translated world as right as possible yet again? How do we avoid error? More practically still, how do we live with inevitable error?

Just as these questions occupied Singer, they will continue to occupy Singer scholars, philosophers, and translators. Singer was not as trusting as God in regard to translation; "I am not going to make the same blunder," he wrote; "all translators must be closely watched."[26] Struggling with his translators personally to get it right was Singer's way of watching. For Singer, whose native tongue necessitated translation and whose career depended upon it, the ultimate justification, however, for struggling so much with translation was not so much fear of being misunderstood, or as he put it, "that if I'm going to be translated one day into Chinese that no one will understand what a Hasid is and what a rabbi is." Singer desired—as directly as possible—to speak his own creation into being in another tongue: "What I do worry about," writes the Nobel Prize winner, "is that my work will be good enough to be translated or to be read, and I work accordingly."[27]

Notes

1.   Isaac Bashevis Singer, "On Translating My Books," in *On the World of Translation* (New York: American P.E.N. Center, 1987), 111.
2.   Naomi Morse, "Values for Children in the Writing of Isaac Bashevis Singer," *Children's Literature: Selected Essays and Bibliographies*, ed. Anne S. MacLeod (1977): 17.
3.   Francelia Butler, "An Interview with Isaac Bashevis Singer," *Sharing Literature with Children* (Prospect Height, Ill.: Waveland Press, 1977), 58.
4.   Singer, "Translating," 110–11.
5.   Alida Allison, "Interview with Libby Shub," unpublished, 1992.
6.   Isaac Bashevis Singer, "On Writing for Children," *Annual of the Children's Literature Association* 6 (1977): 14.
7.   Allison, "Interview."
8.   Allison, "Interview."
9.   Singer, "Translating," 111.
10.   Roderick McGillis, "Reactivating the Ear: Orality and Children's Poetry," *The Voice of the Narrator in Children's Literature*, ed. Charlotte Otten and Gary D. Schmidt (New York: Greenwood Press, 1989), 252.
11.   Allison, "Interview."
12.   Singer, "Translating," 112, 111.
13.   Alida Allison, "Interview with Uri Shulevitz," unpublished, 1993.
14.   Isaac Bashevis Singer, *When Shlemiel Went to Warsaw* (New York: Farrar, Straus & Giroux, 1968), 49.
15.   Singer, "Translating," 110–11.

16. George Steiner, *After Babel* (New York: Oxford University Press, 1975), 62.

17. Grace Farrell, "Belief and Disbelief: The Kabbalic Basis of Singer's Secular Vision," *From Exile to Redemption: The Fiction of I. B. Singer* (Carbondale: Southern Illinois University Press, 1987), 19.

18. Isaac Bashevis Singer, "My Personal Conception of Religion," *Flora Levy Lecture in the Humanities* (Lafayette, La.: University of Southwestern Louisiana, 1982), 1: 3–4.

19. Elie Weisel, *Souls on Fire: Portraits and Legends of Hasidic Masters* (New York: Vintage Press, 1972), 86.

20. Alida Allison, "Interview with Mr. Lo, Secretary, Hong Kong Taoists Society," unpublished, 1973.

21. Steiner, *Babel*, 58.

22. Singer, "Translating," 112.

23. Isaac Bashevis Singer, *Collected Stories* (New York: Farrar, Straus & Giroux, 1981), 14.

24. Singer, "Translating," 111.

25. Steiner, *Babel*, 57.

26. Singer, "Translating," 111, 110.

27. Laurie Colwin, "I. B. Singer: Storyteller," *New York Times Book Review*, 23 July 1978, 24.

Upside Down in the Daytime:
Singer and Male Homosexuality

JOSEPH SHERMAN

Debate over a response in accordance with Jewish Law to the lobby for gay rights has raged in the United States for over 20 years. The problem is either simplified or complicated by the fact that the Torah uncompromisingly prohibits male homosexuality and decrees death as its punishment.[1] Although this punishment may be mitigated, as have other biblical verdicts over the centuries,[2] the prohibition can only be set aside by those who are prepared to set aside Judaism's whole *corpus juris*, the *Halakhah*, itself.

Those who do so—and the debate has called forth several—view the *Halakhah* as a system not absolute but relative to changing social mores, and therefore adaptable to them. Acting on this conviction, a body of Jewish gay activists, under the auspices of the Pacific Southwest Council of the Union of American Hebrew Congregations, constituted the first gay synagogue as a Reform Temple in Los Angeles in 1973, a move that led to the spread of such congregations to New York and elsewhere.[3] For Orthodox Jewish believers, however, the authority of the *Halakhah* is binding for all time and in all circumstances. The majority of rabbis who have contributed responses to the demands of the gay rights movement agree that, unless *Halakhah* is abrogated, the biblical prohibition remains in force, however much a humane, compassionate, or loving attitude towards homosexuals may be advocated.[4]

Between 1962 and 1988 Isaac Bashevis Singer published four stories that examine homosexuality in varied manifestations and from different angles, but all set in the *shtetl* world of the Old Country.[5] Why not set stories with so contemporary a focus of attention in modern-day America where the issue first surfaced and where it continues to arouse controversy after more than two decades?

In a secular society prepared to extend its toleration to widening areas of hitherto strict taboos, the dimensions of the problem are diminished in the degree to which such a society does not regulate itself according to what

---

This essay was written specifically for this volume and is published here for the first time by permission of the author.

it accepts as God-given laws. Singer repeatedly illustrates that if society is not to drift unstoppably into chaos, it needs absolute standards by which human actions can be assessed. Because such a moral conviction can most forcefully be called into notice in a social formation where the categories of sin and virtue have not been blurred, Singer repeatedly recreates a world governed by absolutes. The situational correspondences and parallel consequences in the last two stories of his so-called homosexual cluster, "Two" (1980) and "Disguised" (1988),[6] together offer a considered judgment upon the moral fabric of an emancipated and enlightened Jewish world.

In "Two," Singer chooses a third-person narrator who speaks in one of the favorite voices of Yiddish literature, that of the *maggid*, or itinerant preacher, who shapes moral lessons from the material he selects.[7] This persona enables the writer to interrogate conventional assumptions—not merely of the past, but of the present in relation to that past—and to force on his readers a revaluation of reality's moral dimensions.

"Two" sets up a series of relationships that, evaluated by the traditional criteria of Jewish family values, are unhealthy. A long-delayed male child is brought up as a girl in the formative stages of his life, a conditioning that inevitably muddles the vital question of his sexual identity.[8] Both the child's parents and the home they provide are highly ambivalent. To start with, the parents wait almost the whole of the period permitted by the *Halakhah* for conception within marriage before divorce is made mandatory. Although the Law blames barrenness on the wife, this tale strongly suggests that the fault is not that of Menuha but of her husband, Reb Yomtov, who "had the soul of a female" (33). He is, as his fellow Jews in the study house tease him, "a softy" (34), who appeals to the Godhead not in its awesome (male) manifestation as Creator, Father, and Judge, but in its nurturing (female) form of the Shechinah. Placed where it is, the narrative mention of the Kabbalistic theory that "the virtues of men bring about the union of God and the Shechinah" (33) makes a tart contrast with Reb Yomtov's practice. To the Kabbalists, the perpetual intercourse of the male and female emanations of the Godhead are sustained by holy and proper acts of intercourse in the human realm, the aim of which is ultimately to unite the Shechinah, the sacred bride—sent into exile because of the sinfulness of humanity—with God, the sacred bridegroom, and so accomplish the *tikkun olam*, or restoration of the world, whose harmony will usher in the messianic age. This entire mystical conception is predicated on the union of opposites, of male and female; the married life of Yomtov and Menuha, however, is built on the coupling of like, which breeds not harmony but disruption.

Singer figuratively develops the centrality of this distinction between masculine and feminine by contrasting the relationship between the Hebrew and the Yiddish languages. Reb Yomtov, "drawn more to the matriarchs than to the patriarchs . . . preferred to glance into such volumes as the *Ze'enah u-Re'enah* and *The Lamp of Light* rather than the Gemara, the commentaries, and the Responsa" (34). The former books, designed for the use of women, are written in Yiddish, or *mameloshn*; the latter are the sources of Jewish Law whose study is obligatory for men, in Hebrew and Aramaic, and may therefore be called *tateloshn*. These Yiddish designations connote far more than their rough English equivalents, "mother-tongue" and "father-tongue." First they oppose the vernacular, acquired easily by ear, to the language of scholarship, learned with difficulty through hard application. By extension, this figurative opposition then contrasts the different ethical and emotional functions assigned by usage and custom to mother and father. Mothers conventionally express love for their children through tenderness and indulgence; fathers through discipline and control. *Mameloshn*, Yiddish, embraces and encourages; *tateloshn*, Hebrew/Aramaic, proscribes and prohibits. The balance of opposites thus personified is normally acted out in the Jewish nuclear family: mother and father traditionally give equilibrium to their children by counterbalancing nurture with discipline, permission with prohibition. In these terms, the union of Reb Yomtov and Menuha is an imbalance, since it creates a family with two mothers.

In numerous other ways Reb Yomtov contradicts the typological role defined for males in Jewish life. His work, "removing the impure fat and veins from kosher meat" (33), is the soft (feminine) complement to the hard (masculine) work of the ritual slaughterer. His physique, his clothing and trinkets, his habits (34) all stereotypically associate him with women rather than with men. His wife, Menuha, evidently wholly comfortable in a home from which masculinity has been effaced, desires a daughter to perpetuate its muliebrity. She hopes to recall, in naming her expected daughter, the comfort of "her dead mother" (33). Hence she and her effeminate husband prepare dainty clothing and eagerly start laying by the beginning of a dowry. The parents' self-deception is compounded by the midwife who confuses the infant's sex at birth, so that the mother, who "grew terribly upset that between a yes and a no a daughter had turned into a son" (34), refuses to accept the determination of mere anatomy. The narrative's introduction of this crucial mistake ironically undercuts its prior assertion that "the powers that decide such things saw to it that they had a boy" (34). These "powers" may have determined the child's physiological gender, but the psychological definition of his sexual identity is left in the hands of his parents.

Given the androgynous name of Zissel "after a great-aunt" (34), the growing child is dressed in girl's clothes and encouraged to wear his "elegant curls" long and have them braided by his mother. Confronted with the harsh discipline of *tateloshn*, personified in the cheder teacher "with his white beard, the whipping bench and the whip" (34), Zissel flees to the soft encouragement of *mameloshn* soothingly uttered by a rebbetzin with whom he studied "willingly" (35). Plaintively longing to be a girl, Zissel gets a wholehearted sympathy from his mother: "You were supposed to be . . . What a shame, you would have made such a lovely girl" (35).

At this point the narrative voice intrudes a disturbing observation: "Time, which often is the implement of destiny, did its work" (35). Is the boy's subsequent homosexuality the will of "destiny" or the consequence of his parents' misguided choice? What is the interrelationship between the will of his parents and the will of God? This tale interrogates how far Zissel is to be judged a sinner through his own volition—the Orthodox Jewish standard by which all homosexual activities are evaluated and condemned—or how far he acts under duress as the victim of an unbalanced upbringing.[9]

Too late to rectify their own false nurture yet shocked by its consequences, his parents try through punishments and name-calling to correct the "nature" they themselves have fostered. "Against his will," Zissel is dragged back to cheder and "father-language"; his girlish garments are forcibly exchanged for those unequivocally male-determinant (35). Treated differently from other boys by his teachers, mocked by his peers, coerced into the painful position of "[suffering] anxiety and all kinds of doubts," Zissel grows bashful of undressing before other males because he was "convinced . . . that the signs of manhood were a disgrace" (36). Secretly indulging in cross-dressing, gazing "enviously" at the women in their finery in the synagogue's gallery, Zissel predictably finds solace in locking himself away to recite "a prayer in Yiddish from his mother's prayer book" (36). Once again he escapes from the "father-language" of rebuke and correction to the "mother-language" of comfort and consolation.

Significantly, after the first four paragraphs of the story, Reb Yomtov disappears completely. Even his nominal male-father presence is effaced by the female-mother, the ubiquity of whose possessions, regularly and repeatedly used by Zissel, defines her dominance. Since social convention attends only to physical appearance, not to emotional reality, busy matchmakers see Zissel as worthy of the best offers, but his mother's influence remains paramount: she hinders any redefinition of Zissel's sexual identity by making all the proposed brides she looks over objects of ridicule (36). She has made Zissel dependent upon continual cosseting to the extent that he comes, as a matter of course, to find young men sexually attractive, turning from his earlier companionship with young women because he now recognizes threatening competition in their flirtatiousness (37).

The youth to whom he is drawn is himself rendered sexually ambivalent through being identified by his mother's name as Ezriel Dvorah's, a device that subtly stereotypes him to conventional perception as another "mummy's boy." His physical attractiveness is enhanced by the immaculateness of his dress and his "big-city" behavior. Both in this tale and in "Disguised," traits such as these are made to connote not only connection with European enlightenment, but also corruption by it; worldly sophistication is shown in time to promote moral decadence. Before polish has hardened into vice, however, such refinements make Ezriel highly desirable in small-town eyes: in the study house "the other students competed to be his study partner," and "girls rushed to the windows and stared at him from behind drawn curtains" (37). Embodying the world and the flesh, Ezriel's glamour offers a continual temptation to eschew the spirit: "When Ezriel spoke, everyone stopped reading the text to listen. When it was time to take a walk . . . several boys were always ready to accompany him" (37). Drawn to delicate men, he chooses Zissel for his partner, and holy studies immediately lose all value except as an excuse for physical proximity.

Singer's tale exploits the conviction that in a tradition-bound Jewish world, peer and community pressure eliminated the expression of homosexuality through a process of behavioristic conditioning. Therefore, in seventeenth-century Poland, Rabbi Joseph Caro's earlier prohibition against men being secluded together was lifted by Rabbi Joel Sirkes on the grounds that homosexuality was unknown in Eastern Europe.[10] But Ezriel, fresh from a big city susceptible to "enlightenment," defines a counter-behavior that strikes at the root of traditionalism. His goading simply drives Zissel, sexually sundered from *shtetl* norms, to openly subvert them. Betrothing himself to an attractive and highly eligible girl as a conscious act of revenge against the man he really desires, Zissel, in his self-absorption, takes the first step towards casting off all the restraints of the Law. Ezriel and Zissel, as if playing a game of "dares," drive each other to acts progressively more and more morally undermining. To respond in kind, Ezriel engages himself to "a local girl [who] was homely" (38). Having no real interest in normative marriage, he deliberately chooses a bride whose plainness bespeaks his disdain both for women and for heterosexuality. This exploitation of custom and convention to pursue a forbidden agenda accentuates the vulnerability of the Law in the face of "modern" self-definitions. The cornerstone of its perpetuation, marriage, is here used as a stick with which homosexual lovers beat each other.

Because the narrative aims to show how far psychological imbalances can, if not readjusted by morally positive acts of choice, descend rapidly into sin, it steadily compels a shift in the reader's sympathies. Zissel as helpless child invites compassion; as an emerging adult, his acts of free choice become problematic. On his wedding night, "Zissel was overcome by trembling" because "he could not do what he knew he was supposed to" (38). Empathy for the cause of this painful situation, which our knowledge of Zissel's warped childhood must awaken, is now blunted by our knowledge of the motives that drove him to contract this marriage in the first place. By exploiting the innocent, Zissel moves not only towards sin himself, but towards becoming the cause of sin in others.

Here, as so often in his work, Singer is concerned to identify how far personal backsliding affects the moral condition of the world. Zissel's progressive descent is presented unsparingly. Yet the limited awareness of the *shtetl* is equally unsentimentally perceived. The grossly superstitious reaction of the mothers of both bride and groom to the absence of conception

in this marriage ridicules the folly of assuming that "nature" exists indepen-
dently of nurture: seeking remedies from sacred and profane sources respectively, the eager grandmothers-to-be find that "the cures recommended by
both the rabbi and the witch were the same" (39). The problem, however,
slowly formulates itself as one less of cure than of moral choice: Ezriel
and Zissel lay waste all around them because they build their homosexual
relationship on a series of frauds.

Ezriel's marriage predictably collapses and he goes "back to his mother"
from whose home he writes to Zissel "[i]n an elaborate handwriting and a
Hebrew full of flowery phrases" (39). Both in presentation and style, his
letter manifests not deep feeling but wanton self-indulgence, making a
demand which it knows will not be refused. Ezriel feels better able to seduce
through manipulation of written rather than spoken words—and ironically
enough through the written words of the Hebrew—not the Yiddish—
language. The *Haskalah*, or Jewish Enlightenment, of which Ezriel is so
flamboyant a product, has transformed Hebrew from the "father-language"
of the Law whose discipline Zissel once fled, into the language of the world
whose enticements Zissel now embraces.

Ezriel's intention, and the means he employs to encompass it, illustrate
Singer's abiding animus against the corrupting influences of the *Haskalah*.
Concluding with the biblical phrase "they yearned one for the other," this
high-flown and meretricious *maskilic* correspondence reveals the "secrets of
their hearts" to be desire of the flesh, which is consummated "at an inn
lying between Tomasow and Frampol" (40). The physical emblematizes the
psychological: like the place, the condition is one of betweenness, the action
one of chicanery. Ezriel uses the Torah as a screen for wrongdoing, telling
his mother that "he was going to enquire about a teaching position" and
taking with him prayer shawl and phylacteries (40). Zissel, suppressing the
potentially redeeming emotions of "heartache and shame" (39), steals both
his bride's dowry and her jewelry. At this precise moment, the tale's narrative
voice explicitly transforms Zissel from victim into agent: his consciously
chosen actions nullify the mitigating circumstances of his deforming childhood. Employing his youthful inclination towards cross-dressing as a "trick"
to flee the responsibilities of his marriage, he succeeds in hiding not only
from others but from himself: "When he caught a glimpse of himself in the
mirror, he hardly knew his own face" (40). Having surrendered totally to
the *yetzer ha'rah*, or Evil Inclination, he willfully rejects all claim of morality
in pursuit of self-gratification: "Zissel walked past the market and saw from
afar his wife pushing her way towards the butcher's block. He pitied her,
but he had already broken the commandments that forbid a man to dress
in women's clothes and to steal, and he hurried along" (40).

This pursuit of sin is underscored in a simple narrative detail. When
Ezriel and Zissel studied in the yeshiva they would walk together down
"Synagogue Street" (39); on his way to his tryst, Zissel gets a lift on "Church

Street" (40). The area of the forbidden opens out from small things to greater. Inevitably they return to Ezriel's "big city" where, more easily concealed, sin has greater opportunities to enlarge itself. Here, as elsewhere in his work, Singer employs a well-established convention in Yiddish fiction, in which "the city embodies the possibilities of enlightenment, assimilation, anonymity, and radical alienation."[11] Thus, in Lublin, unmolested, "the pair lived for several years together, indulging themselves to their heart's desire" (41). Explicit moral condemnation juxtaposes the word "indulged" against the fact that the wives they have abandoned without divorce are in Jewish law adjudged *agunot* (41), forbidden to remarry and hence condemned to wasted lives. Evading the net cast by the law in behalf of those they have wronged enmeshes these "two" even more tightly in a net of their own devising.[12]

To complete his transvestitism, Zissel "plucked some of [his beard], singed the rest, and from time to time committed the transgression of shaving" (41) while impersonating an observant Jewish wife. As Singer spells out elsewhere,[13] deception of this kind leads automatically to self-deception: "Zissel became so involved with his female cronies he often forgot what he was." But this is a game bought with stolen money and played in borrowed time. Their material circumstances diminish in proportion as their moral decay increases. Ezriel's beauty fades into "wrinkles in his forehead and . . . grey threads in his beard"; his fastidious dress yields place to "a patched gaberdine and a ratty fur hat." The physical emptiness of Zissel's pots of boiling water displayed to disguise nonexistent Sabbath preparations manifests the spiritual emptiness of their lives. Unvarnished poverty becomes the correlative of simulated piety: "It was true that the two had broken the law, but they hadn't abandoned their faith in God and the Torah" (42). This highly ironic narrative observation serves pointedly to separate sign from significance. It calculatedly reminds readers that Judaism, by affirming that God, the Torah, and Israel are one, uncompromisingly insists that its package is all or nothing; actions, not intentions, determine the moral quality of every individual life.

Both personal and communal depravity is bred by the attempt of these "two" to enact gender roles in the confusion of gender, and to exercise the functions of normality in the context of what the narrative unswervingly presents as abnormality. His brief attempt at earning his own living having failed, Ezriel demands the privileges of traditional Jewish manhood without any of its responsibilities. To support him, Zissa, now referred to in the feminine, unwillingly accepts appointment as the ritual bath attendant (43). A series of inversions that corrupt the whole community is thus set in motion by an act of role reversal supposedly affecting only the personal happiness of "two." Responsibility for regulating *taharat ha'mishpachah*, the purity of the family, is now entrusted to one who, as a man, mocks both the purity of the Divine and the innocence of the human. The intimate secrets of wives and brides are confided to one, himself the betrayer of a wife, who despite all his "adroitness" violates that Law designed to preserve the Covenant of Israel, while his partner "could now sit around in idleness . . . He was not yet forty, but he had fallen into a melancholy" (43–44). Singer repeatedly assigns this condition of "melancholy" to those who abandon Torah discipline for secular laxity. Ezriel is rendered impotent because he has no part to play in the society he inhabits. His enraged fear, provoked by Zissel's gossip, that their masquerade is threatened because his lover might come to feel male sexual urges through daily exposure to female nudity, underscores the extent to which, unstable themselves, their deception threatens the stability of society as a whole.

With the appearance before Zissel of the "dazzling flesh" of Reizl, the "ravishing virgin of seventeen" who is about to become a bride, "what Ezriel most feared came to be. For the first time in his life Zissel felt desire for a woman" (44). As this "desire turned to passion," Zissel's sexual identity dramatically reasserts the male, a confusion foregrounded by the narrative's repeated interchange of the two forms of his name to highlight the danger of sexual shuffling.

As so often in Singer's fiction, the catastrophe is emblematically anticipated in natural forces descriptively invested with the power of evil. An unprecedented blizzard "howled around corners as if a thousand witches had hanged themselves"; despite massive attempts at heating, all houses remain cold; no one ventures out because, as Ezriel, with unconscious irony, warns Zissel, "demons were afoot outside" (45). Knowing that Reizl is "scheduled to come to the bath that evening," Zissel, now wholly at one with such demons, is determined to indulge lust behind a pious mask, and goes out, "putting himself at God's mercy." Such mercy, in the form of a natural warning against proceeding, is perhaps shown him when he is blown into a snowdrift. But in Singer, such warnings are ambiguous. The bitterest of ironies ensures that Zissel is rescued from certain death by Reizl herself. The narrative consciousness is pessimistically aware that, as the Talmud teaches, "All things are in the hands of Heaven except the fear of Heaven,"[14] and the guilty destroy themselves at the expense of the guiltless. A young couple's eagerness to pleasure themselves in the sanctified act of marital union hastens the simultaneous destruction of both sacred and profane.

The powers of evil mockingly set their own stage: the desolation of the *mikvah* on this most menacing of all nights makes it the potential locale not for purification but for profanation. Because she instinctively discerns their evil intention, Reizl has long recoiled from Zissel's unwholesome attentions. Now her fear "of the dismal powers that hold sway over such places" (46) is well founded. The voice of Satan has urged Zissel to "Assail and defile," an urge central to Singer's perception of the nature of sin: once an individual willfully succumbs to one unnatural impulse, all the rest follow of their own. But the evil that drives Zissel on also permits no escape from its consequences—he is dragged to death by the chaste wife he has affronted. His abandonment to viciousness erodes all sympathy for him as the power of the *mikvah* asserts itself as inviolate: it prevents the rape by drowning both rapist and intended victim.

The world without is symbolically made to reflect the deed committed within: the moon emerged "pale as the face of a corpse after ablution, its light congealed upon the shrouds of night" (46). Entering the bathhouse, Reizl's husband and his coachman find that "the echoes of their voices" do indeed proceed "from a ruin"—the ruin of virtue by one who has been living out what is now recognized as a "shameless farce" (47). The shocking discovery that "the bath attendant was male" leads to a fresh act of horror, the murder of Ezriel. The sins that he and Zissel have committed, the narrative structure suggests, have become a general moral pollutant. Moments before his death, in freezing cold, lit by a candle which "cast ominous shadows," Ezriel sits "searching his soul . . . consumed by gloom" (47). His appalled awareness of the hopelessness of a life sundered from its most energizing influences must confront violent death as its only possible termination.

Each step of Ezriel's brutal lynching is a savage parody of punishments once handed down by the Sanhedrin: "half his beard" is torn out, because his conduct has vitiated the object of the Divine prohibition against shaving; his ritual garment, another outward sign of his lip service to the commandments, is "snatched off"; he is beaten "with a cudgel" in a travesty of the chastisement prescribed for a transgressor against religious law. This is certainly not presented as justice: Ezriel's assailants are "ruffians," their voices are "violent," their steps are "heavy" (47); what they do is as much a violation of the Law as the behavior they attack. But it is shown to be the ineluctable consequence of false choice. Ezriel shares the fate of Zissel, who, having set the Law at naught in pursuit of self-gratification, mocks marriage, steals to live a homosexual life maintained through transvestitism and depilation, and yields to lust, attempted rape, and effectual murder. Zissel and Ezriel's attempt to live as pious Jews is rendered a *brachah levattalah*, a broken or empty blessing, approaching mockery of God, since it is impossible, as the events of the tale show, to live the Truth while practicing a lie.

Their bodies, as perfunctorily prepared for burial as the Law will permit, are "buried beneath the fence late at night" in the place reserved for those who offend beyond the power of rabbinical courts to pardon. Then suddenly the narrative seems to dip ambivalently. Their unidentified and dishonored mound, "soon overgrown with weeds" (47), is discovered one morning marked by a board that mysteriously appears from nowhere bearing the famous inscription from 2 Samuel (1:23): " 'Lovely and pleasant in their lives and in their deaths they were not divided' " (47). Someone "who . . . was never discovered" evidently so much admired the courage of the dead pair in "coming out" as to make a public statement in support of it, since such a message can be addressed only to the living, not to the dead.

Is the tale now inviting a belated though equivocal sympathy for these homosexual lovers? Closer reflection dispels the illusion. The board and its slogan are instead exposed as the tale's crowning narrative irony: one, more-over, that is consciously intertextual, since the same quotation completes the epitaph on the gravestone of Jacob and Wanda/Sarah and forms the concluding paragraph of Singer's novel, *The Slave*, which lyrically celebrates the morally transforming power of heterosexual love. In this case, by contrast, while they may not be divided in death, the lives of Ezriel and Zissel were founded on falsehood, built on betrayal, rent by discord, and destroyed by violence. The tale's concluding sentence, listing four impossible conditions under which the board might have survived "to this day" (47), rounds out the tale's determination to de-romanticize this relationship, and to uncom-promisingly present it as an abuse of free choice and a defiance of God's Law.

The second of the two tales, "Disguised," effectively dramatizes a Tal-mudic opinion that *mishkav zakhur*, lying with men as with women, is defined as "abomination" because a married man with homosexual tendencies will abandon his wife and disrupt his family in order to indulge his forbidden lusts.[15] So replete is "Disguised" with Talmudic comment on sexual sin that, even more obviously than does "Two," it takes on the aspect of a moral homily on Proverbs 2:19—"None who come to her return, nor do they reach the paths of life"[16]—the very text that Singer deliberately puts into the mouth of Pinchosl, the homosexual husband he creates here (57). Starting from the premise that entering into a homosexual relationship is an act of volition, the narrative seeks to investigate the degree of individual culpability involved.

The story is recounted from the perspective of Temerl, the *agunah*. Like the abandoned wives in "Two," she, too, is made an innocent dupe. The question in both stories—unanswered but consistently demanding—is why, having first married and then chosen a homosexual lifestyle, the hus-bands abscond without giving their wives the divorce that would set them free? Since under Jewish law divorce is comparatively easy, all such husbands need do is to send a *get* by messenger. Do they fail to do so out of contempt for women? Or are they merely too self-absorbed? Not only inexplicable, the behaviour of the men concerned is also inexcusable, since, apart from exposing the potential tyranny of patriarchy, predictably none of the wives in either tale is left with children who might give purpose to their otherwise empty lives. Pinchosl's abandonment of Temerl "left her with nothing but an ache in her heart" (49).

Unlike the wives in the first tale, who fade into mute victims of deceit and cowardice, Temerl fights for her right to a fulfilling life by going in search of her strayed husband. Yet her very independent-spiritedness emphasizes the powerlessness of women in the patriarchal Jewish world. When her husband leaves her, the townspeople's cross-examination is grounded in an unassailable conviction that abandonment must be the wife's fault. The moral advantages to be gained from living according to absolute standards are shown to be offset by the social disadvantages of gender inequality, and by the inability of an ideal to control individual freedom of choice. The moral absolute is only socially operative as long as individuals abide by its discipline. This is why it is so easy for a husband to walk out on his wife, and why it is so difficult for an abandoned wife to regain her freedom.

Pinchosl is presented as a striking antithesis to Zissel in the first tale. On the face of things, he has been lavishly fortunate. Both insignificant and commonplace, without looks, money, or brilliance, he is taken in marriage by the young, beautiful, and devoted daughter of a remarkably generous rich man. The emotional and material circumstances of his married life appear to offer an enviable completeness. Yet he is unaccountably moved by secret urges that leave him dissatisfied. So "a few months" after the wedding, he flees "in the middle of the night," like Ezriel taking with him "his prayer shawl and phylacteries," but, unlike Zissel, refusing to steal his wife's dowry (48–49).

Since Pinchosl is specifically presented as neither a thief nor a voluptuary, the mystery of his disappearance calls forth a generalized narrative observation that, while admitting an incapacity to understand human motives, leaves open for further exploration the question of moral culpability: "People often say that one cannot understand the ways of the Almighty. Yet the ways of human beings can be just as perplexing" (50). Here, as throughout this tale, conventional expectation is confounded. Where Zissel in the first tale chooses to hide his secret life in the big city, and thus becomes one with those corruptions with which the city is conventionally invested, Pinchosl elects to live disguised in the small town of Kalisz. Set side by side, Singer's two thematically linked narratives ironically demonstrate that the nonnormative does not in reality express itself in cliches of place or practice. Yet the predictably superstitious explanation, "the demons had captured him" (50), is again figuratively true. Pinchosl falls victim, as did Zissel, to the demons of homosexual desire and is driven to live a lie.

Temerl's discovery that "each human being had his own desires, his own calculations, and sometimes his or her own madness" (52) exposes a world in which the *Halakhah* tries to govern the ungovernable, order the chaotic, and structure the amorphous. The question placed squarely before us, however, is not why the *Halakhah* fails to accomplish all of this, but what happens to a world from which its attempt is removed? The effectiveness of the *Halakhah* lies in the hands of individuals; but remove the fear of God that motivates them to obey it, and the partial order it imposes vanishes in aggregating disorder. Since this is how Singer consistently perceives contemporary life, he deliberately encodes his judgment of it in a re-creation of vanished *shtetl* morality.

In the Old Country, which valued holy living, there existed a standard by which actions were measured and their consequences judged. In the New Country, which values unrestricted individual freedom, human actions, having reference neither to an absolute standard nor to the common good, cease to have meaning. It is certainly not by narrative chance that among countless grotesque stories of aberrant human behavior, Temerl hears also "of men who escaped to America, where, she was told, it was nighttime when it was daytime in Poland, and where people walked upside down" (52). Read figuratively, this presentation of "modern" America castigates a moral relativism that turns day into night and, ethically speaking, makes people "walk upside down."[17] By deliberate contrast, therefore, when a man she charges in "old" Poland with being her strayed husband turns out to be someone else, Temerl is "sentenced to pay a fine of eighteen groschen for suspecting the innocent and giving a stranger a bad name" (53). While in monetary terms the fine is nominal, its moral significance is enormous, upholding as it does the need for absolute justice. Temerl's charge is thoroughly investigated, evidence is tested, and a judgment given according to a law that recognizes no distinction between the civil and the moral. In consequence, in a truly Jewish world, to reapply Singer's metaphor, people walk upright in the daytime.

When Temerl finally encounters her strayed husband dressed as a woman, she cannot comprehend what she sees except as insanity: "Are you mad, possessed by a dybbuk?" (54). Her only response to his determination to "confess the whole truth" is to demand whether he has "God forbid, forsaken [his] faith" (55). When he tells her explicitly that "I'm not a man anymore—not really, not for you . . ." all she can believe is that he has been physically maimed. Hearing Elkonah's name and learning of Pinchosl's liaison with "Him" make no impression on her conscious mind; invited by Pinchosl to go back with him to "where we live," she demands, "Who is the 'we'? Did you find another woman?" (56). An attitude that would nowadays be dismissed as inconceivable naïveté is placed in a context that not only makes it perfectly credible but also implies a condemnation of a world gone mad.

Pinchosl's citation from the Talmud[18] to explain his conduct (56) moves the narrative even closer to homily. This piece of Talmudic advice is chiefly concerned with preventing the public profanation of God's name by a scholar who, by gratifying his evil impulses, would make a mockery of holy study for others as he has done for himself. Although it naturally hopes in this way to set stumbling blocks before the commission of sin, the Talmudic recommendation does not concern itself with the effects of sin upon the sinner himself. What those effects are can be seen in Pinchosl's subsequent conduct. His hesitant shifts of emotion when he confronts the wife he has wronged reveal the formerly "learned and law-abiding" Pinchosl to be less than comfortable with the situation into which his own lusts have driven him. When he offers Temerl refreshment in his seedy home, and they are "sitting and drinking like two sisters" (58), he is by turns brazen and contrite: "This was . . . a worldly man who reminded her of the adventurers described in the storybooks she used to read before she married . . . He repeatedly apologized for his sins and the sufferings he had caused her and her parents. He even joked and smiled—something he had never done in former times" (57).

The steady acquisition of worldliness is shown to be the inevitable concomitant of abandoning the fear of God, as Pinchosl himself acknowledges: "I can regret but not repent. Those who are trapped in our net can never escape" (57). The truth of this Midrashic precept, dramatized earlier in "Two" and repeated here, is confirmed with the appearance of Elkonah: tall, handsome, foppish, he "proved to be like one of those who are referred to in the Talmud as profligates for the sake of spite."[19] In person, conduct, and values, he embodies unbridled depravity. Not content with disregarding the Law himself, he perverts its institutions for others, outrageously offering to give Temerl a divorce himself "in order to save Pinchosl a costly trip." In response to Temerl's shocked question, "Have you no fear of God at all?" he boasts merely of seducing yeshiva boys and of the indispensable help afforded him in this pursuit by Pinchosl who, uneasily enough in his lover's presence, continues to speak "with the humility of a Jew" (58).

In this tale's homosexual relationship there is no demonstration of "loving selfless concern" often urged today; we see only dominator and dominated. With Elkonah's arrival, Temerl's initial question to Pinchosl, "Are you someone's servant or slave?" (54–55), is revealed to be literal truth. The pretzels he bakes in his self-chosen womanish role are not only a means of livelihood, but also an emblem of his lover's insatiable fleshly appetites, which his own passions have enslaved him into gratifying. These febrile urges have driven him to exchange comfort as Temerl's husband for drudgery as Elkonah's "wife," a role reversal that demands abandoning learning in favor of pimping and discarding a woman's magnanimous devotion for a man's egocentric promiscuity. His "marriage" to Elkonah can only be a torment, something Pinchosl himself wryly recognizes when he affirms that "passions . . . are Gehenna on earth, perhaps the Gate to Hell" (57).

Temerl's repeated conviction that Pinchosl is "utterly mad" confirms the truth of yet another Talmudic maxim: "No man sins unless he is overcome by a spirit of madness."[20] The narrative establishes the destructiveness of Pinchosl's behavior both through his own self-awareness and through his lover's blasphemous hedonism. Yet it also adduces for Pinchosl—as it did for Zissel—some extenuating circumstances. To be sure, Temerl's generously given and faithfully honored oath to keep Pinchosl's secret shows up the meanness of Pinchosl's original faithlessness. But this contrast is tempered by two ambivalences.

First, Pinchosl's desperate desire to keep his secret bespeaks both fear and guilt, emotions arguably inspired as much by a troubled conscience as by dread of social censure. Second, Temerl's willingness to sustain his lie suggests that she still retains some of the affection he once awakened in her. Although to the end she sees him as part of the World of Lies built on abuse of free choice, her dying words, "Who knows? Perhaps I will meet this madman once again in Gehenna," also convey Judaism's awareness that, as its burial service proclaims, "there is none righteous upon earth." Her unwavering acceptance of the Jewish tradition that every human soul will, on account of its moral imperfections, spend 11 months in Gehenna before being admitted to Paradise simultaneously acknowledges both the universality of sin and the compassion of an all-knowing God. What sets Temerl free from the burden of earthly secrecy is her recognition, on her deathbed, that "the place where I am going is called the World of Truth." There, finally, will be no place for "disguise."

The narrative pity that recognizes Pinchosl's inability to help himself is finally not mitigating, however. Unhappy and unfulfilled as he was with Temerl, he is little better off with Elkonah, in whose conduct his mistreatment of Temerl rebounds upon him. Impelled neither by upbringing nor by social pressure, he is driven to seek an alternative lifestyle, which leads to aggregating deception and perversion—inescapably part of the price he must pay for his freedom of choice. Temerl herself has sufficient maturity of judgment to point out the contrast between what he has chosen and what he enables her to choose again for herself (58).

The different capacities for growth of their respective choices is unambiguously contrasted at the end of the tale: Pinchosl fades out, presumably statically bound to the servitude of Elkonah's dissipated sensuality, while Temerl ripens into a pious matriarch, attended at her deathbed by "a rabbi and . . . the elders of the burial society . . . surrounded by her sons, daughters, and grandchildren, as well as friends and admirers from the region" (59). However much of a tempered compassion there may be towards the compulsions that drive Pinchosl on, his election of the nonnormative is unequivocally presented as life-denying by contrast with Temerl's participation in a moral schema that equates the law of nature with the will of God.

Presented as unique case histories, both tales broaden out into general examinations of the consequences of free choice misapplied. For Singer, at the end of his career as much as at its beginning, God's presence or absence in the world is made manifest in human choice and action. Each of these two late tales denies individuals the right to live outside or beyond community; each directs attention to the consequences for both individuals and communities when the absolutes of *Halakhah* are removed. The focus of these tales is less upon deviation from sexual norms than upon the degree to which such deviation damages the well-being of others; they do not reject male homosexuality per se as much as they repudiate modern doctrines of selfishness.

In making this repudiation, Singer does not hesitate to speak openly in the voice of the moralist. Introducing *The Death of Methuselah*, the 1988 collection in which "Disguised" first appeared, he boldly restates the artistic credo he first enunciated in his Nobel Lecture 10 years before: "Art must not be all rebellion and spite; it can also have the potential of building and correction."[21] This assertion exposes Singer's unceasing attacks over many years upon didacticism in fiction as essentially a criticism of artistic form rather than of moral content, a reaction more against crude techniques than against ethical emphasis. In every important respect, these two tales reiterate the abiding artistic and moral concerns of Singer's whole creative output; they do and they say, in miniature, everything done or said in all his major work. And this, quite explicitly, is to affirm through fiction the ancient teaching of Sa'adiah Gaon: "Sin is not sinful because God forbade it, but God forbade it because it is sinful."[22]

Whether or not he was deliberately responding to the furor over American Reform's accommodation of homosexuality, for Singer the moral confusion inherent in the debate, as indeed in the problem that aroused it, is symptomatic of the ethically inchoate condition of the modern world. Such confusion presents itself to Singer's creative imagination as the contemporary rebuilding of Babel with the arrogance of reason on the site of enlightenment. Rephrasing in the slippery language of doubting men what was once accepted with perfect faith as the unambiguous Word of the Divine, and reconstructing according to relativistic caprice what was once incontestably understood as the Revealed Will, modern Jewish society has, as Singer's tales pessimistically dramatize, come to speak in a confusion of tongues that makes each person unintelligible to another, and God incomprehensible to all.

Notes

1.   The prohibition is found in Leviticus 18:22: "Thou shalt not lie with mankind as with womankind; it is abomination (*to'evah hu*)." The punishment is prescribed in Leviticus 20:13: "And if a man lie with mankind, as with womankind, both of them have committed abomination (*to'evah asu*): they shall surely be put to death (*shneyhem mot yumatu*); their blood shall be upon them."

2.   Two such, against the ordeal of jealousy for the suspected adulteress (Numbers 5:11–31) and the stoning of the rebellious son (Deuteronomy 21:18–21), are cited, with the relevant mitigating Talmudic judgements, by Robert Kirschner, "Halakhah and Homosexuality: A Reappraisal," *Judaism* 37, no. 4 (Fall 1988): 458.

3.   See Norman Lamm, "Judaism and the Modern Attitude to Homosexuality," in *Encyclopedia Judaica Yearbook 1974* (Jerusalem: Keter, 1974), 205. How the existence of this original gay synagogue, Beth Chayim Chadashim, "test[s] the outer limits of Judaism" is outlined in one of the earliest, and subsequently much-quoted, pieces of personal testimony

by one of its first rabbis, Janet Ross Marder: "The Impact of Beth Chayim Chadashim on My Religious Growth," *Journal of Reform Judaism* 32 (Winter 1985): 33–37.

4.   These responsa have been cast in accessible secular form as essays published in the pages of Jewish scholarly journals, notably *Judaism*, which has actively promoted and sustained the debate. Some of the most vigorous, in chronological order of appearance, are Hershel J. Matt, "Sin, Crime, Sickness, or Alternative Life Style? A Jewish Approach to Homosexuality," *Judaism* 27, no. 1 (Winter 1978): 13–24; Robert Kirschner, "Halakhah and Homosexuality: A Reappraisal," *Judaism* 37, no. 4 (Fall 1988): 450–58; and Samuel H. Dresner, "Homosexuality and the Order of Creation," *Judaism* 40, no. 3 (Summer 1991), 309–21. *Judaism* has also published a wide-ranging symposium on the subject: "Homosexuals and Homosexuality: Psychiatrists, Religious Leaders, and Laymen Compare Notes," *Judaism* 32, no. 4 (Fall 1983): 390–443.

5.   These are, in chronological order and, as far as I have to date been able to ascertain, in original place of publication in English, as follows: "Yentl the Yeshiva Boy," *Commentary* 34, no. 3 (September 1962), reprinted in *The Spinoza of Market Street and Other Stories*, 1964; "Zeitel and Rickl," in *The Seance and Other Stories*, 1968; "Two," in the *New Yorker*, 20 December 1976, reprinted in *Old Love*, 1980; "Disguised," in *The Death of Methuselah and Other Stories*, 1988.

6.   The texts to which I refer, and from which page references to quotations used are cited parenthetically in my essay, are the following: "Two," in *Old Love* (London: Jonathan Cape, 1980), 33–47, and "Disguised," in *The Death of Methuselah and Other Stories* (New York: Farrar, Straus & Giroux, 1988), 48–60.

7.   This voice was developed to a remarkable degree in the work of Ayzik-Meir Dik (?1807–93), a formative influence on the shape of modern Yiddish fiction. To what extent Dik's narrative techniques, including those of parody and intertextuality, have influenced Singer's is a fascinating area that still awaits detailed critical investigation.

8.   In his adulatory collection of Singer anecdotes, Paul Kresh reports the following exchange, about "Yentl the Yeshiva Boy," between Singer and his students at Bard College during October 1975—approximately one year before "Two" appeared in English—which has relevance to the present discussion:

But why did Isaac pick a strange girl like Yentl as the heroine of his story?

"I am interested always in the exception—you might say, almost, in freaks. Because through the exception we can learn more about ourselves, about normal people."

Isaac wants everybody with a question to have a turn. A young man points out that Yentl's mother is dead when the story starts and that her father laments that Yentl isn't proficient in domestic matters and says God should have made her a boy. How could a father say such a thing to his own daughter? Isaac says he has heard fathers say such things to their children. He has known parents so eager to have a girl that when a boy was born they dressed him as a girl and gave him a girlish name. Dr. [Justus] Rosenberg points out that Rilke was made to dress like a girl until the age of puberty and ended up a homosexual.

Paul Kresh, *Isaac Bashevis Singer: The Magician of West 86th Street* (New York: Dial Press, 1979), 11.

9.   As Singer's tale poses it, this question becomes a fictional dramatization of the vexed debate over how far the *Halakhic* category of *ones*, or duress, advanced in mitigation of prohibited sexual acts committed under the compulsion of uncontrollable passion, can or should be applied to homosexual acts. The *Halakhic* parameters of this debate and its sources are cited and outlined by Norman Lamm, "Judaism and the Modern Attitude to Homosexuality," 202–4; Hershel J. Matt, "Sin," 16–17; and Robert Kirschner, "Halakhah," 451–52.

10.   For fear of lewdness "in our times" (in "our countries," Spain and Palestine), [in the sixteenth century] Rabbi Joseph Caro (1488–1575) from Safed prohibited two men from being secluded together; this ban was lifted in Poland by one of that state's greatest Talmudic

scholars, Rabbi Joel Sirkes (1561–1640), a century later. For sources and discussion, see Norman Lamm, "Judaism," 196–97.

11. Anita Norich, *The Homeless Imagination in the Fiction of Israel Joshua Singer* (Bloomington: Indiana University Press, 1991), 50.

12. Singer's often-used image of sin as a net from which there is no escape has close affinities with Rabbi Akiva's exegetical comment on Genesis 4:7: "If thou doest well, shall [thy countenance] not be lifted up? and if thou doest not well, sin coucheth at the door; and unto thee is its desire, but thou mayest rule over it." The Midrash records Rabbi Akiva as commenting thus: "At first [sin] is like a spider's web, but eventually it becomes like a ship's rope." *Midrash: Genesis Rabbah* 22:6, translated and annotated by A. Freedman, 2 vols. (London: Soncino, 1951), 185. The same image is used in identical circumstances in "Disguised."

13. He does so explicitly in "Yentl the Yeshiva Boy," where cross-dressing produces this consequence: "[Yentl] lay there thinking outlandish thoughts that brought her close to madness. She fell asleep, then woke with a start. In her dream she had been at the same time a man and a woman, wearing both a woman's bodice and a man's fringed garment . . . Only now did Yentl grasp the meaning of the Torah's prohibition against wearing the clothes of the other sex. By doing so one deceived not only others but also oneself. Even the soul was perplexed, finding itself incarnate in a strange body." *Short Friday and Other Stories* (New York: Fawcett Crest, 1980), 169–70.

14. *Niddah* 16b; *Berakoth* 33b. The second of these citations reads in English translation as follows: "R. Hanina further said: 'Everything is in the hands of heaven except the fear of heaven' [i.e., all a man's qualities are fixed by nature, but his moral character depends on his own choice.]" Babylonian Talmud: *Berakoth*, translated and annotated by Maurice Simon (London: Soncino, 1948), 210.

15. This explanation is offered by the *Tosafot* and Rabbi Asher ben Yechiel in commenting on *Nedarim* 51a, where the Talmudic discussion seeks an exact definition of the Hebrew word *to'evah*, abomination. See Norman Lamm, "Judaism," 197, and *Nedarim*, translated by H. Freedman (London: Soncino, 1936).

16. This verse is quoted in the following Talmudic discussion of those converted to idolatry: "Scripture says, *None that go unto her return neither do they attain the paths of life*. But if they do not return, how can they attain [the paths of life]?—What it means is that even if they do turn away from it they will not attain the paths of life." Babylonian Talmud: *Abodah Zarah* 17a, translated and annotated by A. Mishcon and A. Cohen (London: Soncino, 1935), 86.

The rabbis, using this verse as their prooftext, consistently link the sins of lust and idolatry as a moral quagmire from which there is no escape. Malbim's commentary on Proverbs 2:15–19 makes explicit a connection that Singer exploits: "The dangers pictured here are . . . two-fold: the moral dangers of dissolute living . . . and the hazard of heresy . . . The first kind of sin, the sexual sin, shortens life, debilitates physically and leads only to death; while the second, the sin of heresy, involves a man in distortions of truth—it leads him down winding paths from which he can never return to the high road." *Malbim on Mishley: The Commentary of Rabbi Meir Leibush Malbim on the Book of Proverbs*, abridged and adapted into English by Charles Wengrov (Jerusalem: Feldheim, 1982), 27–28.

17. This metaphor was commonly used by early Eastern European Jewish immigrants to the United States to describe the shock of their encounter with New World Judaism. Thus Jonathan D. Sarna entitles his 1982 English translation of Rabbi Moses Weinberger's scathing critique of Jewish observance in New York, first published in Hebrew in 1887, "People Walk on Their Heads." Some of Weinberger's remarks in his book startlingly anticipate Singer's own attitude a century later: "We do not believe that American Judaism can hope for much . . . Such is the nature of innovations these days: today it allows a man to do this, and tomorrow that. In the end he denies all, and makes of everything lofty, holy,

and sublime an everlasting ruin . . . this, the new world, is a world turned upside down. People walk on their heads in Columbus's land, not on their feet." *People Walk on Their Heads: Moses Weinberger's Jews and Judaism in New York*, ed. and trans. Jonathan D. Sarna, (New York: Holmes and Meir, 1982), 65, 78. I am grateful to Dr. Ida Cohen Selavan, Judaica Librarian of the Klau Library, Hebrew Union College, Cincinnati, for calling my attention to this book and to the illuminating parallel it makes.

18.   *Kiddushin* 40a: "R. Il'ai the Elder said: If a man sees that his [evil] desire is conquering him, let him go to a place where he is unknown, don black and cover himself with black [his sombre garments may subdue his lust], and do as his heart desires [if he is still unable to resist], but let him not publicly profane God's name [by sinning where he is known]." Babylonian Talmud: *Kiddushin*, translated and annotated by I. Epstein (London: Soncino, 1936), 199.

19.   Babylonian Talmud: *Abodah Zarah* 26b, translated and annotated by A. Mishcon and A. Cohen (London: Soncino, 1935), 131–32.

20.   Babylonian Talmud: *Sotah* 3a, translated by A. Cohen (London: Soncino, 1936), 7.

21.   Isaac Bashevis Singer, "Author's Note" to *The Death of Methuselah and Other Stories* (New York: Farrar, Straus & Giroux, 1988), viii.

22.   Sa'adia, *Emunot VeDeot*, 933, translated by S. Rosenblatt (New Haven: Yale University Press, 1948).

Judaism, Genius, or Gender: Women in the Fiction of Isaac Bashevis Singer

Nancy Berkowitz Bate

In 1955 when she was 15 years old, Letty Cottin Pogrebin lost her mother to ovarian cancer. She describes sitting shiva:

> One night, about twenty people are milling about the house but by Jewish computation there are only nine Jews in our living room. This is because only nine men have shown up for the memorial service. A minyan, the quorum required for Jewish communal prayer, calls for ten men.
> "I know Hebrew." I say, "You can count me, Daddy."
> I meant, I want to count. I meant, don't count me out just because I am a girl.
> "You know it's not allowed," he replies, frowning . . .
> In those first weeks after losing my mother I needed to lean on my religion, rock myself in Hebrew rhythms as familiar to me as rain. But how could I mourn as a Jew if my Kaddish did not count? . . . The answer is I could not. I refused to be an illegitimate child in my own religion. I could not be a ghost in the minyan. If I did not count, I would not stay. I mourned as a daughter, and left Judaism behind.[1]

Like Pogrebin, Isaac Bashevis Singer's heroines are coerced into making a Sophie's choice. Evelyn Torton Beck writes that Singer is misogynous. He "sees the world as essentially male-centered,"[2] and portrays women almost entirely in terms of their relationships with men. Singer's work, however, reflects the temper of his time and his community. In his society, communal continuity and stability were consistently given priority over individual fulfillment. Despite this fact, his oeuvre displays a potent sympathy with those independent women whose ambitions could not be accommodated by the Jewish community. Singer acknowledges the predicament of women and illuminates it with sensitivity and humor.

Jewish women in early twentieth century Eastern Europe were unequivocally second-class citizens. Women could not be counted in a prayer quorum

This essay was written specifically for this volume and is published here for the first time by permission of the author.

or lead a service. "Like the minor, the deaf-mute, and the idiot, they could not serve as witnesses in a Jewish court, except for a few specified cases."[3] The life of a Hassidic Jew was guided by " *mitzvot*," commandments written in the Torah and interpreted in the Talmud. The Jewish women of Singer's era had long been viewed as peripheral Jews, because they were exempt from many positive, timebound *mitzvot*. These *mitzvot* include hearing the Shofar on Rosh Hashanah, praying the three daily services, wearing a prayer shawl and phylacteries, and Torah study. Women had been " 'excused' from most of the positive symbols which, for the male Jew, hallow time, hallow his physical being, and inform both his myth and his philosophy."[4]

Of course women could opt to perform *mitzvot* that were incumbent upon men, but according to the Talmud, "Greater is he who is commanded and carries out an act, than he who is not commanded, and carries it out" (*Kiddushin* 31a). Therefore, the *mitzvot* optionally performed by a woman could never give her equal status with men whose *mitzvot* were obligatory.

Women's few obligatory *mitzvot* were closely connected to physical goals and objects. The lives of women in the *shtetl* revolved around physical objects and corporeal experience—cooking, cleaning, childbearing, and child rearing. Those *mitzvot* that were almost exclusively the province of the Jewish woman included the provision of kosher food for her family, the kindling of Sabbath candles, and postmenstrual visitation to the ritual bath in order to enable her husband to have intercourse with her. These *mitzvot* aided and reinforced the lifestyle of the community and the family, but did little to cultivate the relationship between the individual and God. Because women lacked an "independent spiritual life to counterbalance the materialism of [their] existence, the mind of the average woman was devoted to physical considerations: marriages, deaths, dinners, clothes, and money. It was, thus, natural that Jewish men should have come to identify women with *gashmiut* [physicality] and men with *ruhniut* [spirituality]."[5]

This identification of *gashmiut* with the female saturates Singer's work. For example the "Slaughterer," who wanted to see the "higher spheres, [where] there was no death, no slaughtering . . . no stomachs and intestines," supposed that his daughters "ate too much and were getting too fat . . . they combed each other's hair and plaited it into braids. They were forever babbling . . . and they laughed. They looked for lice, they fought, they washed, they kissed . . . Why was it necessary to clothe and adorn the body so much, Yoineh Meir would wonder."[6]

Yoineh Meir never considered teaching his daughters Torah. "Whoever teaches his daughter Torah teaches her *tiflut* [nonsense or obscenity]," said the Talmud (*Sotah* 20a). Despite this prohibition, another of Singer's characters, Reb Todros, does teach his daughter Torah. Yentl, of "Yentl the Yeshiva Boy," loved to study the Torah, although Torah study by women had been discouraged for centuries. The *Shulhan Arukh*, a source widely consulted in Singer's era, says, "The sages have commanded that a man should not teach his daughter Torah, because most women do not have the intention of truly learning and they turn the teachings of the Torah into nonsense in accordance with their limited understanding" (*Shulhan Arukh, Yoreh De'ah, Hilkhot Talmud Torah* 246:6).[7]

Within the confines of her time and place Yentl could not accommodate both her womanhood and her beloved Torah, so she embraced the Torah and concealed her womanhood from her community, from the man she loved, and from herself. When her father dies, she cuts her hair and dresses as a man. The tragedy of her story lies in the suppression of Yentl's sexuality and gender identity, in her exile from community, and in the sorrow she bequeaths to those who have loved her.

Yentl, like the reader, believes that cross-dressing will merely disguise her superficially. But she finds herself transformed viscerally. Role-playing can be a self-fulfilling prophecy. Singer explains: "to make believe is real power . . . life itself is a play . . . we put on clothes and we make believe almost that this is what we are. We forget our nakedness and we see ourselves as always dressed. When you wear a mask long enough, it becomes a part of your face."[8]

In "Yentl" Singer says: "Only now did Yentl grasp the meaning of the Torah's prohibition against wearing the clothes of the other sex. By doing so one deceived not only others but also oneself."[9] After months of immersion in the exclusively male subculture of the Yeshiva, Yentl gradually acquires the gestures, the mannerisms, the thought patterns of a man. When the story began, Yentl, for the first time, had found herself in the company of young men. She had noticed "how different their talk was from the jabbering of women . . . but she was too shy to join in" (133). The young men had teased her and had called her "bashful. A violet by the wayside" (133). After months in disguise, Yentl undergoes a metamorphosis. She speaks "in a singsong, gesticulate[s] with her thumb, clutche[s] her sidelocks, pluck[s] at her beardless chin, ma[kes] all the customary gestures of a yeshiva student. In the heat of argument she even seize[s] Avigdor [her study partner] by the lapel and call[s] him stupid" (154).

Yentl's perception of Hadass, an eligible young woman, reveals a similar transformation. Initially, Yentl says Hadass "must consider herself a beauty, for she was always in front of the mirror, but, in fact, she was not that good-looking" (136). Avigdor asks Yentl, "She doesn't appeal to you?" "Not particularly" (136) is Yentl's ironic, heterosexual reply. Months later Yentl looks at Hadass "as she stood there—tall, blond, with a long neck, hollow cheeks, and blue eyes . . . Her hair, fixed in two braids, was flung back over her shoulders. A pity I'm not a man" (139), Yentl thinks. She regards Hadass with the eyes of a man and, influenced by her *gashmiut,* finds herself attracted to a beautiful woman. Yentl impulsively, perhaps involuntarily, says to Hadass, "You're beautiful . . . everyone wants you . . . I, too, want you" (141). Yentl is losing her heterosexual orientation, but she cannot conceive of having a homosexual attraction to a woman, and believes, "I must be going mad" (142). Frustrated that as a man she cannot marry Avigdor, whom she adores, Yentl marries Hadass and deceives her into believing their homosexual intercourse is a typical marital relationship. Eventually, Yentl can no longer endure her own duplicity and leaves the *shtetl* to study Torah elsewhere.

According to the narrow sex role definitions of her era, Yentl can live neither as man nor woman, homosexual nor heterosexual. No outlet affords her both intellectual and emotional fulfillment; no niche exists for her in the *shtetl*. Yentl's gender-identity crisis and her *gashmiut*, leave her friends Avigdor and Hadass in a joyless union. Singer does not misogynistically fault the women or the community, however, but the Creator who assembled the world haphazardly. "Even Heaven makes mistakes" (132), declares Reb Todros.

Singer implies that women with ambition and talent are divine errors. Only divine fallibility could account for Yentl's love of Torah. Viewed through a telescope filtered by contemporary ethics, Singer's implication is misogynous; but the *shtetl* community of the early twentieth century was not overly concerned with gender ethics. Singer intends his stories to resurrect a vanished world. He is consistently, intentionally, anachronistic. His works transport the reader to Singer's own childhood. For centuries talmudic Judaism had sustained numerous islands of Jewish civilization in the great sea of European Christendom. Singer's intense loyalty to the Hassidic Judaism of his parents precluded his ever suggesting that the Talmud could be ignored without the trespassor suffering dire consequences. Singer's characters cannot safely jettison such cargo.

The author is not misogynous in the context of his time and place. On the contrary, he is hypersensitive to the anguish he observed in the lives of his sister, his mother, and the female characters of his stories. He demonstrates the impossibility of a woman reconciling her intellectual ambitions with talmudic Judaism, and he never simplifies the conundrum by offering a solution to it. Still today, Orthodox women are struggling with the apparent injustices endemic to talmudic Judaism.[10]

Talmud study was integral to daily life throughout Singer's formative years. Singer's father, Menahem, loved the Talmud and the Torah. He was an intensely spiritual individual and leery of any contact with women. Singer saw his father turn away from any woman who approached him for fear that the very sight of a woman, her physicality, or *gashmiut*, would distract him from the path of righteousness and somehow compromise his spiritual nature. On the other hand, Singer saw his mother, Bathsheva, as a source of love, wisdom, and sustenance for his family.

She was a rationalist. He was aware of her great intellect, and she certainly influenced the creation of Yentl. "Once I heard her say about the Yiddish writer David Berglson that he tried to imitate Knut Hamsun . . .

I saw my brother's eyes light up and he exclaimed, 'Mother, you understand literature better than all our critics!' "[11] But unlike Yentl, Bathsheva dedicated her life to her family, though she may have chafed under her domestic burdens. In fact, Singer's nephew Maurice Carr writes that "Bathsheva carries in her womanly frame a manly spirit . . . The better to express her grievance against Jehovah, the bungling Maker of her misbirth, she is all the more meticulous in her observance of His divine commandments."[12] Singer recounts:

> My mother was, even at that time, an ardent feminist, or a suffragist as they called them then. Whenever she read about the cruelties in war, she would say that only women could end these murderous events. Her recipe was that all women should unite and decide not to live with their husbands until they had resolved to make peace once and forever. My mother elaborated on this idea many times, and my brother answered her, "Neither men nor women will ever unite. Nature always accomplishes what it had intended, that all life must fight for its existence." My mother's narrow face became pale, and she said, "In that case, there will never be peace in this world."[13]

The contradiction between Menahem's response to women and Singer's admiration of his mother defines the contradictions in Singer's vision of women. As Edward Alexander puts it: "Women often figure in his stories as the embodiment of the sensual principle which distracts men from the life of piety or the life of intellect." But women also demonstrate the "creative principle capable of restoring life to men . . . in whom the springs of life have been dried up."[14] It is the woman's *gashmiut* that empowers her as either an obstacle to or enabler of man's spirituality.

This polarity is sustained in Singer's vision of man's relationship to woman and is underscored in the *Kabbala*, which serves as a subtext for Singer's work.[15] Union with a woman frequently leads to "either of two antithetical culminations: a vision of chaos, as in *Satan in Goray* . . . or 'The Destruction of Kreshev,' [or 'Yentl'] or a vision of order and faith, as in 'Short Friday' or 'The Spinoza of Market Street.' "[16] In the *Kabbala*, woman again takes on two roles: either that of the Shekhina, a manifestation of peace and piety, or of Lilith, the embodiment of chaos. "The loving embrace of the King and His Queen the Shekhina secured the well-being not only of Israel but also of the whole world . . . When the Jerusalem Temple was destroyed . . . the Shekhina-Matronit . . . went into exile . . . God . . . let the place of His departed Queen be taken by Lilith."[17] These opposing partners of the Godhead parallel Singer's dual visions of woman, as a distraction from piety and intellect or as the facilitator of the pious, intellectual life. In the *Kabbala* the pious union of husband and wife and/ or the performance of certain prayers and rituals lead to serenity and order in the heavenly realm as well as here in the earthly realm, while the sinfulness of Israel leads to turmoil on earth and in the heavens.

Singer recognizes the internal and external conflicts engendered by the ambitious, assertive, independent woman, but regards her as a source of upheaval and a threat to communal stability. That such a woman can never find a niche in the community of the *shtetl* or within the milieu of the Jewish neighborhood is in keeping with the only communal context Singer knew during his formative years. Not only does Singer castigate the community for its time-bound inflexibility, but he also directs his criticism and considerable sarcasm toward the ultimate source of sexism in the *shtetl*: God. Singer's stories cast a gauntlet at the feet of the Creator:

> "He created the world in six short winter days and has been resting ever since. There are those who are of the opinion that He didn't even work that hard."
> "Do you mean by that He wasn't the First Cause?" . . .
> "Who else is the First Cause? He is a jealous God. He would never delegate such power. *But being the cause and keeping order are different things altogether.*" (emphasis added)[18]

In "The Dead Fiddler," a brilliant woman strains the communal strictures that imprison her, sowing the seeds of communal disintegration. Liebe Yentl, the only daughter of a wealthy couple, Reb Sheftel and Zise Feige, had no household chores to distract her from study and introspection. She was inordinately bright, sensitive, and paranoid: "Her head was full of whims and fancies . . . She averted her eyes from slaughtered fowl and from meat on the salting board . . . She had no friends in Shidlovtse. She complained that the girls of the town were common and backward; as soon as they were married, they became careless and slovenly. Whenever she had to go among people, she fasted the day before, for fear that she might vomit. Although she was beautiful, clever, and learned, it always seemed to her that people were laughing and pointing at her."[19]

When Liebe Yentl's fiancé, Ozer, dies, she overreacts. Having only once laid eyes on Ozer, she "fell ill from grieving. Her mother heard her sobbing in the dark . . . She drank whole dippers full [of water] . . . As though . . . a fire were raging inside her, consuming everything" (35).

She is burning with two conflicting desires: to fulfill her potential for drama, comedy, music, and a frank, uninhibited sexual appetite; and to conform to the expectations of her parents and society by marrying. Ozer's death highlights Liebe Yentl's quandary, catalyzing her hysterics. When Liebe Yentl is again betrothed, a dybbuk, Getsl the dead fiddler, enters her, in effect choosing for her the first option. She abandons her role as a chaste Jewish maiden in order to express a complex and compelling array of talents.

Liebe Yentl has been coerced by community standards into choosing her Judaism, her genius, or her gender. She opts for genius. Only in the guise of a demon can Liebe Yentl's wit, talent, and wholesome lust be applauded by the townspeople who would have otherwise excoriated her. As

Getsl the fiddler or as Beyle the whore, Liebe Yentl is able to exhibit her talents and to express an exuberant sensuality that would never have been permitted to her as a modest Jewish matron. Under the stringent restrictions of talmudic Judaism, a *shtetl* woman could never reveal these qualities.

As a demon, Liebe Yentl can tyrannize her parents, criticize the community's hypocrisy, and engage in unfeminine behavior: drinking, boasting, and dirty-joke telling. Graphically manifesting her *gashmiut*, she expresses an unrestrained corporeality, a sexuality untrammelled by talmudic laws. In the guise of Getsl or of Beyle, Liebe Yentl says she can "smell a man a mile away" (43); she downs brandy like water, says the "Worka rabbi can kiss me you know where" (48), labels holy amulets "sacred toilet paper" (43), and "[tears] off her shift and exhibit[s] her shame [genitals]" (53). She "sang ribald songs and soldier's ditties" (42), hurled insults at the townsfolk, boasted of lechery, and recited quotations from the Torah, "all of it in singsong and in rhyme" (40).

Liebe Yentl's father and brother desert the chaotic household. Her mother is too sick to hold the townspeople at bay, and they "break the door open and enter" (41), shattering the sanctity of the home. Blurring the traditional separation of the sexes, men and women commit sacrilege by dancing together to demon's music and mock the sanctity of marriage by arranging a demons' wedding.

"The Dead Fiddler" illustrates the author's ambivalence about the role of women in the Hassidic community and in society as a whole. Singer may well have believed that women's ambitions were potentially dangerous. "The Dead Fiddler" accurately reflects the fears of unrestrained female sexuality that were pervasive in Hassidic communities and in Western society. Liebe Yentl's possession has triggered the disintegration of her family, rocking the foundation of community, much as, in Singer's Hassidic and anxious view of it, any woman's overwhelming passions, if given free rein, might corrupt a whole society.

That Liebe Yentl has been possessed on the occasion of her betrothal is no coincidence. Like the "enlightened" young women of Singer's era, Liebe Yentl regards marriage in the world of the *shtetl* as oblivion—a monotonous, claustrophobic existence. When her two demons agree to marry, their wedding songs illustrate Liebe Yentl's ambivalence about marriage. She compares marriage to death and her future husband to a corpse.

> Weep, bride, weep and moan,
> Dead men fear to be alone . . .
> Corpse and corpse, wraith and wraith,
> Every demon seeks a mate.
> Angel Dumah, devil, Shed,
> A coffin is a bridal bed. (51)

Her fear of marriage is underscored when, as Beyle, she screams at her mother, "Better a rotten fiddler than a creep from Zawiercia!" (52). (Shmelke Motl, Liebe Yentl's betrothed, was from Zawiercia.)

Liebe Yentl's only escape from life as a miserable housewife is the dybbuks' domain, the alternate reality of Death—what the dybbuks call the "World of Delusion" (56). This is the only world where Liebe Yentl's sensitivity and wit can reach their full potential. For I. B. Singer this "world of delusion" was clearly a possibility. He said, "It has been shown by Salomon Maimon and the neo-Kantians that . . . existence is nothing but a category of thinking . . . philosophers have finally made us realize that 'reality' is only reality from our point of view, from the point of view of our senses, of our consciousness."[20] Liebe Yentl's demonic possession renders an alternate world, the "World of Delusion," accessible to mortal human beings, to the reader, and to the townsfolk who, because they have not died, are limited to experiencing this dimension of reality solely through their senses.

How aptly Virginia Woolf has described Liebe Yentl's predicament and its tragic outcome:

> Any woman born with a great gift in the 16th century would certainly have gone crazed, shot herself, or ended her days in some lonely cottage outside the village, half witch, half wizard, feared and mocked at. For it needs little skill in psychology to be sure that a highly gifted girl who had tried to use her gift for poetry would have been so thwarted and hindered by other people, so tortured and pulled asunder by her own contrary instincts, that she must have lost her health and sanity to a certainty.[21]

Reading storybooks, "secretly . . . borrowing from her father's bookcase" (34), and walking the Gentile streets alone had given Liebe Yentl a broader, more worldly perspective than the typical *shtetl* maiden.

Similar to "Yentl," in its depiction of a brilliant mind imprisoned in woman's body "The Dead Fiddler" echoes descriptions of Singer's own mother and sister. His mother had a "brain capable of storing all those volumes of Torah, Talmud, and Kabbalah, not to mention that burden of agonized grievance she carries around with her against Jehovah her Maker."[22] Like Liebe Yentl, Singer's sister, Hinde Esther, whom he called "quite a talented authoress,"[23] also "suffered from hysteria and had mild attacks of epilepsy. At times she seemed possessed by a dibbuk."[24] When Hinde Esther asked her mother what she should be when she grew up, Batsheva answered, "What can a girl be?"[25] Hinde "had already acquired some modern ideas, and read Yiddish newspapers and books, longed for a romance, not an arranged marriage."[26] Nevertheless Hinde Esther's marriage was an arranged one. She cried beforehand, "I'd rather go into exile."[27] Liebe Yentl echos that plaintive cry.

The injustices suffered by Singer's mother and sister profoundly affected him. In "Yentl" Singer accepted the tyranny of the community, but with "The Dead Fiddler" he acknowledged the inability of the Hassidic community to compassionately accommodate women who could not find satisfaction in the role of wife and mother. He has since genially conceded that "the people who wrote the Talmud didn't know about the Women's Liberation."[28]

Singer utilized his dybbuks to expose the inhumanity of ranking dogma above individual well-being. He scathingly portrays the gross inadequacy, the almost sadistic insensitivity, of the male Hassidic response to divergent and/or marginal women typified by his mother, his sister, and Liebe Yentl. The Hassidic men, in their petty rivalry to exorcise the dybbuks, stand in stark contrast to Zise Feige, Liebe Yentl's mother. "Torturers, you're killing my child!" ("Dead Fiddler," 53) she cries. The Hassidim of Radzymin, of Shidlovtse, and of Worka exploit Liebe Yentl merely to validate their respective dogmas and extend their respective spheres of influence. They are remarkably untroubled by the tragedy endemic to the young woman's rejection of her identity.

Liebe Yentl's father, Reb Sheftel, epitomizes the Hassidic attitude. Before the dybbuks ever emerged, Zise Feige had recognized that her daughter's behavior was eccentric. She shared her concern with Reb Sheftel, her pious husband. He responded with "a rule for everything . . . his only reply was, 'When, God willing, she gets married, she will forget all this foolishness' " (34–35). More committed to his piety than to his daughter, Reb Sheftel views marriage as the solution to any young woman's problem. In the guise of Getsl, his daughter rebukes him, "You think you're so strong because your beard's long? . . . Better an open rake than a sanctimonious fake . . . You may have the Shidlovtse schlemiels fooled, but Getsl the fiddler has been around" (39). Reb Sheftel, following the instructions of his Radzymin rabbi, hangs amulets around his daughter's neck, and she responds by screaming: "Tell the Radzymin rabbi that I spit at his amulets" (43). Defiantly, Liebe Yentl ties elflocks in her father's beard.

Continuing to mock provincial Hassidic rivalries, the author candidly describes the puerile, spiteful response of the Worka Hassidim. They were "bitter opponents of the Radzymin rabbi, [and] celebrated that day with honey cake and brandy" (44). Later, the "Hassidim of the Radzymin rabbi had heard the news that the Worka talismans had failed, and they came to gloat" (54). Close to death, Liebe Yentl defies her father, a Radzymin Hasid, by capitulating to the rival Worka Hassidim. In the guise of Beyle she finally declares that the "Worka rabbi is not the Radzymin schlemiel" (48). The followers of the Worka rabbi literally bind the nude maiden to their will. When Hassidic Judaism ties her up, Getsl agrees to leave Liebe Yentl alone. "Finally, several of the Hassidim caught Liebe Yentl's hands and feet and tied her to the bed with their sashes. Then they slipped the Worka rabbi's amulets around her neck" (53). In a poignant double entendre Beyle Tslove reproaches Getsl for leaving before their wedding night: "Imp, you made a fool of a Jewish daughter all for nothing!" (55)

The violent rape of spirit that Singer has elaborated hardly appears to be a hearty endorsement of the Hassidic tradition. Singer condemns the inadequacy of the Hassidic response to a woman in agony, and his portrayal of that response accentuates its cruelty.

The significance of the demonic in this story is related to "exile and the problem of meaning."[29] Liebe Yentl, in her self-imposed isolation, is exiled from the community. Why was Liebe Yentl ever born? Perhaps to fulfill herself and provide a degree of enlightenment for the skeptics of her town. If only for a few months and in disguise, she was everything she was capable of being. Every facet of a complex and creative individual scintillated and beguiled us from the stage of Liebe Yentl's sickbed. The Greek chorus of the town's rabble reveled in her virtuosity. For this she lived. On a superficial level Liebe Yentl gained nothing from her possession. She never found an acceptable outlet for her talent. She refused to marry and died poor and alone; but on a subliminal level the ordeal of demonic possession apparently galvanized her courage. Her unequivocal rejection of marriage constituted an open rebellion against the community that had bound and silenced her.

Contrast Yentl, who took a quintessentially Jewish approach to absurdity, to injustice. She immersed herself in Torah and in the slim chance for redemption her study might have afforded her. Her love of Torah transcended all other passions. For Yentl the Torah was

> a Tree of Life to them that hold fast to it,
> And everyone that upholds it is happy
> Its ways are ways of pleasantness,
> And all its paths are peace.[30]

For Liebe Yentl, however, it was through her possession by supposed demons that, ironically, she exhibited her Divine gifts, her creativity, her facility with language, her musical ability. It was her storytelling, like Singer's, that opened to the town's rabble a window to an alternative titillating "World of Delusion" where empirical reality "hangs by a thread".[31]

Notes

1. Letty Cottin Pogrebin, *Deborah, Golda, and Me: Being Female and Jewish in America* (New York: Crown Publishers, 1991), 43–50.

2. Evelyn Torton Beck, "I. B. Singer's Misogyny," *Lillith*, no. 6 (1979): 35.

3. Paula Hyman, "The Other Half: Women in the Jewish Tradition," in *The Jewish Woman: New Perspectives*, ed. Elizabeth Koltun (New York: Schocken Books, 1978), 106.

4. Rachel Adler, "The Jew Who Wasn't There: Halakhah and the Jewish Woman," in *On Being a Jewish Feminist: A Reader*, ed. Susannah Heschel (New York: Schocken Books, 1983), 13.

5. Ibid., 15.

6. Isaac Bashevis Singer, "The Slaughterer," in *The Seance and Other Stories* (New York: Farrar, Straus & Giroux, 1968), 21, 22–23.

7. As translated by Rachel Biale, *Women and Jewish Law* (New York: Schocken Books), 37.

8. Grace Farrell, ed., *Isaac Bashevis Singer: Conversations* (Jackson: University Press of Mississippi, 1992), 197.

9. Isaac Bashevis Singer, "Yentl the Yeshiva Boy," in *Short Friday and Other Stories* (New York: Farrar, Straus & Giroux), 140; hereafter cited in the text.

10. On this see Blu Greenberg, "Is Now the Time for Orthodox Women Rabbis?" *Moment* 18 (December 1993): 50–53, 74; Haviva Krasner-Davidson, "Why I'm Applying to Yeshiva U," *Moment* 18 (December 1993): 54–55, 97.

11. Isaac Bashevis Singer, *Love and Exile* (Garden City, N.Y.: Doubleday and Co., 1984), xxxii.

12. Maurice Carr, "My Uncle Yitzhak: A Memoir of I. B. Singer," *Commentary* 94, no.6 (December 1992): 26.

13. Singer, *Love and Exile*, xxxii.

14. Edward Alexander, *Isaac Bashevis Singer* (Boston: Twayne Publishers, 1980), 135.

15. For an extended discussion of Singer and Kabbalah, see Grace Farrell Lee, *From Exile to Redemption: The Fiction of Isaac Bashevis Singer* (Carbondale: Southern Illinois University Press, 1987), especially chap. 2.

16. Morris Golden, "Dr. Fischelson's Miracle: Duality and Vision in Singer's Fiction," in *The Achievement of Isaac Bashevis Singer*, ed. Marcia Allentuck (Carbondale: Southern Illinois University Press, 1969), 26.

17. Raphael Patai, *The Hebrew Goddess*. 3d enl. ed. (Detroit: Wayne State University Press, 1990), 159–60. "The myth of Lilith the child-killer remained a potent factor in the lives of the tradition-bound Jews down to the 19th century," explains Patai, 240.

18. Isaac Bashevis Singer, "The Warehouse," in *The Seance and Other Stories* (New York: Farrar, Straus & Giroux, 1968), 134.

19. Isaac Bashevis Singer, "The Dead Fiddler," in *The Seance and Other Stories* (New York: Farrar, Straus & Giroux, 1968), 34; hereafter cited in the text.

20. Richard Burgin, "Conversations with Isaac Bashevis Singer," in *Isaac Bashevis Singer: Conversations*, 245.

21. Virginia Woolf, *A Room of One's Own* (San Diego: Harcourt Brace Jovanovich, 1957), 49.

22. Carr, "Uncle Yitzhak," 29.

23. Singer, *Fun der alter un nayer heym* (Of the Old and New Home) 6 June 1964, quoted in Anita Norich, "The Family Singer and the Autobiographic Imagination," *Prooftexts* 10 (1990): 106n, 14.

24. Isaac Bashevis Singer, *In My Father's Court* (New York: Farrar, Straus & Giroux, 1966), 151.

25. Clive Sinclair, "Esther Singer Kreitman: The Trammeled Talent of Isaac Bashevis Singer's Neglected Sister," *Lilith* (Spring 1991): 8.

26. Singer, *Father's Court*, 153.

27. Ibid., 155.

28. Grace Farrell Lee, "Stewed Prunes and Rice Pudding: College Students Eat and Talk with I. B. Singer," *Contemporary Literature* 19, no. 4 (Autumn 1978): 456.

29. Farrell Lee, *From Exile to Redemption*, 32.

30. Adapted from Proberbs 3:17 in Rabbinical Assembly of America and the United Synagogue of America, *Sabbath and Festival Prayer Book* (United States of America, 1973), 136.

31. Singer, "Dead Fiddler," 51.

CONTRIBUTORS OF NEW ESSAYS

◆

David H. Hirsch is professor of English and Judaic Studies at Brown University. He has published widely on American literature and on the literature of the Holocaust. In his book *Deconstructing Literature: Criticism after Auschwitz*, he examines the moral and ethical implications of deconstruction and postmodernism in the wake of the Holocaust. With his wife, Roslyn Hirsch, he has translated from Polish *Auschwitz: True Tales from a Grotesque Land*, by Sara Nomberg-Przytyk, and from Yiddish *In the Sinai Desert*, by the poet Abraham Sutzkever, and a collection of short stories written in the Lodz Ghetto by Isaiah Spiegel, entitled *Ghetto Kingdom*.

Alida Allison received her Ph.D. in comparative literature from the University of California, Riverside. She is an assistant professor at San Diego State University. With Terri Frongia, she wrote and edited *The Grad Student's Guide to Getting Published* (1992) for Simon and Schuster. With the support of the 1992 Children's Literature Association Research Fellowship, she has completed *Isaac Bashevis Singer: His Childhood Memoirs and Children's Stories* for Twayne Publishers. Professor Allison is director of SDSU's 400-member Children's Literature Circle.

Joseph Sherman is senior lecturer in the Department of English, University of the Witwatersrand, Johannesburg, South Africa, where he specializes in modern Yiddish literature, which he reads in the original. He has published essays on Singer in the *Journal of Narrative Technique*, *Prooftexts*, *Judaism*, and *English Studies in Africa*. His books include two annotated reclamations of important works of South African Yiddish literature, entitled *From a Land Far Off*, a selection of South African Yiddish short stories, and *Oudtshoorn: Jerusalem of Africa*, a monograph on the Yiddish world that lay at the center of South Africa's international ostrich feather industry at the end of the nineteenth century. He is currently writing a book on Singer's novels, and his translation of *Shadows on the Hudson* is forthcoming from Farrar, Straus & Giroux in the fall of 1996.

Nancy Berkowitz Bate holds a degree from the University of Michigan and is currently a graduate student at Butler University.

Grace Farrell is the Rebecca Clifton Reade Professor of English at Butler University, Indianapolis. Winner of four National Endowment for the Humanities awards, she has published essays primarily on nineteenth- and twentieth-century American fiction in journals including *American Transcendental Quarterly, Boulevard, Contemporary Literature, Cross Currents, Essays in Literature, Journal of Religion in Literature, Modern Language Studies, Novel,* and *Southern Literary Journal.* She has contributed chapters to *Poe's Pym: Critical Explorations, Companion to Poe Studies,* and *Critical Essays on Anne Tyler.* Her books include *From Exile to Redemption: The Fiction of Isaac Bashevis Singer, Isaac Bashevis Singer: Conversations,* and an edition of Lillie Blake's nineteenth-century novel, *Fettered For Life.*

Index

♦